SPY PILOT

SPY PILOT

FRANCIS GARY POWERS, THE U-2 INCIDENT, AND A CONTROVERSIAL COLD WAR LEGACY

FRANCIS GARY POWERS JR.
AND KEITH DUNNAVANT

FOREWORD BY SERGEI KHRUSHCHEV

 Prometheus Books

59 John Glenn Drive
Amherst, New York 14228

Published 2019 by Prometheus Books

Cover image of Powers in front of F-84 circa 1952 © 2018 Associated Press;
Soviet photo of US spy plane
Cover design by Jacqueline Nasso Cooke
Cover design © Prometheus Books

Inquiries should be addressed to
Prometheus Books
59 John Glenn Drive
Amherst, New York 14228
VOICE: 716–691–0133 • FAX: 716–691–0137
WWW.PROMETHEUSBOOKS.COM

23 22 21 20 19   5 4 3 2 1

Library of Congress Cataloging-in-Publication Data

Names: Powers, Francis Gary, Jr., 1965- author. | Dunnavant, Keith, author.
Title: Spy pilot : Francis Gary Powers, the U-2 incident, and a controversial Cold War legacy /
    Francis Gary Powers Jr. and Keith Dunnavant.
Other titles: Francis Gary Powers, the U-2 incident, and a controversial Cold War legacy
Description: Amherst, New York : Prometheus Books, 2019. | Includes index.
Identifiers: LCCN 2018040315 (print) | LCCN 2018045041 (ebook) |
    ISBN 9781633884694 (eBook) | ISBN 9781633884687 (hardback)
Subjects: LCSH: Powers, Francis Gary, 1929-1977. | U-2 Incident, 1960. | Prisoners of war—
    Soviet Union—Biography. | Air pilots, Military—United States—Biography. | Powers,
    Francis Gary, Jr., 1965- | Powers family. | United States. Central Intelligence Agency. |
    Cold War. | BISAC: HISTORY / Military / Other. | POLITICAL SCIENCE / Political
    Freedom & Security / Intelligence. | BIOGRAPHY & AUTOBIOGRAPHY / Military.
Classification: LCC DK266.3 (ebook) | LCC DK266.3 .P66 2019 (print) |
    DDC 327.1273047092 [B] —dc23
LC record available at https://lccn.loc.gov/2018040315

Printed in the United States of America

To my mom and dad for their unconditional love. I would like to dedicate this book to my wife, Jen, and our son, Trey, who provide me with daily inspiration. I love you. And also to my sister, Dee, for her support over the years. I love you too.

—Francis Gary Powers Jr.

To my uncles who served their country honorably during the Cold War: Roy Evans (US Air Force), Carroll Hughes (US Navy), Robert Andersen (US Air Force), and Alvin Hughes (NASA).

—Keith Dunnavant

CONTENTS

AUTHORS' NOTE

In the interest of clarity, after the introduction, the narrative of *Spy Pilot* unfolds in the third person. Once Francis Gary Powers Jr. is born in 1965, the book is written in first person from his perspective.

FOREWORD

by Sergei Khrushchev

F or more than two decades, I have watched Francis Gary Powers Jr. work tirelessly to honor and preserve the memory of his father, an ordinary American who was caught up in extraordinary circumstances.

I, too, have made great efforts to honor and preserve the legacy of my father, Nikita Khrushchev.

This is something Gary and I have in common.

During those difficult days of the Cold War, when my father led the Soviet Union (1953–1964), he managed to avert nuclear disaster while working with American presidents Dwight D. Eisenhower and John F. Kennedy. He helped move the two superpowers toward peaceful coexistence. Not peace, but peaceful coexistence.

Still, it was an acknowledged fact that both countries spied on each other. The war of secrets was important in helping East and West avoid armed confrontation.

It is interesting to me how two spies destined to be linked forever in the history books were treated very differently by their respective countries.

In 1957, Colonel Rudolf Abel was captured by American authorities in New York City and rightly convicted of espionage and sentenced to a long prison term.

In 1960, after being shot down while flying a U-2 spy plane over the Soviet Union, Francis Gary Powers was rightly convicted of espionage and sentenced to a long prison term.

Both men were patriots who loved their country, believed fervently in their nation's ideals, and worked for the cause of world peace, before running out of luck.

When these two Cold War figures were exchanged in 1962, in a deal orchestrated by American lawyer James B. Donovan, their fates quickly diverged.

Upon his return to the Soviet Union, Abel was awarded the Order of Lenin, the USSR's highest civilian honor, and the state established a pension for him. He was considered a hero of the Soviet people.

By contrast, Powers returned to the United States under a cloud of suspicion.

Fortunately, Gary has dedicated much of his life to learning and communicating the truth about his father, including the writing of this important book about the Cold War.

INTRODUCTION

Sometimes, it is the little things that linger, like the scruff of a father's beard.

Every night, when I was a young boy, my dad came to my room, tucked me into bed, and kissed me on the cheek, the day-long growth of his nine o'clock shadow pressing firmly against my still-smooth skin. There was love in that moment. There was security.

I'll never forget the last time we shared this ritual. It was the night before my world shattered.

In those days, Dad piloted a traffic helicopter for KNBC-TV, the NBC-owned station in Los Angeles. We lived very comfortably in the San Fernando Valley town of Sherman Oaks: father; mother; elder sister, Dee; and me. Life was good.

The first day of August in 1977 was an ordinary workday for my forty-seven-year-old father, but something went terribly wrong. His helicopter ran out of gas and crashed near a golf course in Encino. When someone from the station came to tell the family about the crash, I was left confused, thinking he must have broken a few bones and probably would be confined to a hospital bed for a few days. No one pulled me aside to reveal the awful truth.

Later in the day, with the house full of people and a somber tone permeating the place, I stood behind several adults in the living room, watching Channel 4's evening newscast. Jess Marlow was a giant in Los Angeles television, the personification of the stone-faced, detached anchorman. Hearing from this iconic figure that my father was dead, at the same time much of Southern California learned the news, was shocking . . . and so was watching him choke up and actually shed a tear on live television. There was no crying on television in those days, but

Marlow could not help himself. He had lost a colleague and a friend. I was devastated beyond words. My life would never be the same.

Several adults went out of their way to comfort me, including another dear family friend, the actor Robert Conrad. At one point, Conrad called me on the telephone and gave me what amounted to a pep talk: "Your father was a good man," he said, stressing that, "no matter what you might hear," your dad was a patriot who sacrificed greatly for his country.

"Be proud of him. His legacy is now in you. . . ."

No matter what I might hear?

I tried to process what Mr. Conrad said, but on the day my father died, I was still too young and too sheltered to fully appreciate the burden associated with being Francis Gary Powers Jr., because I didn't really know my father. I didn't know him at all.

I knew the helicopter pilot. The man who patiently helped me with my homework. The man who carefully taught me how to shoot a .22-caliber rifle. The man who gently kissed me good night. But I didn't know what I didn't know.

In time, I would feel compelled to solve the riddle of Conrad's cryptic consolation, to learn the haunting truth about my father.

Chapter One

THE RESTLESS HEART

One morning in the early 1940s, Oliver Powers loaded up his family in his pickup truck and plotted a course for the state line. With his wife, Ida, seated next to him and their children hunkered down in the open-air truck bed, Oliver carefully traversed the unforgiving dirt roads out of the isolated hollow where they lived, near the coal-mining company town of Harmon, Virginia. They were headed for a picnic in neighboring West Virginia, unable to imagine how a seemingly routine outing would profoundly shape the family's story.

Deeply rooted in a hardscrabble corner of Appalachia, far from the prosperity of the industrial age, the Powers clan lived in several different locations through the years, including an old family farmhouse adjacent to a dairy in the picturesque hills near the town of Pound, where Oliver's ancestors had once struggled to make ends meet working the land. "You could sell your produce, your milk, hogs, but to [find anybody to] sell it to, you had to cross that mountain on foot," said lifelong resident Jack Goff, pointing toward the nearby border with Kentucky. "'Cause there wasn't any road." The narrow, steep trail, known as the Buffalo Trace, once was used by Native American tribes who followed the Buffalo herds on their seasonal migration from the fertile grazing lands of the Ohio Valley through Virginia before settling for the winter in North Carolina. Even after the first road was built to connect the hollow to the outside world, the trail remained a source of adventure for the area's children.

After the first of the coal mines opened in 1913, in the nearby company town of Jenkins, Kentucky, James Powers, Oliver's father, worked building houses for the miners, simple little wood-frame structures typically including four or five small rooms sealed by an outer shell of canvas. Coal-fired stoves heated the rustic domiciles—the precious rocks purchased, like most other necessities of life, at the nearby company-owned store. The surging demand for coal produced thousands of jobs across the area, paying as much as $7 per day, good money during the years of the Great Depression and World War II. In the context of that time and place, coal mining equaled opportunity beyond farming, even as it also represented a trap that swallowed many lives whole.

Oliver landed his first mine job in his late teens. It was difficult work, with danger forever lurking in the sweet mountain air, peril beyond the gradual debilitation of all that coal dust accumulating in the lungs. When two pieces of heavy equipment collided underground, violently slamming him against a wall, he was lucky to escape with his life. "There wasn't room for his pelvis to turn over," said Goff, whose life was closely entangled with the Powers family. "It sort of crushed him, and he didn't walk straight after that."

Hardened by the mining life, frustrated by his circumstances, Oliver could be "gruff and loud," recalled his daughter, Jan Powers Melvin, born while her father served a hitch in the US Army. She was six months old when she was introduced to Oliver for the first time; the baby girl immediately started bawling in apparent fright. "We knew he loved us, but he wasn't the type of man to easily show affection." Still, as a grown man with a houseful of kids, he remained remarkably deferential to his own father, demonstrated by his habit of hiding his lit cigarette whenever a disapproving James walked into the room.

Like most mine wives, Ida, who was slightly heavyset and usually trying to lose weight, took pride in her toughness in the face of all those daily hardships. But she could be very loving. Deeply religious, she made sure the family regularly attended services at the Church of Christ, which required a significant commute when they lived in Harmon. A good neighbor who was always eager to help, she was usually the first one to show up at someone's house when a new baby was on the way.

At various times, especially during the Depression, the mines shut down or cut back on personnel, leaving Oliver without a way to adequately provide for his family. On occasion he would run some moonshine, but eventually he opened a shoe-repair shop, first as a side business and then as his full-time occupation, escaping the mining life for good. He dreamed of a better life for his children, especially his only son.

Francis Gary Powers, born on August 17, 1929, at the hospital in the nearby community of Burdine, Kentucky, just two months before Wall Street crashed, grew up knowing how it felt to go to bed hungry. He saw the desperation in his parents' eyes, unable to help. Years later, he remarked about how the mining life "made people like my mother and father old before their time."[1]

Shaped by parents who engendered in him a strong sense of right and wrong and left him free to roam the surrounding countryside, Francis grew up empowered by a sense of gathering independence, hunting, fishing, swimming, and spelunking in the distant hills. Sometimes he hiked to a favorite spot, the top of a high cliff overlooking the surrounding valley, and let his thoughts drift to faraway places, beyond the overarching mines, which he saw "poisoning everything."[2] Doted on by his five sisters, he became, by his own estimation, "something of a loner."[3] If he was not outside doing something physical, he could often be found in his room reading, especially books dealing with history.

Young Francis could be an irritating brother, such as the times when Jan, two years younger and shorter, endured his childish picking, victimized by his much longer arms. Sometimes she tried to "smack" him, but he was always able to keep her at arm's length. And he could also be their protector. One day when they were very young, Jan, Jean, and Francis were walking through a nearby pasture. They didn't see the bull until he started chasing them. "Scared the daylights out of us," Jan said. The Powers kids ran all the way home, with Francis pulling Jan forcefully by the hand, up onto the cement steps of their little house, just ahead of the rampaging animal. Once they reached the safety of a closed door, they could look out the window and see the mad cow snorting ominously but harmlessly on those cement steps. "That was a close call we'd never forget," Jan said.

Without extra money for luxuries such as vacations, the children recognized their day trip to West Virginia early in World War II as a rare treat. Several hours into their adventure, in Princeton, they happened upon a county fair, where a pilot was offering airplane rides in a little Piper Cub for the princely sum of two dollars and fifty cents. Oliver looked at Francis. He could see the gleam in his fourteen-year-old son's eyes.

Three-quarters of a century later, Joan, relaxing in her modest house several miles from the old farm on the outskirts of Pound, remembered the pivotal moment like it had happened that very morning. Her eyes brightened at the way her father indulged her brother. "Anything Francis wanted," the elderly lady said with a girlish laugh, "Oliver was going to get it for him." She paused and smiled. "You know how it was. He was the only son."

Working steadily, the patriarch of the clan felt good about his ability to splurge on his boy, who soared through the clouds for several loops around the surrounding countryside, never to be the same.

"There was a lady pilot doing the flying and she must've liked Francis, because she kept him up there longer than he had paid for," Joan said. "I guess she could see how much he liked it. Well, I never will forget. He's standing at the back of the truck with the biggest grin on his face and says, 'I left my heart up there.' I was only 9 or 10 and I didn't quite understand. I thought he had fallen in love with that lady pilot!"

The experience struck a nerve deep inside Francis.

"It was quite a thrill," he recalled many years later. "I was so nervous, just shaking all over, because it was such a thrill to me."[4]

What Oliver could not have guessed then was that the flight would alter not just his son, but American history.

During the final year of the war, Oliver landed a good-paying job in a defense plant in Detroit. The father and his son moved first, until he could send for Ida and the girls, having secured two small adjoining apartments in an area near the industrial center of River Rouge. The wide-eyed country folks felt like strangers in a foreign land, encountering skyscrapers, streetcars, and the bustle of urban life. For the first time, the Powers family owned an icebox, with daily deliveries of ice to fill it, which made them feel prosperous. Thrown into a big-city melting pot, they became acquainted with people from vastly different backgrounds.

On his way home from school, Francis encountered a large bunch of white boys beating up on one small African American child. "He took the black boy's part [and] started helping him fight the rest of 'em," Jan recalled. Relating the incident to his sister, Francis said, "It just wasn't fair for all those big boys to be picking on one little boy, no matter what his skin color was."

Not long after the Japanese surrendered, the Powers family moved back to the farm, where Francis played left guard on the Grundy High School football team and joined his best friend, Jack Goff—who would one day marry his sister Jean—in various adventures. As younger boys, they had sent off some box tops from their corn flakes and formed a Junior Airplane Spotters club, carefully watching the distant skies and learning to tell the difference between the various American military planes of the day, such as the P-51 Mustang and the P-47 Thunderbolt. This activity remained a favorite pastime after the war, along with picking wild strawberries—"The cattle grazed those hills, but they'd leave the strawberries alone," Jack recalled—and exploring caves. They got to know the game warden, who helped them locate new caves to explore; the boys delighted in the pulse-pounding excitement of crawling through the dark, not knowing what they would find or how far they could go before the walls became too narrow and they would have to turn back.

As a young man, Francis cut a handsome figure, attracting a steady stream of girlfriends. When he sometimes worked cobbling shoes for his father, business tended to pick up from the young ladies. "My sister and her friends were a little older than me," recalled Liz Boyd, the daughter of a coal miner, "and they took their shoes in all the time just so they could see him. He was quite a good-looking man."

Francis developed a reputation as a pool shark, according to his buddy Jack, who later owned a pool room next to Oliver's shoe shop and was something of a pool shark himself. Francis worked as a lifeguard at the local swimming pool, and he earned good money one summer by helping dig a train tunnel for the coal company. But like many sons of coal miners, he was driven by one especially powerful urge: to escape.

Determined that his son would transcend the dead-end life that had ensnared him, Oliver began planning for Francis's future when he was still a young boy. He was going to become a doctor. After all, doctors earned good money. They didn't have to spend their days in a big black hole, filling their lungs with soot. They didn't have to struggle for everything. To Oliver, it was that simple.

At first, Francis dutifully bought into his father's grand plan, which led him to East Tennessee's Milligan College, located about 100 miles south, where he pursued a premed curriculum in the years immediately after World War II. Two or three times during the school year, he took the bus home or jumped a train car, usually hitchhiking part of the way. To help pay for his education, he worked a series of jobs, even accepting part-time employment—against Oliver's wishes—in the same mine where his father toiled for decades.

One summer he landed a job on a crew building a tipple, a large structure used for loading the extracted coal into railroad cars. "Best job I ever had in those days, in terms of [earning] money," he said.[5] The work was grueling and long: ten hours a day, seven days a week.

Francis was working toward something, but not toward the life his father wanted for him.

"I had been talked into [becoming a doctor] by my dad," he said. "He wanted me to be a doctor [and I] was an obedient son. But I soon realized, I was not doctor material. . . . Didn't think I was cut out for it."[6]

Although he graduated from Milligan on schedule in 1950, Francis rebelled against his father by turning his back on medicine, enlisting in the US Air Force after the Korean War broke out. Oliver was deeply disappointed, but his boy was determined to follow his heart into the wild blue yonder.

After basic training at Lackland Air Force Base in San Antonio, Texas, Francis was assigned to duty as a photo technician, which allowed him to take the second flight of his life. Boarding the Douglas DC-3 to Denver, he grabbed one of the window seats in the first row, so he could look out over the wing. Several months later, he was accepted into the Aviation Cadet program and methodically worked his way through the various stages required to become a fighter pilot. An attack of appendicitis delayed his training for several months, causing him to miss combat in Korea. He graduated from the flight program just before the armistice was signed in 1953. Only later would it become clear that the illness had played a large role in making him available for a very special assignment.

By the time he arrived at Turner Air Force Base in Albany, Georgia, in July 1953, Francis had stopped calling himself Francis, in all but official matters. Most of his friends outside rural Virginia now knew him as Frank, which he thought sounded more manly, and Frank Powers quickly distinguished himself flying the F-84 Thunderjet, a once cutting-edge plane headed toward obsolescence.

Developed by Republic Aviation, the F-84 was one of the earliest American jet fighters, featuring an Allison J35 turbojet engine and capable of exceeding 600 miles per hour. The aircraft played a large role in the Korean War, particularly as a tactical bomber, but it had proven no match in air-to-air combat against the Soviet Union's revolutionary, swept-wing MiG-15, which was eventually countered by a US Air Force game changer, North American Aviation's swept-wing F-86 Sabre.

When Powers reported for duty with the 508th Strategic Fighter Wing, part of the Strategic Air Command (SAC), the Pentagon was busy developing a new use for the latest version of the Thunderjet: dropping nuclear bombs.

Eight years after the top secret Manhattan Project successfully harnessed the power of the atom, leading to President Harry Truman's fateful decision to order the dropping of the world's first two atomic bombs on the Japanese cities of Hiroshima and Nagasaki, which swiftly ended World War II, the nuclear arms race with the Soviet Union colored every aspect of American defense and foreign policy. The Cold War represented a new brand of tension and risk. Never before in the history of the world had two powerful nations, after spending years stockpiling weapons and perfecting delivery systems, been capable of destroying each other in a matter of minutes. All across America, public-school teachers empowered by Civil Defense authorities regularly led students through so-called duck and cover drills, which became as ubiquitous as poodle skirts and ducktails. Beyond the harsh reality that such defensive maneuvers would have proven useless in a direct hit from a thermonuclear blast, the routine reflected the palpable anxiety infusing the otherwise-placid fifties: Someday, the communists might decide to push the button and ignite World War III.

Nowhere was the philosophical and military standoff of the Cold War more routinely evident than in the divided city of Berlin, Germany.

Since being carved up by the victorious nations of World War II, the onetime Nazi capital had served as the tense frontier between East and West. When the Soviets blockaded highway and rail traffic into free West Berlin in 1948–1949, in an attempt to force the United States, Great Britain, and France to withdraw, the Allies mounted a massive resupply effort to become known as the Berlin Airlift. It was the first test of Western resolve in the face of Soviet aggression, and the Soviets eventually blinked.

By the mid-1950s, with a large contingent of US and Soviet forces permanently stationed on opposite sides of the border, creating a powder keg between superpowers waiting for a struck match, the contrast between the zones was stark: freedom and prosperity on one side, tyranny and poverty on the other. Each year, thousands of East Germans fled communism by slipping across the border, forced to escape with only what they could carry. The Soviet-backed East German government began to consider remedies to stop this mass exodus.

Like many Americans who understood what the city represented, Francis Gary Powers dreamed of someday seeing Berlin.

While preparing for his role in the unthinkable, which included detailed training about the handling of nuclear weapons, briefings about US strategy in the case of war, and instructions on where to report in case of a high-threat alert, Powers participated in survival training at two different bases. He learned how to use a parachute, subsist on limited rations for an extended period, and resist brainwashing from the enemy. He believed in being prepared but hoped he would never have to use any of his newly acquired knowledge.

Like Powers, Ohio native Tony Bevacqua was determined to become a pilot. The Air Force initially turned him down, because he had attained only a high-school diploma, causing him to start out as an enlisted man, painting insignias on T-6s and B-25s. When the supply/demand curve turned in his favor, producing a temporary relaxation of the rules, Bevacqua quickly moved through Aviation Cadet training, eventually winding up at Turner, where he shared a four-bedroom house about two miles from the front gate with three other pilots: Wes Upchurch, Vic Milam, and Frank Powers.

Tony considered Frank "a very good pilot" who was "very precise and detail oriented." He especially admired the man's abilities on the gunnery range, where he won several competitions while utilizing the F-84's .50-caliber guns in steep dives.

Over beers at the officer's club, the two friends talked about women and sports and their shared appreciation for flying fast airplanes and driving fast cars. They laughed about the unsuspecting airliners they frequently lined up on, as part of their routine attack simulations.

"Frank was a personable guy and fun to be around," Bevacqua said. "By the time I got there, he was spending a lot of time with Barbara."

About a month after arriving at Turner, a cashier at the post-exchange took a shine to Frank and introduced him to her daughter, who worked as a cashier at a nearby Marine base. Beautiful and full of life, eighteen-year-old Barbara Gay Moore was Frank's kind of girl. They hit it off immediately. The romance quickly turned serious, and Frank put a ring on her finger, but he became increasingly troubled by her erratic behavior and excessive drinking.

"I'd go on these trips and I'd find out she's gone out with other men," Powers confided many years later. "She wouldn't wear the ring. I was quite suspicious and rightfully so."[7]

When he was assigned for some temporary duty at Eglin Air Force Base, the massive testing facility along the Gulf Coast in northwest Florida, Barbara agreed to drive down to meet him for the Fourth of July weekend. When the appointed time arrived, she didn't show up. Without any way to contact her, Barbara's fiancé was at once concerned and mistrustful. She eventually showed up two days later—"an entire day and night unaccounted for."[8] They argued and she made up some story.

Frank was not the type to share too much, but Bevacqua could see his friend wrestling with a dilemma.

"She was a handful, and their relationship was pretty rocky," Bevacqua said. "But Frank clearly loved her and thought he could make it work."

After several broken engagements, the couple eventually decided to marry as quickly as possible. Because Barbara wanted her brother to preside over the ceremony, they hastily drove to the small town of Newnan, located about 150 miles north of Albany, Georgia, where Jack Moore was the pastor of Lovejoy Memorial United Methodist Church. The preacher hustled to make the necessary arrangements, including engaging the services of local photographer Joe Norman and asking a friend for a rather big favor.

"I got a call from Jack, who said his sister was marrying this fellow later in the day," recalled Johnny Estep, who owned a local concrete business and served in the National Guard with the preacher. "It all happened in a hurry and he needed a best man, because he didn't know anybody in town. Wasn't any more complicated than that."

When the small wedding party convened in the living room of the Methodist parsonage, located five blocks east of the courthouse square at 129 East Broad Street, Estep shook hands with the groom, whom he had never met, and wished him well. It was April 2, 1955. No members of the Powers family were in attendance. The ceremony was over in a matter of minutes, after which Mr. and Mrs. Francis Gary Powers rushed off to their honeymoon.[9]

"Never realized I was part of history until many years later," Estep said in 2015.

Scheduled to complete his four-year hitch in the Air Force toward the end of 1955, First Lieutenant Powers began making inquiries with several major airlines, seduced by the thought of flying a Douglas DC-6 or a Lockheed C-121 Super Constellation to exotic locales. Now that sounded like a great way to make a living. But none of the carriers showed any interest in hiring him, so he extended his commission indefinitely, energized by the opportunity to keep flying and happy to be bringing home more than four hundred dollars per month. It sure beat shoveling coal.

Several weeks after his buddy Frank told him he was planning to make a career of the Air Force, Bevacqua arrived at their house one night and noticed that Frank's bedroom was empty. All of his belongings were suddenly gone. Usually, if a pilot was reassigned, he would be given time for a rollicking send-off at the officer's club and would leave a forwarding address for his mail. But Frank had not said a word to anybody.

"He just disappeared."

Chapter Two

OPEN SKIES

On May 1, 1954, Nikita Khrushchev assumed his position of authority outside Lenin's and Stalin's Mausoleum in the heart of Moscow, alongside many of his top generals and members of the politburo, as a large crowd of cheering citizens lined the streets. Eight months after rising to power as the First Secretary of the Communist Party of the Soviet Union, following the death of Joseph Stalin, Khrushchev carefully watched the traditional May Day parade of tanks, troops, antiaircraft guns, and airplanes. Included among the display of Soviet military might was the new Myasishchev M-4 Molot ("Hammer") long-range bomber, which pleased him greatly. He knew the Americans were watching.

Even as the Boeing B-52 Stratofortress, a massive eight-engine monster designed to deliver nuclear payloads and provide a new level of deterrent, moved toward operational status in 1955, many American military and political leaders believed the Soviet Union was closing the gap in the arms race, particularly in the deployment of long-range strategic bombers. The so-called bomber gap became a source of intense debate and a political burden for President Dwight D. Eisenhower, especially when word began to leak to the West about the M-4, which was seen as a significant leap forward in Soviet technology.

The possibility that the new weapon could pose risks to the US strategic arsenal created grave concern in certain circles in Washington. How many of these planes did the Soviets have? Where were they based? How would the United States know if it had suddenly fallen behind in the arms race?

While pushing for additional spending on bombers and other remedies to maintain American superiority, hawks in Congress, the Pentagon, and the media pressured Eisenhower to address what they saw as a gathering vulnerability. Some even suggested that by not acting decisively, the old general was risking the possibility of a communist sneak attack, tapping into the bitter memories of a generation shaped by Pearl Harbor.

By November 1954, Eisenhower knew what he had to do. It was the sort of risk only a president could authorize.

William J. "Wild Bill" Donovan understood the power of a secret. As the head of the Office of Special Services (OSS) during World War II, Donovan proved to be a formidable asset for the Allied cause. The former Justice Department official, who was greatly influenced by Great Britain's MI6 spy agency, assembled a network of clandestine operatives, established training programs for espionage and sabotage, and coordinated once-disparate activities into a cohesive message to be consumed by the president and other decision makers. He also landed on Utah Beach on the day after D-day, defying orders from his superiors.

Moving inland with one of his agents, Donovan and the other man were suddenly pinned down by German machine-gun fire.

"David," he said, turning to his colleague, "we mustn't be captured. We know too much."[1]

"Yes, sir," responded Colonel David K. E. Bruce.

Donovan then asked him a question that went straight to the heart of the matter.

"Have you the pill?"

At this, the OSS's commander of European covert operations admitted that he had not brought the agency's specially concocted suicide pill.

"Never mind," Donovan said. "I have two of them."

The man who practically invented American spying would one day be recognized as the father of the Central Intelligence Agency (CIA).

Two years after the war ended and the OSS was disbanded, the dawn of the Cold War convinced powerful members of Congress and the Truman administration that the country needed a permanent clandestine service, which led to the founding of the CIA. Many OSS veterans wound up with positions of importance and authority in the CIA, including one of Donovan's most trusted operatives: former corporate lawyer Allen W. Dulles, who served as the agency's director from 1953 to 1961 and profoundly shaped its culture.

The younger brother of the towering John Foster Dulles, who served as Eisenhower's secretary of state, Allen was among the small group of Eastern intellectuals who helped shape postwar American foreign policy, especially with regard to what they perceived as the existential threat of communism. While John Foster, whom Eisenhower would eulogize as "one of the truly great men of our time,"[2] extended America's dominance through the projection of the soft power of diplomacy, Allen represented not just the ultimate spy who trafficked in the exploitation of secrets but also the feared enforcer from democracy's home office.

Largely invisible to the American public, the CIA emerged as one of the most powerful institutions in Washington, maneuvering in the shadows against the Soviets and frequently exceeding its intelligence-gathering mandate to become an instrument of covert foreign policy, staging coups in third-world countries including Iran, Guatemala, and the Congo. In an age when the epic clash between East and West trumped every other consideration, even the preservation of democracy, installing friendly governments was often justified as the price of blocking Soviet aggression and influence.

All too eager to cultivate his image as a power broker and that of the agency as an instrument of American will, Dulles once advised a journalist to think of the CIA as "the State Department for unfriendly countries."[3]

The case of Iran demonstrated how the imperatives of the struggle for Cold War advantage sometimes produced unintended consequences. By working with the British to covertly undermine a democratically elected government and reaffirm Mohammad Reza Pahlavi, the latest in a line of royals known as the Shah, as the country's all-powerful leader in 1953, the United States gained a steadfast ally. The coup would pay huge dividends through the years, but the Shah's hardline tactics eventually produced significant dissent, which helped foment the Islamic Revolution of 1979.

The battle for secrets was deeply embedded in the arc of the Cold War, starting with the act of espionage that enabled the Soviet Union to explode its first atomic device in August 1949, effectively launching the arms race. In 1953, American citizens Julius and Ethel Rosenberg were convicted and executed for passing Manhattan Project secrets to the Soviets, providing a widely publicized object lesson about the power of acquired knowledge to tilt the international order.

When the Pentagon began to worry about the possibility of a "bomber gap," the CIA was tasked with investigating the situation.

The resulting estimate was based on "knowledge of the Soviet aircraft-manufacturing industry and the types of aircraft under construction ... and included projections concerning the future rate of build-up on the basis of existing production rates and expected expansion of industrial capacity," Dulles recalled in his memoir.[4] The CIA estimated that the Soviets would produce hundreds of M-4s in the coming years.

The large contingent of American agents scattered across the world, using fake names and awash in spy-craft, routinely risked their lives to obtain vital intelligence about Soviet assets, capabilities, and plans. But human intelligence was not the answer to every problem.

Harry Truman wrestled with this dilemma as far back as 1947, authorizing a series of border-skirting missions in modified fighters, bombers, and even balloons, with mixed results. Several aircraft were lost at sea, and a Navy plane went down over Siberia. His successor could see the stakes rising. Eisenhower needed to know what the Soviets had, before they surprised him with something big.

The possibility of building a series of reconnaissance airplanes and routinely flying over the heart of the Soviet Union to photograph military assets arrived in the Oval Office several days after the midterm elections. This idea was first proposed by James Killian, the president of the Massachusetts Institute of Technology, who chaired a special commission that had been formed to consider the sort of weapons needed to protect the country from another Pearl Harbor, and Edwin Land, the founder of Polaroid.

No one played a more critical role in advocating for the aerial surveillance than Allen Dulles, who recalled, "Without a better basis than we had for gauging the nature and extent of the threat to us from surprise nuclear attack, our very survival might be threatened."[5] The man who sent operatives into dangerous situations and routinely pushed third-world leaders around was never cavalier about the projection of American power. In fact, after it was all over, Khrushchev paid Dulles a telling compliment: "Despite all of Dulles's blind hatred for communism, when it came to the possibility of war being unleashed, he remained a sober politician."[6]

After carefully studying the proposal and determining that the potential rewards far outweighed the risks, Dulles told the president: "Difficulties might arise out of these flights but we can live with them."[7]

For Eisenhower, a grandfatherly figure who reflected traditional America's middle-of-the-road impulses, the need to gather information about the Soviet military buildup cast a large shadow across his presidency. The rivalry would largely define his years in the White House. Shortly after entering office in January 1953, he had used the veiled threat of nuclear weapons to bring North Korea and Red China to the bargaining table, which resulted in an end to the hostilities. Still, the man who managed the enormous military and political challenge of the D-day landings, one of the pivot points of the century, proved a reluctant warrior in the White House. During those tense years, Ike moved forward with modernizing the country's nuclear forces, which led to a large number of tests in the Nevada desert and on isolated islands in the Pacific, and he partnered with Canada to form the North American Air Defense Command (NORAD), to provide constant monitoring of the distant skies. But he understood the horrors of war and was determined to avoid overt confrontation at all costs, especially with the Soviets, realizing that any direct collision between the superpowers could quickly spin out of control.

Understandably concerned that the Soviets might see the provocation of an invading spy plane as an act of war, Eisenhower approved the plan with one big condition: No missions were to be flown by military pilots. This directive was supported enthusiastically by Killian and Land, who had encouraged the CIA to take the lead, but frustrated the Air Force generals who had shepherded the initiative. Ike was adamant. In the event that one of the planes was ever shot down, he wanted the White House to have plausible deniability.

As a boy in Michigan, Clarence L. "Kelly" Johnson sometimes hiked to the top of a bluff with his younger brother, Clifford, to fly kites during a thunderstorm. "I think he thought he was Ben Franklin," Clifford said with a smile many years later.[8] "He learned a lot about how the wind worked." In time he would learn to harness the forces of nature for more ambitious purposes.

Educated as an engineer at the University of Michigan, Johnson happily accepted a job as a tooler, earning $83 per month during the depths of the Great Depression, just to get his foot in the door at the still-nascent Lockheed Aircraft Corporation, which had been bought out of bankruptcy by a group headed by Robert Gross. He quickly rose through the ranks, solving a critical aerodynamic problem with the Electra, one of the most successful airliners of the first era of commercial aviation, and designing the Hudson bomber for the British, famously reworking the blueprint to satisfy his clients during a lost weekend in a London hotel.

"Kelly was very smart and very driven," said Pete Law, one of his longtime engineers. "He was the sort of man who figured out a way to get things done, regardless of the obstacles."

By 1943, his P-38 Lightning was playing a significant role in the Pacific War, demonstrated by US Army Air Force Major Richard Bong's forty kills. With the military in desperate need of new and more powerful aircraft, the thirty-three-year-old Johnson cast a large shadow at the fast-growing aircraft company headquartered at the Burbank Airport.

With word leaking out about the Germans developing the world's first jet-powered aircraft, the Messerschmitt ME 262, which everyone recognized as a potential game changer in the skies over occupied Europe, Johnson landed a contract with the Pentagon to build America's answer. Understanding the stakes and the need for performance and secrecy, he convinced Robert Gross, the Lockheed chairman, to let him move into a new hangar, separated from the rest of the company. "I wanted a direct relationship between design engineer and mechanic and manufacturing ... without the delays and complications of intermediate departments," he said.[9] With black-out drapes covering the windows and complete authority vested in one man, the Advanced Development Projects division, which initially included a lean staff of twenty-three engineers and a small number of technicians and mechanics, quickly grew into Kelly Johnson's private empire. During a cryptic telephone conversation, a member of the staff made a joking reference to the rickety moonshine still in the popular *Li'l Abner* comic strip. Soon everyone in the know started referring to the secret hangar as the Skunk Works, which became the most fabled factory in aviation history.

Unencumbered by layers of management questioning his every decision, and mostly left alone by the Army Air Force, Johnson and his small team required only 143 days to design and manufacture the first XP-80, eventually to be known as the P-80 Shooting Star. It was a singular achievement, validated in the successful first flight by Tony LeVier, a onetime barnstormer from Minnesota who had dreamed of flying for one of the airlines but flunked his physical. He became a test pilot instead, destined to make twelve first flights for Lockheed, emerging as a legend in a shadowy world. "Tony was the greatest American test pilot of all time," said his friend and protégé Bob Gilliland, who in 1964 became the first man to fly the SR-71 Blackbird.

The risks associated with testing an unproven machine, especially as aviation negotiated the treacherous transition from propellers to jet engines, could be seen during one of LeVier's early flights. Moments after takeoff, the engine exploded and blew the tail off. "I thought I had bought the farm," LeVier said.[10] He somehow landed the craft but spent several weeks in the hospital, his spine severely injured. He was soon back at work, however, putting his life on the line in the next version of Johnson's new jet.

Various problems needed to be solved to make the P-80 reliable, including the especially menacing threat of compressibility, which Johnson had first encountered while building the earlier P-38 Lighting fighter. The violent buildup of air ahead of the plane, which could overwhelm a pilot's ability to maintain control or even break it into pieces, needed to be mitigated with various structural alterations and a strict adherence to flight procedures. Mastering air flow and the art of creating machines capable of sustaining such pressures represented foundational discoveries, building blocks to be applied in the design of more-sophisticated aircraft in the years ahead.

The F-104 Starfighter grew out of Johnson's discussions with pilots and other Air Force officers during a trip to the warfront in Korea but would not be ready until after the conflict ended. The sleek machine, which looked like a silver bullet, was a quantum leap in fighter design. At a time when the early success of the Soviet-made MiGs led to a conventional wisdom that the future belonged entirely to swept-wing aircraft, the counterintuitive Starfighter featured very small trapezoidal wings—the perfect size determined during excessive model testing at Edwards Air Force Base—and a compact fuselage. The result was an extremely fast airplane, the first fighter capable of reaching Mach 2—two times the speed of sound. Although the F-104 would have a checkered safety record, it was embraced not only by the US Air Force but also by a long list of

NATO and other Allied countries that made it their primary fighter in the middle years of the Cold War. While strengthening Johnson's ties to the Pentagon, the Starfighter also demonstrated his ability to push right up to the edge of what was possible with innovative ideas.

By consistently producing planes that flew faster and higher, with increasingly more complex requirements—driven by patriotism and a sense of mission that he once explained as, "be quick, be quiet, and be on time"—Johnson and his engineers dealt with the various consequences of extending the frontier, which tested their ability to find creative solutions. Johnson was well on his way to widespread acclaim as one of the greatest aviation designers ever to wield a slide rule. "The Leonardo da Vinci of American aviation," said Bob Gilliland, who tested the Starfighter. Hall Hibbard, one of his superiors, once admiringly said, "That damned Swede can actually see air!"[11]

The CIA needed just such a visionary to build its first spy plane.

Long before the solution to the problem arrived at the White House, Johnson was pushing his friends at the Pentagon to give him a crack at such a project. As Chris Pocock noted in his book *The U-2 Spyplane*, nearly one year before Eisenhower gave the go-ahead, on November 30, 1953, Jack Carter, a recently retired US Air Force colonel who worked in the planning department at Lockheed, addressed an "eyes only"[12] memo to his boss, Gene Root, a prominent figure who would eventually lead Lockheed's missile and space division. Outlining the sort of aircraft he believed the military needed to overfly the Soviet Union, he said he believed that a single-seat plane capable of attaining altitudes of between 65,000 and 70,000 feet would be able to avoid Soviet defenses until about 1960. This, as it turns out, was a rather-astute and prescient estimate. Urging his company to design and build such an aircraft, Carter told his superior, "The corporation would be directly contributing to the solution of one of the most vital and difficult problems" facing America's strategic defense.[13]

In December, according to the once-classified program logs he maintained, Johnson began discussions with the Air Force about modifying the F-104 design to "get the maximum possible altitude for reconnaissance purposes."[14] The final design, known as CL-282, retained some semblance of the Starfighter fuselage but looked like a very different airplane.

After Johnson's design was initially rejected as too radical by the Air Force, authority over the program passed to the CIA (although the Air Force would supply the engine), which was more receptive to the proposal. The key meeting took place over lunch in Washington on November 19, 1954, twelve days after Eisenhower's tentative approval of the project, with Johnson being grilled by Allen Dulles; one of his longtime deputies, Lawrence Houston; Secretary of the Air Force Harold Talbott; and Air Force General Donald Putt.

The discussion was frank. At one point, someone asked Johnson why he thought he could get such a cutting-edge airplane in the air within nine months when other defense contractors insisted such a timetable was too ambitious.

"He has proven it three times already!" Putt interjected, referring to the P-80, P-80A, and F-104.[15]

When the five men shook hands, Lockheed took a step into the shadowy world of espionage.

"I was impressed with the secrecy aspect and was told that I was essentially being drafted for the project," Johnson wrote in his diary.[16]

As the CIA took over security of the Skunk Works, sealing the perimeter with serious-looking plainclothes men carrying automatic weapons, and arranged to fund Lockheed's $35 million contract through a dummy company, Kelly selected a special team and finalized his blueprints for a revolutionary aircraft. He started searching for an isolated place to test it.

The CIA refused to consider Edwards Air Force Base, the massive facility in California's high desert where Chuck Yeager had broken the sound barrier in 1947, which transformed the once-dusty outpost into a center of test pilot activity; or the nearby Lockheed facility in Palmdale known as Plant 42. Both were secure, but not secure enough. The

Company, as the CIA was known, wanted a new base where its new plane and new pilots could disappear.

LeVier suggested an isolated patch of dirt in Nevada. At the controls of a small plane on April 12, 1955, he gave the decision makers, including Johnson and the CIA's Richard "Dick" Bissell Jr., their first glimpse of the area around a dry lakebed that was wide and straight enough for takeoffs and landings. "We didn't even get clearance," he said, "but flew over it, and within 30 seconds, we knew it was the place."[17]

Since it was located adjacent to the Nevada Test Site, where many of the early atomic bombs were exploded, with ominous mushroom clouds visible from the distant horizon, the land was not exactly prime real estate for civilian development. "Site was a dandy," Johnson wrote, "but will take much red tape to get cleared."[18] This was Bissell's problem, and he wasn't worried. The proximity to the nuclear proving ground would make it easy for the government to deem the land off limits without too many questions being asked.

Several weeks later, the base, located at an altitude of about 5,000 feet, began to take shape with a 6,000-foot runway, two large hangars, a control tower, several mobile homes, and a mess hall. Because everyone involved with the project needed a top secret security clearance and was forbidden to even acknowledge its existence, the place became known in the shorthand of the pilots, engineers, and spooks as the Ranch, Watertown, Groom Lake, or, Kelly's personal preference, Paradise Ranch. Only years later would it acquire its more mythical name, derived from the government grid system: Area 51.

"Whatever you called it, it was a pretty bleak place," recalled Jake Kratt, one of the first CIA pilots brought into the program.

Bissell knew very little about airplanes, but he now had his own very special air base. A Connecticut-born aristocrat who had taught economics at Yale, his alma mater, Bissell was pulled into government service just before Pearl Harbor. Near the end of the war, he was part of the American delegation to the Yalta Conference in the Crimea, where a dying President Franklin Roosevelt, looking very frail, ceded domination over much of Eastern Europe to the communists. In time, historians would mark the spoils party as the prelude to the Cold War. Bissell came away understanding, long before the blockade of Berlin and the Soviet Union's first atomic blast, that the wartime cooperation with the USSR was transactional and temporary. "I left Yalta knowing I would never believe Stalin to be an ally," he said.[19]

Work with the postwar Marshall Plan to rebuild Western Europe eventually led him to the CIA, where he became one of Dulles's most trusted aides, slipping easily into a covert world where he was expected to fight a war in the shadows while keeping the country's secrets. "There had to be a piece of him that was cold to do what he did," said his son, Richard Bissell III, who learned about his father's most famous accomplishments much later in life.[20] "When you are in the business of getting a foreign leader out of a job—or killed—you have to be." A devoted family man, he nevertheless compartmentalized his world, never letting his wife or children know exactly what he was up to when he was gone for weeks at a time. Like the rest of America, they had no clue about the U-2.

Headquartered at a front company operating out of a civilian office building on E Street near the Lincoln Memorial, and with complete authority over the CIA's first foray into aerial reconnaissance and the clout to pull whatever strings Johnson needed yanked, Bissell did not need to be told that the White House expected him to produce with the aircraft, working under the code name Aquatone. His career was riding on Johnson's ability to deliver on his bold promise.

Feeling enormous urgency, Johnson pushed his team relentlessly and leaned on contractors he saw falling behind schedule, especially the Pratt & Whitney people, who struggled to get the engine performing properly. "Terrifically long hours," he said in one of his program log entries.[21] "Everybody almost dead."

While working through various problems with the power plant, tooling, electronics, pressure suits, aerodynamics, part fabrication, and wind-tunnel testing, the Skunk Works team negotiated the long road from the start of design to first experimental flight in just 243 days. The confidence Bissell and his closest associates—the Air Force liaison officer, Colonel Ozzie Ritland, and the CIA's expert on the Soviet atomic program, Herbert Miller—gained in Johnson, which grew out of their close working relationship, allowed the agency to cede many details to him without micromanaging the Skunk Works, which significantly sped up the aircraft's development. They hit what Bissell once considered an "almost unrealistic date" for the first flight.[22]

Disassembled and loaded into a Douglas C-124 cargo plane for the short flight to the Ranch, the first U-2 was then reassembled in one of the new hangars. Some of the men involved with the program saw it up close for the first time on the runway.

The U-2 was a very different sort of aircraft. Powered at first by a J57 Pratt & Whitney engine, it featured very long wings, stretching more than 80 feet—nearly twice as long as the fuselage—which proved crucial in achieving the proper amount of lift to sustain flight at such a high altitude. When it was parked, the wings tended to droop, a feature exacerbated by a scaled-down set of landing gear—a so-called bicycle configuration, aided on takeoff with an extension known as a pogo, which dropped off as the plane left the ground. No one knew if the engine would operate effectively at such a high ceiling, or if it could cruise steadily enough to provide clear pictures from such an altitude. The whole project represented a step into the unknown.

To achieve the CIA's objectives, including carrying enough fuel to reach the necessary range, Johnson had been forced to sacrifice significant strength and maneuverability. Realizing that every pound saved on the structure represented another pound of fuel, they built the craft out of an ultra-light aluminum, which gave it the feel of a flying tin can, helping it rise to previously unattained heights. The wings sometimes vibrated during turbulence, one of the attributes that could make it difficult to handle. Landing could be tricky, because of the enormous drag caused by the unusual design. "Very light, very fragile, very flimsy," was LeVier's initial observation.[23]

On August 1, the team assembled for the unofficial first flight, which was scheduled as merely a taxi test, with LeVier at the controls to check the engine and the breaks. They experienced some last-minute trouble with the fuel, and after the pilot followed his boss's instructions to rev the engine to 70 knots, the plane leapt off of the dry lakebed and into the air, about 35 feet off the ground. It wanted to fly. LeVier had never known an aircraft capable of gaining flight at such a low speed, and he was simultaneously impressed and unnerved. "The lakebed was so smooth, I couldn't feel when the wheels were no longer touching," he recalled, adding, "I almost crapped."[24] When he touched down and slammed the breaks, both tires blew and the breaks caught fire, which brought out the fire truck.

Now fully acquainted with the lightness of the airplane, LeVier piloted the official first flight three days later, taking the U-2 to 8,000 feet in a driving rainstorm. On the radio with the boss, who was chasing in a C-47, he said the plane flew "like a baby buggy."[25]

Given the inclement weather, they decided to cut the flight short, but when he tried to land it nose first, it began porpoising, or bouncing violently, because of the unusual aerodynamics at play, and he pulled up. Johnson began to sweat, concerned about losing his precious prototype. It took LeVier two more passes, but he finally stuck the landing. He could see the U-2 was not going to be an easy plane to learn how to fly. (Ben Rich, one of Johnson's engineers and the man who would one day succeed him as the head of the Skunk Works, called the U-2 "a stern taskmaster [that was] unforgiving of pilot error or lack of concentration."[26]) But they were in business. That night, huddled in one of the hangars in a place that did not exist, they all drank themselves silly and took turns arm wrestling, celebrating their new baby.

A few weeks after committing to stay in the Air Force, Powers returned from a routine training flight in his F-84 and noticed his name typed onto a sheet of paper on the squadron bulletin board, ordering him to report to a certain major the next morning. His was one of several names. Naturally, he was curious, thinking, *What could this be about?*

The meeting left him with more questions than answers. He learned only that he and the other officers had been identified because they had all achieved exceptional pilot ratings and had been granted top secret security clearances; amassed a certain number of hours in a single-engine plane; and signed up for an indefinite period of service.

Like his colleagues, Powers was offered the chance to take another meeting, if he was interested. He was interested, although he found the whole business rather strange: "The Air Force was not in the habit of arranging outside job interviews for its officers."[27]

The next meeting took place at night, far from the base.

Arriving at the Radium Springs Inn, a motel on the outskirts of town, he knocked on the appropriate cottage door at the appointed time. A dark-haired, medium-build man who appeared to be in his thirties answered the door. He was wearing civilian clothes and was flanked by two other men similarly attired.

Feeling unsure of what he was walking into, the First Lieutenant said, "I was told to ask for a Mr. William Collins."

"I'm Bill Collins. You must be . . ."

Collins paused.

Finally, the Air Force man answered, "Lieutenant Powers."[28]

During the meeting, Powers learned that the men, who never said who they worked for, were recruiting pilots for a special mission that was "risky" but "important for your country."

Immediately intrigued by the opportunity, which stirred his patriotism and his sense of adventure, Frank was disappointed to learn that the assignment would require him to be overseas for eighteen months, without the ability to take his wife. He knew this would never work.

Nine months into his marriage, he was increasingly concerned about Barbara's state of mind. The behavior that had concerned him before their wedding day had not improved. His relatives had already been exposed to her excessive drinking.

Standing in the motel room, Frank doubted they could survive such an extended separation.

To his surprise, however, when Frank went home that night and told his wife what he was allowed to tell her, she was enthusiastic about the opportunity for her husband's advancement, especially when she learned it would pay him, while overseas, the incredible sum of $2,500 per month, about five times the median American income at the time. They talked about what they could do with the money, including buying a house and providing for the children surely to come in the years ahead.

Convinced by Barbara's assurances, Powers took another meeting at the motel, where Collins—not his real name—pulled back the veil on his operation: If the lieutenant passed the various tests, he would be working for the CIA, flying a brand-new top secret airplane that flew higher than any airplane ever produced. At the end of his assignment, he would be allowed to reenter the Air Force at a rank comparable to his peers, his time with the agency counting toward his military service.

His heart racing with excitement, Powers then heard the sentence that would define the rest of his life:

"Your main mission will be to fly over Russia."[29]

Not long after this meeting, he packed up his clothes and other belongings and moved out of the Albany house. After completing some paperwork, he was honorably separated from the Air Force, becoming a civilian once more. No one could know exactly what he was up to—not even his wife, although he was allowed to tell her that he was to make reconnaissance flights near the Russian border—and the boys at Turner were left to wonder, too caught up in their own lives to linger too much on one pilot's sudden vanishing act.

Toward the end of January 1956, Frank flew to Washington under an assumed name, complete with a fake identification card, and checked into the DuPont Plaza Hotel, feeling the full weight of his career choice. He was now entering the realm of spies.

By this time, Kelly Johnson and his dedicated team of skunks had routinely taken the U-2, code named Angel, above 70,000 feet, higher than any other aircraft in the world, which the experts believed made it invisible to Soviet radar and invulnerable to Soviet defenses. (Their various altitude records remained secret for years.) They had demonstrated a range of roughly 4,000 miles, which meant it could fly deep into the USSR and out again without needing to refuel.

With four versions of the plane in the air, nine more being assembled, and seven more on the drawing board, Lockheed and the CIA continued to work through various problems, including achieving the proper calibrations to ensure the engine, updated through several versions, and fuel pump worked effectively at such a high ceiling. The engine problems persisted and would take time to solve.

During one flight near the Mississippi River, Jake Kratt experienced a flame-out. Learning on the spot, he descended to around 30,000 feet—aware that trying to light in the thin air at maximum altitude could burn it out—and eventually he reignited the burner, only to suffer another engine failure. This time he had no luck getting the burner to start. Leaning on the plane's glider-mimicking characteristics, he allowed it to sail through the air for several hundred miles while heading toward the Ranch, before landing at an Air Force Base in New Mexico. Never one to leave a thing to chance, Dick Bissell, when informed of the impending touchdown, placed an urgent telephone call to the commander of the base, carefully instructing him to move the special aircraft to a remote part of the base and to secure it with a tarpaulin and an armed guard. No one was to see it.[30]

Unaware that six other pilots were already training at the Ranch, Powers was called to Collins's hotel room in Washington, where he joined several others for the big reveal. The agency man reached into his briefcase and pulled out a black-and-white photograph as the pilots moved in to study it closely. "It was a strange-looking aircraft, unlike any I had ever seen . . . [with a] remarkably long wingspan. . . . A jet, but with the body of a glider," Powers recalled.[31]

As Collins answered various questions, a table-top radio blared. Frustrated that he could not hear clearly, Powers reached over and turned it off. He was surprised when Collins, too, stopped making noise. At that time, Powers was still unaware of even the most basic spy-craft—until it dawned on him that the radio was filling the room with noise for a reason. Embarrassed, he reached over and turned the radio back on, and the spook continued his briefing.

Looking closely at the photograph, Powers liked one thing about the aircraft immediately. It was a single-seater, and like most fighter pilots, he preferred to fly alone.

Utilizing the fake name Francis G. Palmer, and a phony address, he flew all over the country for several months, undergoing extensive physicals at Lovelace Clinic in Albuquerque, New Mexico, as well as psychological tests, security clearances, and pressure-suit fittings. They tested him in the suit in a high-altitude chamber, attached various probes to his body, and stimulated a wide variety of physical reactions to make sure he was not prone to seizures, blacking out, or panic. None of the activities took place in a government building, because it was a completely black operation, and none of it could be traced back to Washington, in case they were being watched by the Soviets. They made him take a lie-detector test. They introduced him to various aspects of spy-craft, including the importance of avoiding noticeable patterns, to make it difficult for an operative to be tailed, which is the reason why a particular Company trip flew him and several others from Washington, DC, to St. Louis, Missouri, to Omaha, Nebraska, and back to St. Louis, before arriving in Albuquerque, New Mexico.

Eventually Frank wound up at the Ranch, where he was finally introduced to the airplane and began developing the skills he would need in the dangerous days ahead. He learned the U-2's various limits and idio-syncrasies, including the delicate hand required to land it, while carefully managing the wing angles, especially when confronted with high cross-winds. He saw how the plane kept climbing as the fuel burned off, and how at a certain altitude, he could pull the throttle all the way back to idle and it would remain at 100 percent power. He became acquainted with the dangerous intersection known as the "coffin corner."

"Down at sea level, you had a huge margin between the fastest the airplane could fly and the slowest it could fly, around 200 miles per hour," he said.[32] "But when you are at max altitude . . . your fastest and slowest speed come to a point where, you're flying it as slow as you possibly can without stalling and you're going almost as fast as you can without getting into severe buffeting. If you speed up, you're in trouble. If you slow down, you're in trouble. Takes a lot of attention and personal control."

Harry Andonian, who tested the plane for the Air Force, said, "That was one of the most difficult aspects of flying the U-2. The coffin corner could be very tricky. You had very little margin for error."

As part of the need to reduce weight, the Skunks Works had opted not to include an ejection seat, which meant if a pilot decided to abandon the aircraft, he would need to bail out.

High-altitude flight required the same sort of nylon pressure suits then being worn by the test pilots heading for the edge of space in experimental craft at Edwards; these suits were designed as a black project by the David Clark Company, maker of women's braziers. Because of the peculiarities of such high-altitude flight, pilots spent significant time learning to deal with the confinement.

Among the various features of the aircraft Powers learned to master was the self-destruct mechanism. In the event he ever felt the need to bail out, he knew exactly which two buttons to push to activate the explosive charge designed to destroy the camera. The secret of the U-2 needed to be protected at all costs.

During his training, Powers took several days off and traveled to Virginia to see the family. Stopping by to visit his new brother-in-law Jack Goff, he suggested they go hunting for rabbits.

"Found that kinda strange," Jack said. "I don't hunt rabbits and I never know of him to hunt rabbits."

Jack wondered if this was a desperate effort for his friend to reconnect to the place he had escaped.

Still, Jack grabbed two rifles and they headed out across the field behind his house, bound for the nearby woods.

At one point, when they were far from the house, all alone in the woods, Francis turned to him and said, "Jack, I want you to know something. If anything happens to me, I want you to know, I was doing what I thought was best for the most people. . . ."

Was he talking about his decision to leave Pound? Was he talking about something he had done?

Jack just nodded. "Okay," he said, perplexed but somehow understanding that his friend was speaking purposely in a riddle.

They stepped carefully through the tall grass, keeping a sharp eye out for rabbits.

About two weeks before LeVier began testing the U-2, in late July 1955, President Eisenhower traveled to Geneva, Switzerland, for a summit conference with Anthony Eden, the prime minister of the United Kingdom; Edgar Faure, the prime minister of France; and Nikolai Bulganin, the premier of the Soviet Union, who appeared on behalf of Khrushchev. (At this time, in the Soviet system, Khrushchev was not officially the head of state, but no one doubted who called the shots.) During the meeting, Eisenhower presented a radical proposal, calling on the world's two superpowers to exchange detailed maps of all military installations and to allow reconnaissance flights of each other's territory. The meeting was cordial, widely interpreted as the beginning of a thaw in the Cold War, but the so-called Open Skies policy was immediately dismissed by Khrushchev, who branded it nothing more than an "espionage plot."[33]

If the Soviets had taken up the White House on this idea, the U-2 might never have been needed and Francis Gary Powers's life most certainly would have taken a very different turn.

Eleven months later, the CIA was prepared to open the skies without Khrushchev's permission.

Not content to simply be invisible, someone in Washington decided it would be better for the U-2 to hide in plain sight. When the first detachment of planes and pilots were deployed to the joint US Air Force and Royal Air Force base Lakenheath in England in May, the National Advisory Committee for Aeronautics (NACA), the forerunner of the National Aeronautics and Space Administration (NASA), issued a press release announcing a program to conduct weather research with the new plane, whose existence had been a secret. The U-2 was now the center, instead, of an elaborate lie. When he heard the news, Johnson was livid, writing in his journal, "A stupid shambles!"[34] Fortunately the release generated no attention.

Despite the British initially agreeing to host the first operational U-2 wing, known as Detachment A, the deal became a casualty of an embarrassing attempt at espionage when a British frogman was caught spying on a Soviet ship. Prime Minister Eden and his cabinet got cold feet about the American espionage about to commence from their airspace, and retracted their approval, necessitating a hasty relocation to the NATO base in Wiesbaden, West Germany, where Chancellor Konrad Adenauer gave his stamp of approval.

Around this time, twenty-year-old pilot Michael Betterton found himself volunteered into a classified assignment. Young, unattached, and eager to chase some adventure, he didn't ask many questions. When he reported to Wiesbaden, the colonel in charge said, "Nice to meet you, lieutenant. Welcome to the CIA!"

Betterton flashed a puzzled look. "What's the CIA?"

Growing up in the agricultural community of Visalia, in California's San Joaquin Valley, Betterton had never heard of America's spy agency. Over the next seventeen months, as a support pilot mostly flying the U-2 pilots and agency leaders around the continent in a C-54, he became deeply involved in his country's biggest secret.

"It was unbelievable to me that I was being swept up in this life," Betterton said. "Of course, I couldn't tell my family or friends."

On June 20, 1956, Carl Overstreet, a Virginia native who had been stationed at Turner, took off from Wiesbaden and headed east. Within minutes he was flying a surveillance mission through East Germany, Poland, and Czechoslovakia, testing the new camera and electronic intelligence systems. Twelve days later, Jake Kratt and Glen Dunaway flew similar missions through Iron Curtain countries. All returned safely without incident.

Overflying the Soviet Union would require presidential approval, and as the Company men waited for the "go" signal, the delay was colored in irony.

In the wake of the Open Skies rebuff, General Nathan Twining, the US Air Force chief of staff, who would later be appointed chairman of the Joint Chiefs of Staff, happened to be in Moscow as a guest of the Soviet military. During an air show, he was allowed to witness a formation of M-4 bombers, whose existence had launched the chain reaction leading to the U-2 overflights.

On July 4, when Hervey Stockman soared toward the stratosphere and headed into the rising sun, eventually crossing the border into the USSR, the Cold War veered off in a dangerous new direction. No one could predict the end game with any certainty.

This was somehow a step beyond covert agents utilizing phony documents, tiny cameras, bugging devices, blackmail, and propaganda in the perpetual search for secrets and leverage.

One operative could easily be disavowed, but if anything should go wrong, it would be difficult for Washington to explain an aircraft so clearly designed for high-altitude reconnaissance, especially in the event that the plane and its high-tech spy pilot, wielding a camera like a bayonet, were ever blasted out of the sky. Often displaying ambivalence about the program, which on one level violated his beliefs about the way civilized nations should act toward one another during peacetime, Eisenhower once conceded, "Nothing would make me ask Congress to declare war more quickly than a violation of our airspace by Soviet aircraft."[35]

Stockman, a native of New Jersey who had flown P-51 Mustangs in World War II, penetrated deep into Soviet territory on his first flight. The resulting photographic intelligence, which began to lay a foundation for a deeper understanding of Soviet capabilities, was greeted with tremendous enthusiasm by Eisenhower and Dulles. Stockman landed safely. But one thing did not go according to plan, and Johnson was not happy.

"Well, boys," he told senior members of his Skunk Works team. "Ike got his first picture postcard. . . . But goddamn it, we were spotted about as soon as we took off. . . ."[36]

Contrary to CIA assurances, the U-2 was not invisible to Soviet radar at 70,000 feet. From the earliest flights, the Soviets carefully tracked the incursions. Sometimes MiGs were dispatched. "You could see the contrails beneath," Kratt recalled. "But we felt reasonably safe, because we didn't think they could reach us." The latest model, the MiG-19, could climb no higher than about 55,000 feet, well below the U-2's maximum ceiling.

Enraged, Khrushchev launched a protest with the American government, but he was powerless to prevent such violations of his territory. He said nothing publicly.

In August, before shipping out for his overseas deployment as part of the Detachment B, or Detachment 10-10, to the Incirlik Air Force Base in Adana, Turkey, Powers made a trip to see the family in Pound. Following orders, he said he would be conducting weather experiments, which his sister Jan thought odd. "Why do you have to go all the way over there to study the weather?" she asked, teasing him. "We have weather here."

Beyond the thrill of handling such an innovative aircraft and flying off to the edge of the sky, Powers was driven by the desire to do something patriotic for his country. Profoundly marked by the experience of living through World War II, he understood how fragile freedom could be. It had always bugged him that he had not made it to combat in Korea. Now he saw the struggle with the Soviets in the starkest terms and felt fortunate to be a part of an effort considered so vital to the nation's security.

Sometimes he flashed back to those early meetings with William Collins and how his life pivoted toward another reality.

"All my life I've wanted to do something like this," he had told the agency man.[37]

All his life he would live with the consequences.

While stationed in Turkey, Powers and the other pilots in the "weather detachment" lived in small trailers on a corner of the base, far from the regular US Air Force flight line. Some enterprising aviators attached lean-tos, which they called camel bars. Security was tight. They often wandered into town and rubbed elbows with the local Turks, sometimes venturing off into the countryside and on toward the pristine Mediterranean beaches on motorcycles. They hunted ducks, snorkeled, drank beer. "Frank was a real outgoing guy ... happy-go-lucky when he wasn't flying," recalled camera technician John Birdseye, who sometimes bowled with Powers and his wife at a primitive bowling alley in a modified Quonset hut. "Like all those pilots, [when it was time for a flight] he was a businessman with a mission."

In the fall of 1956, Detachment A was reassigned to Giebelstadt Air Force Base in Bavaria. Unlike bustling Wiesbaden, the tiny base at Giebelstadt, which had housed one of the few squadrons of ME 262 jets at the end of World War II, was isolated and easy to camouflage. It became a perfect hiding place for the U-2.

At the start of Powers's overseas assignment, Barbara moved in with her mother in Georgia, following through on their original plan, so they could save money for a house. But she became restless and eventually moved to Europe to be closer to him, in violation of CIA wishes, apparently living for a time in Paris. Michael Betterton liked Frank and could see his wife exerting influence that undermined him with his superiors. "[Powers] spent a lot of time with us because he would come up for a while and then go on to see her," Betterton said. "I know [the agency security people] were not happy about [her presence in Europe] and talked to him about it." Barbara eventually moved to Athens, landing an office job at an Air Force base, which allowed Frank to visit frequently.

With Soviet agents prowling around looking for details on the program, Barbara's personal weakness represented a glaring vulnerability.

"Barbara was a security risk," said Joe Murphy, who worked as a security specialist for the CIA, and had known Frank since the early days at the Ranch. "The fear was that she would lose control of herself out in public . . . draw attention to herself . . . blow the whole operation."

During a trip back to the United States with her husband, when they visited Pound, Barbara got drunk and starting spouting off about her frustration at not being able to live with her husband. "They don't want me telling what I know," she said, which sounded like a threat to members of the family, who didn't know what they didn't know.

Struggling to control his wife, Frank began thinking about divorce.

Less than two months into Powers's deployment, Egyptian President Abdel Nasser nationalized the Suez Canal, sparking a major confrontation with Britain, France, and Israel, with the Soviets threatening to intervene on the side of the Egyptians. In his first mission, Powers was dispatched to the area. His trip revealed a rapid buildup of British and French forces around the island nation of Cypress, confirming Paris's duplicity. President Eisenhower felt blindsided.[38]

A succession of U-2 flights out of Incirlik gave the White House a bird's-eye view of the unfolding invasion, though only a select circle knew the source of the intelligence. Saber-rattling by Khrushchev threatened to spilt the Western alliance over the issue, but, ultimately, Washington believed that the desire by two colonial powers to assert their dominion was not worth risking World War III. Eisenhower pressured his allies to withdraw, a capitulation which greatly diminished Britain and France.

The U-2's role would not be declassified for years, but the CIA's ability to look down from the top of the world and see through the fog of war was rife with symbolism.

Some weeks later in November 1956, Powers made his first flight over the Soviet Union.

Reflecting on the experience many years later, he said, "You were apprehensive of the unknown. It was the not knowing that got to you. Were they even aware that I was up there?"[39]

He did not see any signs of jets or missiles.

Even though it was sent out infrequently, the U-2 was quickly winning big fans at the CIA and the Pentagon.

In early 1957, General Curtis LeMay, the firebrand head of Strategic Air Command (SAC), decided to deactivate his F-84 wing, which left Tony Bevacqua, Powers's onetime roommate, open for a new assignment. A superior asked him, "How'd you like to fly something I can't tell you a darned thing about?" Intrigued, he immediately replied in the affirmative, thinking that if he rejected the opportunity, he might face a fate worse than death for a fighter pilot: transfer to a bomber squadron.

After several weeks of physical and psychological tests at Wright-Patterson Air Force Base in Dayton, Ohio, and being fitted for a pressure suit in New Haven, Connecticut, he remained in the dark about his new aircraft. "With the suit, I knew it was going to be a high flier," he recalled.

Minutes after stepping out of an Air Force transport plane at March Air Force Base in Riverside, California, he was directed onto another plane with civilian markings, joining several other Air Force pilots. About an hour later, the plane, piloted by Lockheed test pilot Ray Goudy, landed in a remote area. A member of the ground's crew yelled, "Welcome to Groom Lake."

Emboldened by the CIA's success with the U-2, the Air Force was forming its own squadron.

"Holy cow," Bevacqua thought when he saw the U-2 for the first time, starting the training that would have him soloing in a matter of weeks. "What is that?"

"It sure looked odd," he recalled.

At this time, he was completely unaware that his friend who had disappeared was flying the same aircraft.

In his proposal to the president, Edwin Land, the founder of Polaroid, had spoken very optimistically about the potential of the reconnaissance program to peel back the veil shrouding Soviet capabilities. Within a few months, he was proven correct. The photographs taken by the U-2 allowed the CIA to map vast areas of the USSR, bringing many once-hidden military installations into view.

Like various other aspects of the aircraft, the cameras were designed especially for the project. They were meticulously honed to reduce weight and keep working throughout a long flight, and they utilized a Mylar film recently perfected by Kodak. "The cameras required a lot of attention, especially the shutters, which often stuck shut," explained Birdseye, who learned the peculiarities produced by dramatic changes in temperature and other influences and how to work the problem. Once the film was rushed into the hands of the skilled interpreters, a wealth of previously hidden knowledge about the closed society informed the president, whose desk was often overflowing with large black-and-white prints, demonstrating another important discovery.

Once the evidence began to accumulate, the agency reached an important conclusion: There was no "bomber gap."

The Cold War took an unexpected turn when Jimmy Bozart dropped his change.

While making his collections one day in the summer of 1953, the paperboy fumbled his money onto a staircase. When he reached down to pick it up, he noticed one of the nickels was split in half, revealing a hollow opening. Upon closer inspection, he found what was later determined to be a tiny piece of microfilm, containing a coded message, which his father turned over to a New York City police officer. Eventually the nickel wound up in the possession of the Federal Bureau of Investigation, which determined that Bozart had stumbled onto a Soviet spy ring.[40]

Four years later, the clue helped lead the FBI to a Brooklyn artist who was in actuality a KGB agent engaged in espionage concerning America's nuclear arsenal.

Colonel Rudolf Ivanovich Abel, the most important Soviet spy to be apprehended since the Rosenbergs, denied everything. He was quickly convicted and sentenced to thirty years in a federal penitentiary. He might have been executed, if not for the clever defense waged by his attorney, James B. Donovan, who argued: "It is possible that in the foreseeable future an American of equivalent rank will be captured by Soviet Russia or an ally. . . . At such time an exchange of prisoners through diplomatic channels could be considered to be in the best interests of the United States. . . ."[41]

The intense media coverage of the trial scarcely mentioned the possibility of an exchange, which seemed far-fetched.

Even as the Abel case cast a temporary spotlight on the battle for secrets, giving Americans another reason to be distrustful and fearful of the Soviets, a tiny aluminum ball emitting an ominous beep proved even more alarming. On October 4, 1957, when the USSR launched Sputnik, the world's first artificial satellite, the technological superiority it demonstrated made Americans feel vulnerable. Soon the United States would join the space race, but it was the anxiety regarding a potential military application of the rocketry that cast such a distressing pall upon one of the century's greatest scientific achievements.

Within months, the Soviets announced the development of their first intercontinental ballistic missiles, which were capable of delivering nuclear weapons launched from the USSR by remote control. "Now the bomber and fighter can go into museums," Khrushchev crowed.[42] American politicians began talking about a "missile gap," which eventually signaled new activity for the U-2.

The Soviets were desperate to learn about the U-2.

The same month Sputnik was launched, while driving to work at Giebelstadt, where his cover job was overseeing the base gym, First Lieutenant Betterton saw a suspicious car parked on the side of the road near the end of the runway. With a U-2 surveillance mission scheduled to launch later that morning, on a flight path that would take it right over the car, and aware that the KGB was snooping around trying to find their secret base, the agency pilot, dressed in his US Air Force uniform, turned right and headed for trouble.

Pulling up next to sedan, where he saw two burly men wearing heavy overcoats, he tried to engage them in conversation.

"Are you lost?" he said in English.

They grunted but didn't answer, so he pressed on.

"This is a dead-end road. It doesn't go anywhere. . . ."

"Can I guide you back to the highway?"

It was possible the mystery men were there to commit an act of sabotage, but, more likely, they were stationed near the end of the runway to take photographs of the secret plane.

Concerned about what the Soviet agents might do if he left them alone long enough to alert agency security, Betterton, who was unarmed, decided the best course of action was to annoy them. So he kept talking. Finally, after about ten minutes, they gave up and drove away.

Not long after, the security chief thanked him for his actions and chided him for taking such a foolish chance with two men who might have killed him. The CIA was starting to make arrangements to shut down its operation at Giebelstadt and transfer most of the pilots to Incirlik. (Some eventually wound up with the new Detachment C in Atsugi, Japan.) The risk of KGB surveillance in West Germany was now too great. The disbandment of Detachment A would make it much more difficult for the

Company to reach the interior of the Soviet Union, which significantly increased the risks associated with the overflights.

Jake Kratt wound up in Incirlik, where he lived two trailers down from Powers. "That's when I first met Frank," said Kratt, who never became a close friend but remembered him as a "a good pilot . . . [who was] like the rest of us, focused on doing his job."

In 1958, at the end of his first eighteen-month deployment, Powers signed a new contract with the CIA and obtained permission to move his wife to Turkey. They decided to give it another try.

As the space race emerged as yet another proxy for the Cold War, the leaders of the superpowers were at least starting to communicate. During a visit to a model American home exhibit in Moscow, Vice President Richard Nixon, while lingering in the kitchen, engaged in an impromptu televised debate with Premier Khrushchev about the relative merits of capitalism and communism. The two politicians were equally forceful but pleasant.

Not once did Khrushchev talk about "burying" the West, avoiding the violent verb that had caused a walkout of US-allied ambassadors in 1956. (The leader was talking about industrial progress, not military action, but the distinction was largely lost in translation.) Around this time, during an address to the Twentieth Congress of the Communist Party, Khrushchev angered hard-liners in his own country by denouncing some of Stalin's more brutal tactics, which he characterized as a "deviation" from Marxism-Leninism. But 1956 was also the year of the Hungarian Revolution. When an uprising ignited by student protesters threatened the communist government in Budapest, Soviet tanks rolled in and crushed the revolt, demonstrating Moscow's determination to maintain its iron grip on the Eastern bloc.

Two months after the so-called Kitchen Debate, in September 1959, the Soviet leader visited the United States. He was alternately charming (while riding on a train; chatting with supermarket shoppers; visiting factory workers; schmoozing with Hollywood stars, including Frank Sinatra; full of smiles and back-slapping) and confrontational (when he felt he had been insulted by an anti-communist civic leader at a banquet in Los Angeles).

"Our rockets are on the assembly lines already!" he thundered from the dais, as the room of dignitaries turned deadly quiet. "Our rockets are on the launching pads! It is a question of war or peace."[43]

He was not smiling.

When security concerns caused him to be turned away at Disneyland, he started cracking jokes but was clearly enraged at the thought that he could be locked out of the home of Mickey Mouse.

The first state visit to the United States by a Soviet leader helped set the stage for a planned summit meeting in Paris in May 1960. Khrushchev also invited Eisenhower to Moscow later in his final full year in the White House. Hopes for achieving a new era of harmony were tempered, however, by a brewing crisis in Berlin.

Increasingly concerned about the Soviets' progress in developing and deploying their ICBMs, which had escaped the view of the U-2s, several key advisors, including Dulles and Bissell, encouraged Eisenhower to approve additional overflights in the winter and spring of 1960. As usual, he was conflicted. By this point, the U-2 had secured a treasure trove of intelligence, making Washington incredibly knowledgeable about Soviet capabilities. Why push their luck? The CIA and Kelly Johnson were already at work on a new spy plane, a strange-looking bird offering the promise of much-faster speeds and higher altitude, along with a vastly reduced radar cross-section. The age of the spy satellite was also dawning, offering reconnaissance photographs from the edge of space. Perhaps they should wait until these next-generation vehicles became operational.

With Paris looming, and with many experts believing it was only a matter of time before Soviet fighters and surface-to-air missiles achieved the range to shoot a U-2 out of the sky, Eisenhower worried about the potential impact of a lost aircraft "when we were engaged in apparently sincere deliberations."[44] What if the Soviets got lucky, he wondered, and made him look duplicitous?

Khrushchev's recent silence concerning the incursions may have contributed to a false state of security, but as Dulles later said, "Since he had been unable to do anything about the U-2, he did not wish to advertise the fact of his impotence to his own people."[45]

Ultimately, Eisenhower, believing the need to gather the intelligence and gain leverage for the summit trumped the potential risks, approved additional overflights to work the missile problem. After a successful mission on April 9, which the Soviets tracked and tried to shoot down, and with the Paris summit scheduled to commence on May 16, the president ordered a final deadline: One last flight, but under no circumstances was an incursion to take place after May 1.

When the agency determined the objectives and decided to conduct the flight out of the Incirlik-based detachment, Frank Powers was selected to fly the mission and began making preparations.

Because he would be flying deeper than ever into denied air space—totaling about nine hours—Washington had arranged to launch the mission out of a base in Peshawar, Pakistan, roughly 2,000 miles closer to the Soviet border.

While packing for the trip during the last week of April, Frank struggled to put Barbara out of his mind. Living in the same trailer had not affected her drinking. Several days earlier, while partying with some of the other pilots and wives, she had stumbled on the dance floor and broken her leg, necessitating a cast. It was just the latest indication that his wife suffered from a serious problem, which he did not know how to handle. He tried to put it out of his mind. He would deal with her when he got back.

After he arrived in Pakistan, the flight was scrubbed twice—once because of intense cloud cover over the target zones, which would have rendered the U-2 camera useless—leaving him to kill time in the hangar reading and playing poker with members of the large support crew that had traveled from Incirlik. It concerned him to learn that his usual plane was being temporarily grounded because of routine maintenance issues.

This caused him to use an aircraft with a history of mechanical problems, one of which had previously necessitated an emergency landing in Japan.

With the deadline looming, "everybody was eager to get in the air, including Frank," said Jake Kratt, one of the backup pilots on hand in case Powers became ill.

On the night before the flight, Frank slept fitfully on a hangar cot. Not long after his 2 a.m. wake-up call on May 1, he started discussing the weather and his variety of landing options with his commanding officer, Air Force Colonel William M. Shelton, who surprised him with a question. "Do you want the silver dollar?"[46]

Since the early days of the program, U-2 pilots had been given the option to carry along a specially designed poison pin hidden inside a silver dollar. Once dislodged from the coin, the pin could be used to prick the skin, causing death by asphyxiation. Like many of his contemporaries, Powers routinely declined to carry the suicide device. This time, however, facing the longest flight so far over the Soviet Union, Frank made a snap decision and slipped the dollar into the pocket of his outer flight suit.

After going through his two-hour preflight breathing ritual, isolation in a pure oxygen environment to prepare for the long flight and prevent the debilitating ailment known as "the bends," Powers, wearing his pressure suit and helmet, carefully stepped up the ladder with the assistance of a colleague and into the plane, locking into his seat around 5:20 a.m., with departure scheduled for 6. The sun had been up for nearly an hour, and it was already very hot. To try to give his friend a little shade, one of the other pilots took off his shirt and held it over the cockpit.

Because of the unusual situation, President Eisenhower needed to personally approve the flight. As six o'clock came and went without word from the White House, and the morning sun turned the open cockpit into an oven, sweat soaked through Frank's long johns and rolled down his face.

Chapter Three

MAYDAY

The warning signs were flashing.

In arguing for what became the April 9, 1960, flight, code named Square Deal, to originate from Pakistan, Air Force Colonel William Burke expressed the opinion that penetrating the USSR from this area presented "a reasonable chance of escaping detection by the Soviet air defense system."[1] On this, Burke, the acting director of the Development Projects Division, was proven wrong. Soon after U-2 pilot Bob Ericson crossed into Soviet territory, he was tracked by Soviet radar, ringing alarm bells throughout the defense establishment.

Despite seeing contrails of MiGs beneath him, Ericson successfully completed his mission and secured evidence of Soviet ICBM deployment near Plesetsk, about 700 miles north of Moscow. The gamble paid off. Khrushchev was especially angered by the timing of the flight, since preparations for the summit were already underway. He watched with frustration, believing his military bungled several opportunities to shoot the U-2 out of the sky.[2] He said nothing, which emboldened the White House. "This was virtually inviting us to repeat the sortie," recalled George Kistiakowsky, Eisenhower's science advisor.[3]

For nearly four years, the CIA had prowled the skies above the USSR with impunity.

But the steady improvement in Soviet defenses was reaching critical mass.

"By the beginning of 1960," Bissell conceded many years later, "we were all growing concerned about the U-2's future and there was considerable discussion of how long it might be before the Soviets developed the capability to shoot one down."[4]

Especially troubling was the technical progress embodied in the SA-2 missile, rapidly being deployed across the Soviet Union. In a confidential assessment dated March 14, 1960, Burke advised Bissell, "The SA-2 Guideline has a high probability of successful intercept at 70,000 feet providing that detection is made in sufficient time to alert the site."[5] This was a key proviso. While the SA-2 had apparently achieved the ability to reach the U-2's maximum altitude, its effective firing zone and maneuverability remained unknown, turning the possibility of a direct hit into a complicated math problem. The CIA's analysts remained skeptical of the Soviet guidance systems, which gave the pilots a measure of reassurance.

"Because of the speed of the missile and the extremely thin atmosphere, it was almost impossible to make a connection," Powers said. "This did not eliminate the possibility of a lucky hit."[6]

In the context of a clear linkage between early warning and missile danger, a memorandum written by Burke on April 26 reflected the elevated level of risk: "Experience gained as a result of Operation Square Deal indicates that penetration without detection from the Pakistan/ Afghanistan area may not be as easy in the future as heretofore."[7]

The policy makers in Washington knew they were playing a very dangerous game by sending Francis Gary Powers into this vortex.

Like the other pilots, Powers began to worry about the growing potential of Soviets defenses. Discussing the situation many years later, he said, "Four years is a long time. . . . They know you've been flying over their country for four years. . . . I figured [if the roles were reversed] we in this country would be working night and day to develop something to try to stop [such incursions]. It's getting to about the point where you can expect things to happen."[8]

One of the primary reasons the agency pushed for an additional flight before the deadline was to get another look at the Plesetsk facility, to judge the Soviet ICBM progress. Aware that the angle of the sun in the northern latitudes could distort the U-2 pictures starting in midsummer, Bissell feared, "If a flight could not be conducted [between April and July], the opportunity would be lost for an entire year."[9]

Because telephone communications between Washington and Peshawar could not be secured, the White House arranged to transmit the president's order through Morse code early on the morning of Sunday, May 1. While Powers sweated in his pressure suit, believing more strongly with each passing minute that the flight would be canceled, Colonel Shelton waited impatiently with an aide inside a radio van on the taxiway. Due to technical problems likely related to atmospherics, they were unable to retrieve the signal on the assigned frequency.

Eventually tuning to another channel, they picked up a message, slightly truncated from what they were expecting: HBJGO. Convinced that this was the signal they had been waiting for, even though several letters were missing, Shelton stepped out of the van and ran over to the U-2 to deliver the news: The White House had given Powers clearance to fly Mission 4154, code named Grand Slam, over the Soviet Union.[10]

It was around 6:20 when a member of the crew pulled the ladder away and slammed the canopy shut. The pilot then locked it from the inside. As Powers taxied on to the runway and carefully guided the U-2C, model 360, into the air, the J75/P13 engine roared with a distinctive whine. He never lost the thrill of hearing the familiar sound.

Quickly climbing toward his assigned altitude and switching into autopilot for his twenty-eighth reconnaissance mission, he headed toward Afghanistan and initiated a single click on the radio. Seconds later, he heard a single click as confirmation. This was his signal to proceed as scheduled, in radio silence.

Determined to pack as much surveillance as possible into one flight, Powers was scheduled to cross over the Hindu Kush range of the Himalayas and into the southern USSR, passing over a 2,900-mile swath of Soviet territory, from Dushambe and the Aral Sea, to the rocket center of Tyuratam, and on to Sverdlovsk, where he would head northwest, reaching the key target of Plesetsk before turning even farther northwest, toward the Barents Sea port of Murmansk. Exiting to the north, he was to land in Bodo, Norway, where a recovery team was waiting to transport the U-2 and secure the pilot. In the case of an emergency, such as running low on fuel, he was authorized to take a shortcut into the neutral nations of Sweden or Finland, which would be sure to cause complications for Washington. But as Shelton remarked, "Anyplace is preferable to going down in the Soviet Union."[11]

The Soviets were especially dangerous if they knew the U-2 was coming. According to an official protest subsequently lodged with the US government by the foreign minister of Afghanistan, for violating their sovereign airspace on the way north, the Soviets provided an early warning of the spy plane's incursion.[12]

While Powers took flight, much of official Washington remained in weekend mode, including the president, who was at rainy Camp David. The inclement weather ruined his plan to play golf, although he eventually worked in some skeet shooting and bowling with his granddaughter.[13]

The Company man dispatched to welcome Powers to Norway, Stan Beerli, the chief of the operations section, expected to see him early in the evening, Bodo time. He assumed his phone was tapped and he was being watched. Like every operative in the field, he was provided a cover story and a way to communicate with the home office in code. When Powers arrived safely, Beerli was instructed to call a certain man in Oslo and tell him they had a great party the previous night.[14]

After flying into the thin, cold air of the stratosphere, Frank was no longer sweating in his pressure suit but he felt his pulse quicken. He always felt a bit uneasy crossing into the USSR. Nine hours was a long time to be in the air, nearly all of it over enemy territory, and the pilot realized he had never been more vulnerable.

Because his sextant—a device used to measure distance based on the angular width between two objects—had been set for a 6 a.m. departure, rendering all of the values off by nearly a half hour, Frank would have to rely heavily on his compass and clock to navigate. For about the first 90 minutes, he encountered heavy cloud cover, which made it more difficult to stay on course.

About the time the sky below turned into a blanket of blue, he saw something in the distance: the contrail of a single-engine jet aircraft, headed in the opposite direction, at supersonic speed. Soon he saw another contrail, heading toward him, at supersonic speed. He assumed it was the same plane, having turned around to follow him.

"I was sure now they were tracking me on radar," he said, relieved by the enormous distance, which reflected the jet's inability to approach the U-2's altitude.[15] "If this was the best they could do, I had nothing to worry about."

The scramble to deal with the invader eventually reached the Kremlin. It was still early morning Moscow time when Premier Khrushchev's telephone rang.

When Rodion Malinovsky, the Soviet defense minister, told him about another American spy plane thundering through the skies and headed toward Sverdlovsk, he flashed back to the "white hot fury" he had experienced during the previous overflight.[16]

After much internal debate, particularly with Foreign Minister Andre Gromyko, who recommended a formal protest and even prepared a preliminary draft to send to the American ambassador, Khrushchev decided to remain quiet. In explaining his rationale to the Presidium of the Central Committee, he said, "What's the sense of [protesting]? The Americans [are] acting this way to emphasize our powerlessness. . . . [Protesting] only encourages their arrogance. What we have to do is shoot those planes down!"[17]

Three weeks later, after forcing an internal investigation into the various failures that he believed had crippled the Soviet response, Khrushchev told Malinovsky: "You must do your very best! Give it everything you've got and bring that plane down!"

After telling his leader that a new SA-2 battery was stationed along the plane's apparent route, Malinovsky said, "We have every possibility of shooting the plane down if our anti-aircraft people aren't gawking at the crows!"[18]

After switching on the camera while flying over the Tyuratam Cosmodrome, the launch site for Soviet space shots which had been confirmed and extensively photographed in previous U-2 missions, Powers worked through a slight course correction and proceeded north, eventually getting a nice view of the snow-capped Ural Mountains, the geographic dividing line between Europe and Asia, to his left. Passing various landmarks, he made notations for his debriefing. When his autopilot malfunctioned—a problem considered significant enough to consider aborting a mission—he switched it off and began flying the plane manually. The choice to head back or proceed was his, but since he was more than 1,300 miles into Soviet territory, he made the fateful decision to keep going. He had gone too far to turn back now.[19]

Almost four hours into the flight, just southeast of Sverdlovsk, while recording figures in his flight log, he felt a thump. A violent shockwave reverberated through the aircraft as a bright-orange flash lit up his world.

"My God," he said to himself. "I've had it now."[20]

Project Aquatone had already endured a string of mishaps claiming several lives.

At the Ranch on August 31, 1956, CIA pilot Frank Grace crashed and died during a nighttime launch, after becoming disoriented in the dark.[21] "He was seen using [a] flashlight in cockpit prior to take-off," Johnson noted in his journal.[22] "A definite no-no."

On April 4, 1957, Lockheed test pilot Bob Sieker lost control of the U-2 prototype at a high altitude.[23] He tried to make it back to base but crashed in the desert, dying from wounds sustained while parachuting to the ground. The subsequent investigation determined that Sieker had experienced a flame-out and that his protective faceplate had blown off his mask, causing him to be "in a bad way from hypoxia."[24]

By pushing so far into the distant skies, toward a multitude of colliding dangers, the team behind the so-called Dragon Lady wrestled with various problems related to oxygen, including a strict adherence to the "pre-breathing" regimen, and experimenting with various changes to the life-support system. They eventually added an ejection seat, which increased weight but helped keep several pilots alive after high-altitude jumps.

Without a trainer or a simulator, catastrophic emergencies were accepted as the price of developing a cutting-edge aircraft. Some pilots managed to land wounded planes or bail out successfully. Others paid the ultimate price.

"It was a dangerous time," said Tony Bevacqua, who worked as an instructor pilot at Laughlin. "You had a new aircraft and new pilots trying to learn how to fly it. Sometimes things went wrong. The U-2 wasn't very tolerant of certain mistakes."

The carnage was not limited to the U-2 pilots. It took a large team of Lockheed personnel, contractors, and spooks to bring Aquatone to life, necessitating a steady procession of C-54 transports between March Air Force Base, Burbank, and the Ranch. Many of the civilians lived in Southern California and commuted daily or weekly. During inclement weather on November 17, 1955, one of the flights failed to clear Mt. Charleston, near Las Vegas. "A very stupid weather crash," Johnson said.[25] All fourteen project employees were lost—including Lockheed engineers Rod Kreimendahl and Dock Hruda—along with all five members of the flight crew. The CIA quickly dispatched a team to secure any top secret documents among the remains and concocted a cover story to protect the secrecy of the U-2 program.[26]

Losing a U-2 over the Soviet Union was the nightmare scenario, and Francis Gary Powers was not dreaming.

Pulling tight on the throttle with his left hand while holding the wheel steady with his right, Powers checked his instruments. Everything looked normal. Then the wing tipped and the nose dropped. Suddenly realizing he had lost control of the aircraft, he felt a violent shudder, which jostled him from side to side in his seat. He believed the wings had broken off.[27]

With what remained of his craft spinning out of control, Kelly Johnson's once-powerful machine was now overpowered by immutable gravity, and Powers reached for the self-destruct button, which worked on a 70-second delay timer, and prepared to eject. Then he changed his mind, pulling his finger back. Slammed forward by the enormous g-forces, in a suit that had inflated when the cabin lost pressurization, he immediately reached a rather-disheartening conclusion: If he ejected from this awkward position, the impact of his legs on the canopy rail would sever both of his legs, because they were trapped underneath the front of the cockpit.

Quickly thinking through his options, as the plane descended below 35,000 feet, Frank jettisoned the canopy, which flew off toward the heavens, and decided to climb out of the cockpit. When he released his seat belt, the resulting force threw him out.

But this solution created another problem: Because he was still tethered to his oxygen supply, and because the g-forces were so severe, he could no longer reach the self-destruct buttons. Even as his faceplate frosted over in the extreme cold, he fumbled in the dark on a bright sunny day, extending his fingers as far as they would go. No luck. Now he had no way to destroy the plane, to keep it from falling into enemy hands.

Somehow he broke free from the oxygen hose and eventually felt a jerk, which yanked him forward. His parachute opened automatically at 15,000 feet and he descended slowly toward the countryside, near a small village.

"I was immediately struck by the silence," he later recalled. "Everything was cold, quiet, serene. . . . There was no sensation of falling. It was as if I were hanging in the sky."[28]

Aware that he could breathe without his oxygen tank, he pulled off his faceplate and continued his descent.

On his way down, he took off his gloves, reached into his pocket, pulled out the map that showed alternate routes back to Pakistan, and ripped it into tiny pieces, which he tossed to the winds. He didn't want such incriminating evidence to fall into the hands of the Soviets.[29]

Then he reached for the silver dollar containing the poison pin. It was a regular-looking straight pin with grooves, which had been dipped in poison, certain to cause almost instantaneous death by asphyxiation. The device was covered by a sheath.

For a moment, he considered whether he should use it. One prick and he would be gone. "A minute or so later ... a horrible minute," he once surmised.[30] Washington could disavow him, although the wreckage of the plane would be difficult to explain.

With his life never more completely in his own hands, caught in a moment that would define him for the ages in many eyes, perhaps his mind brushed upon a twenty-year-old memory, when Oliver told him: "If you kill yourself, you kill a man. . . . A man who dies in sin, he can't be saved."[31]

Instead of using the device, he quickly dislodged it from the coin and the sheath, threw the dollar into the winds, and slipped the poison pin carefully into his pocket.

Looking down, he saw a landscape reminiscent of his native Virginia, including a lake and a forest. He tried to aim for the trees. Perhaps he could slip in unnoticed and plot his escape. But the wind shifted, and he landed in a plowed field on a collective farm instead, barely missing a power line and falling hard near a man on a tractor and another man working with his hands.

The two men ran up to assist him, one collapsing the chute, the other helping the stranger who fell from the sky to his feet.

His clothing contained no markings, so they assumed he was a Soviet pilot.

A car he had seen while floating to the ground pulled up nearby, and two men stepped out. One man was a chauffeur. They helped him take off his helmet and harness.

The locals could see he was dazed, especially as a crowd of children and adults from the nearby village surrounded him, peppering him with questions in Russian, questions he could not understand.

One man held up two fingers, pointed to him and then pointed to the distant sky, where a single red-and-white parachute could be seen drifting gently toward an eventual landing. He was puzzled by the chute but knew it was not connected to his plane. He shook his head.

By this time, he could tell the people surrounding him were starting to grow suspicious, particularly when one of the men looked down and saw the pistol strapped to the outside of his suit.

The man grabbed the weapon, and the pilot made no attempt to stop him. He knew his silence was merely delaying the inevitable.

"Escape would have been hopeless," he recalled, since he was in the middle of the vast USSR, "a long way from the border."[32]

After the Russians loaded his parachute and seat pack into the trunk of the small car, Powers was ushered into the front seat, between the driver and the man with the gun. He didn't need to speak the language to know where they were headed.

After all those hours in the air, Frank enjoyed the cigarette they offered. He felt thirsty, using sign language to let them know he wanted something to drink, and the man behind the wheel pulled up to a house. One of the other men—one of the three or four piled into the back seat—ran inside and quickly returned with a glass of water. The pilot guzzled the water but was still thirsty. He head throbbed—as it often did after being exposed to the pure-oxygen environment for such a long period—and he could feel his heart racing as the car resumed its journey down the bumpy, muddy road.[33]

At one point, the man with his gun began to examine it closely: running his fingers down the barrel, over the prominent letters carved into the metal. He then ran a single finger over the dusty dashboard and spelled out the same letters: U S A.[34]

By the time Powers dropped out of the sky, Moscow was alive with communist pride. As the annual May Day parade of military hardware moved through Red Square, Llewellyn E. Thompson Jr., the American ambassador, focused his eyes on Premier Khrushchev. As usual, Khrushchev was surrounded by key Communist Party and military leaders outside Lenin's and Stalin's Mausoleum as hundreds of thousands of ordinary Russians lined the streets, celebrating their most sacred holiday. The military men were all attired in their dress uniforms, with chests full ribbons, so when one Air Force man, wearing only a regular service jacket, moved through the back of the reviewing stand and approached Khrushchev, Thompson instinctively realized something important was being relayed to the Soviet leader. Only later would he put two and two together.[35]

Leaning in close so he could be heard above the noise of the crowd, Marshall Sergei Biryuzov, the commander of Soviet antiaircraft defenses, whispered in Khrushchev's ear: The U-2 pilot has been shot down and taken prisoner.[36]

Reveling in what he would later recall as an "excellent surprise," Khrushchev congratulated Biryuzov, shaking his hand enthusiastically.[37]

While Khrushchev watched the parade move into its second hour and began plotting his next move, the vise tightened on the American pilot.

At the first stop, in a village with paved streets several miles from the state-owned farm, he was taken into a civic building and searched by a policeman. He was asked to undress. They confiscated some items, including his pressure suit, pack of Kent cigarettes, and lighter. A female doctor examined him, treating some scratches on his leg. She gave him two aspirin tablets.

When Powers was allowed to slip his flight suit back on, he casually patted his pocket. It was still there.

Someone tried to communicate with him in German, but he did not speak German, which was just as well. He still hadn't figured out what he should say.

The CIA failed its pilots by not preparing them to be captured. When he landed on Soviet soil, Powers did not know how Washington planned to respond to his capture or what it would say about his mission. If he had been aware of the planned cover story, at least he could have given voice to the same narrative. Nor had he received any instruction about how he was to act during interrogation.

"I was completely unprepared," he recalled.[38]

Attuned to the details of his environment but unable to understand what was being said by the crowd around him, he noticed a steady stream of men walking through the door, presenting identification cards. Some carried artifacts from his downed plane, including a spool of 72-millimeter film.

The authorities eventually loaded him into a military vehicle featuring two mounted machine guns, and then transported him to the nearby city of Sverdlovsk, where they escorted him into a large government building, where he first encountered men he assumed were agents of the KGB, the Soviet secret police. He took a seat in a nondescript office. The solitary window contained no bars, but from the time he walked into the room, someone was always positioned between him and the window. One would leave; another would take his place. At no time was he ever left with a clear path to the window.

When the new team searched him, they discovered the poison pin, which one of the men carefully placed in his briefcase.

"Are you an American?"

He was shocked to hear English for the first time since leaving Pakistan.

"Yes," he said, realizing it was pointless to deny his nationality.[39]

Despite the lack of any formal training procedures for such a possibility, Powers had broached the subject with an intelligence officer several weeks earlier:

"Let's say the worst happens and I get captured. What do we do? What can we tell these people?"

"You might as well tell them everything, because they're going to get it out of you anyway," the agency man advised.[40]

He was unnerved by this answer, especially considering his knowledge of the way the communists tortured and brainwashed American prisoners during the Korean War.

Suddenly facing the fear of the unknown, but determined not to give up any classified information, he started telling an elaborate lie about flying near the border and somehow getting lost.

The KGB man knew better, but Powers kept spinning as they appeared determined to have him admit that he was a member of the American military.

Eventually, Powers learned that authorities had recovered a cache of personal items, including his wallet, which contained a card identifying him as a civilian employee of the Department of Defense, as well as a Social Security card and a significant amount of currency from several countries. Because he was not returning to base that night, he thought he would need a form of ID, cash, and a change of clothes in Norway. This was the act of a prepared pilot, not a clever spy.

"Someone should have stopped me from taking that," Powers said. "I should have known better myself."[41]

A couple of hours after he parachuted from the sky, he was on a commercial airliner bound for Moscow. He assumed it was only a matter of time before they killed him.

When Powers failed to show up in Bodo at the appointed time, Stan Beerli feared the worst. He relayed an alternate message, launching a chain reaction that eventually reached the Matomic Building in Washington, where the operation was based, at approximately 3:30 a.m. Sunday. Electronic intelligence indicated that Soviet radar tracking of Mission 4154 had ended about two hours earlier.[42] Carmine Vito, the former U-2 pilot who now manned a desk, began trying to find Bissell, placing a call to the home of Bob King, one of his special assistants. "Bill Bailey didn't come home," Vito said. "You better find the man quick."[43]

Aware that his boss was visiting former student Walt Rostow, King struggled to obtain his number during the wee hours of the morning, encountering an uncooperative operator. He was not going to take no for an answer. "It's a goddamned national emergency!" he thundered.[44] By the time King reached Rostow, Bissell had already left to catch a flight back to Washington, unaware of the unfolding situation. After arriving at the headquarters about 3:30 p.m., he began consulting with a small group including Colonel Leo Geary, the US Air Force project officer, and CIA official Richard Helms. They started discussing a cover story, as Bissell felt "a sense of disaster."[45]

General Andrew Goodpaster, the staff secretary to the president, who would one day rise to supreme commander of NATO, broke the news to Eisenhower, who was still at Camp David. "One of our reconnaissance planes on a scheduled flight from its base in Adana, Turkey, is overdue and possibly lost," he said.[46]

The news of the missing aircraft reached Adana early Monday morning, where the housing and administrative officer was dispatched to the Powers trailer. The knocking eventually rousted Barbara from her bed.[47] After hobbling to the door, she said, "This had better be good."[48] Powers's wife was so upset, she required sedation. (The CIA cable concerning the notification said her broken leg had resulted from a "skiing accident."[49]) The CIA arranged for her immediate return to the United States via a commercial airline, along with their German shepherd, Eck.

While Barbara hoped her husband had somehow survived and would eventually come back to her, key members of the Eisenhower administration hoped he was dead. It would be much more convenient for the American government if he were dead.

When Monday morning dawned at the White House without any word, Eisenhower was given every assurance that the plane was likely destroyed and the pilot had perished. Time after time, Dulles and Bissell and several others had insisted he would never have to worry about a live pilot leaving a trail of bread crumbs all the way back to Washington. This belief factored heavily into his decision to undertake such risky provocations, especially with the summit fast approaching. Eisenhower decided to say nothing just yet, waiting for Khrushchev to play his card.

In Islamabad, General Ayub Khan, the strongman leader who had granted broad approval of American aviation activity but had been shielded from direct knowledge of the overflights, received a visit from a CIA operative, who assured him that the United States would make "every effort to minimize any Soviet pressure growing out of the incident."[50] Khan played it cool, asking that a confidential message be passed along to Director Dulles, in which he pledged to "stand by our friends and not let them down on this." Proving he understood Western-style political leverage, he asked for help acquiring an F-104 and upgrading his radar network, to thwart Soviet aggression.

After two days of discussion and fine-tuning, NASA released a cover story approved at the highest level:

A NASA U-2 research airplane being flown in Turkey on a joint NASA-U.S. Air Force Weather Service mission apparently went down in the Lake Van, Turkey area at about 9 a.m. (3 a.m. EDT) Sunday, May 1. During the flight in eastern Turkey, the pilot reported over the emergency frequency that he was experiencing oxygen difficulties. The flight originated in Adana with a mission to obtain data on clear air turbulence. A search is now underway in the Lake Van area. The pilot is an employee of Lockheed Aircraft under contract to NASA. The U-2 program was initiated by NASA in 1956 as a method of making high-altitude weather studies. . . .[51]

A stranger wearing a dark suit walked into Oliver Powers's shoe shop in Norton, Virginia. He asked to speak with the father alone, and the two of them stepped out the back door and into the alley, where the man from Washington broke the news. Francis was missing. Walton Meade, Oliver's son-in-law, happened to be in the shop, and he overheard part of the conversation, which included reference to the cover story. Weather plane. Off course. Walton wasn't buying it, which was a bad sign for the whole plan.

"So just how far over Russia was Francis when he was shot down?" he demanded with a sneer.

The Company man glared at him and walked out the door.

Around this time, Joe Murphy, now stationed in New York City and assigned to another covert project, was driving to Philadelphia for an appointment. He heard the news about a U-2 going down on his car radio and immediately wondered which pilot had been at the controls, thinking whoever it was, he was likely dead. One of the few people in the world who knew the weather-reconnaissance business was a lie, he was "really skeptical about the cover story holding up."

For four days, Khrushchev considered his options. When a session of the Supreme Soviet opened, the various leaders began discussing how to best use the leverage they now enjoyed. "What we had in mind," Khrushchev recalled, "was to confuse and mislead the U.S. government."[52]

At the climax of a long speech to the Supreme Soviet on May 5, Khrushchev paused to great theatrical effect and then announced that his military had shot down an American spy plane, which had invaded Soviet airspace. Defiant and angry, he railed against what he called "aggressive imperialist forces in the United States" who wanted to "undermine" the approaching summit, and he warned of "severe consequences" to East-West relations.

Ambassador Thompson, who had been invited to the session without any explanation and was seated in the balcony of the parliament, unwittingly became a prop in Khrushchev's show. Turning toward the diplomat, Khrushchev asked: "Who sent the plane off? Was it sent without the chiefs of the American armed forces? Was it sent by the Pentagon without the president's knowledge? If it was done without the president's knowledge, the people should know about it!"[53]

He made no reference to the fact that he had been aware of such overflights for nearly four years.

After meeting with his senior advisors, including Allen Dulles, Andrew Goodpaster, Secretary of Defense Thomas Gates, and National Security Advisor Gordon Gray, Eisenhower decided to remain silent and stay with the cover story. "It was agreed by the group that the president should not be personally involved," according to the minutes of the meeting.[54] Instead, the State Department would take the lead. Later in the day, it issued a press release:

> The Department has been informed by NASA that, as announced May 3, an unarmed plane, a U-2 weather research plane based at Adana, Turkey, piloted by a civilian, has been missing since May 1. During the flight of the plane, the pilot reported difficulty with his oxygen equipment. Mr. Khrushchev has announced that a U.S. plane was shot down over the USSR on that date. It may be that this was the missing plane. It is entirely possible that, having a failure in the oxygen equipment which could result in the pilot losing consciousness, the plane continued on automatic pilot for a considerable distance and accidentally violated Soviet air space. In view of Mr. Khrushchev's statement, the U.S. is taking this matter up with the Soviet Government, with particular reference to the fate of the pilot.[55]

The narrative was given voice by White House Press Secretary James Haggerty and Lincoln White, the State Department spokesman, who replied to a question by asserting that there had "never been" any deliberate attempt to violate Soviet airspace.[56]

As long as the pilot was dead and the plane's self-destruct mechanism had worked properly, the White House believed the story would hold up.

Late in the day on May 1, a black sedan with windows concealed by curtains cruised through the streets of downtown Moscow. The driver pulled up to a massive yellow-brick building, stopping in front of two large iron doors. He honked his horn and a guard appeared at a peephole. In a matter of moments the doors opened, allowing the car to enter a courtyard, and quickly slammed shut.

Ushered out of the car, Powers was led onto a pitch-black elevator and eventually into a small room, where he was searched again and ordered to disrobe. He was presented with some old, worn-out clothes, including an oversized, double-breasted black suit and loafers, standard issue for enemies of the state at Lubyanka, the headquarters of the KGB.

The three-hour flight from Sverdlovsk gave Frank time to develop the beginnings of a strategy. When the interrogations began, he decided to tell his Soviet captors what he believed they could easily learn elsewhere, including through the media.

"I'd go ahead and tell them the absolute truth, be just as truthful as I could be, on those things," he explained, "so that when I got to a point that was sensitive and they couldn't know anything about it, I could lie—and they would believe me. Would be willing to believe me, because I'd been truthful in everything else they could prove."[57]

In addition to various questions falling into the realm of biography—such as, "Where were you born?"—the Soviets wanted to know whether he had previously traveled to Norway.

"I told 'em 'yes,' because I assumed they could figure this out [from] passport records and such," he said.[58]

Only later would he learn that this particular confession led to a political backlash in Norway, where the government's participation with American espionage became controversial.

The Norwegians quickly ran scared. Deciding that the Americans "were so inept and unwise" in their handling of the incident, the government decided to fully cooperate with the Soviet investigation into their country's involvement "no matter how much this might offend the State Department."[59] The Pakistani ambassador to Moscow reported to his own government that the Norwegians believed it was fruitless to deny anything to the Soviets because Powers "had made a clean breast of all he knew to the Russians."[60]

The interrogators repeatedly asked him if he had made other overflights, and he repeatedly lied.

He asked to see someone from the US embassy or the Red Cross, but they turned him down, deepening his feelings of isolation and tightening the noose.

While his most persuasive KGB agents worked the US pilot, in a dark place known throughout the Soviet Union for torture and execution, Khrushchev ordered his military to find the wreckage of the plane near Sverdlovsk. In time, Eisenhower felt blindsided with the news that the self-destruct mechanism needed to be activated by the pilot, and that the charge was not sufficient to destroy the entire plane or even the incriminating film. "It was scattered over a wide area," reported Colonel Aleksandrovich Mikahlilov, one of the officers tasked with the important duty of locating the aircraft.[61] "We made sure it was collected and brought to Moscow." (Within weeks, the evidence would be displayed in Gorky Park for all to see, where it drew lines that rivaled the steady procession of visitors to Lenin's and Stalin's tomb. One of the few Americans to see the wreckage was the father of future filmmaker Steven Spielberg, who happened to be in Moscow on business.)

On May 7, while addressing a special session of the Supreme Soviet, Khrushchev sprang his trap. "We have parts of the plane and we also have the pilot, who is quite alive and kicking and confessed to spying for the

CIA," he said, before holding up a large print produced from some of the reconnaissance film.[62]

The news found President Eisenhower at his home in Gettysburg, which looked out onto the Civil War battlefield. He wrestled with the dilemma wrought by his instinct to engage in a cover-up, even as Allen Dulles offered to resign, in order to shield the president. Some of his colleagues thought this sounded like a good idea, but Eisenhower, as Goodpaster said, "isn't in the business of using scapegoats."[63]

Now that the whole world knew the American government had repeatedly lied about the U-2 business, the White House came clean, releasing a statement acknowledging the reconnaissance program had been pursued under "a very broad directive from the president given at the earliest point of his administration to protect us from surprise attack."[64]

When Eisenhower finally acknowledged his direct approval of the overflights, he called the program a "distasteful but vital necessity" to prevent the next Pearl Harbor.[65]

Condemnation was swift. *Time* magazine called Washington's handling of the affair "clumsy and inept."[66] James "Scotty" Reston, the esteemed Washington bureau chief of the *New York Times*, criticized the White House for "bad judgment and bad faith" in issuing "a series of misleading official statements."[67] The *Toledo Blade* called it "the most colossal diplomatic blunder in the nation's history."[68]

To most diplomats and journalists, it was not the least bit problematic that Washington had spied. Both sides spied, after all. But as the *Times* said, "In the Cold War, the guilty person is the one who gets caught."[69]

The trust most Americans placed in their government in 1960 made Eisenhower's duplicity—rooted in what biographer Stephen E. Ambrose called the president's "fetish about keeping the U-2 a secret,"[70] even from key members of Congress—difficult to shoulder, especially when the truth was delivered by the Soviets. The stature Ike enjoyed as an American hero and the personal warmth the vast majority of the country felt for him tempered the feelings of betrayal, but it was a still shock to the whole system.

The country was not quite ready for the cynical age just over the horizon, but in time, the backlash of May 1960 would look like a harbinger.

The debate raging in various quarters could be seen in an essay question placed on a final exam ending the spring term at the Citadel, the South Carolina military college. "I argued that Eisenhower should have told the truth from the beginning," recalled graduating senior David Boyd, who was headed for a commission in the US Army. "He should have said, 'Yes, we did it. What are you going to do about it? We spy on you and you spy on us.' It was the not telling the truth that got him in trouble."

Around 7 a.m. on the morning after Francis Gary Powers became world-famous, his name flashed across newspaper front pages and broadcasts on every continent, Lieutenant Michael Betterton heard a doorbell at his South Florida home. He was getting ready for work. After leaving the CIA, he had returned to regular Air Force duty, flying a KC-97 while attached to the 19th Air Refueling Squadron at Homestead Air Force Base. When he opened the door, he saw two earnest-looking young men in dark suits with skinny neckties and short haircuts. He immediately knew who they were. "They were there to remind me not to talk to anybody, not to tell anybody that I even knew who Francis Gary Powers was," Betterton said. "Well, of course, I knew that without being told. I couldn't even tell my wife." It would be another four decades before he could inform her that he had once worked for the CIA.

Even as key members of the Eisenhower administration believed it was likely Powers had defected, perhaps sabotaging his own mission, the vigorous interrogations continued at Lubyanka, where, completely isolated from the outside world, he began to spiral into a fatalistic despair, especially about his wife and his parents. His mother suffered from a heart condition, and he worried about how she must be suffering with his disappearance.

"No one knows I'm here," he told his captors. "You can just take me out and shoot me and no one will know the difference."[71]

They brought in Western newspapers, including the *New York Times*, and started reading passages to him, to prove that the outside world knew he had been captured. He doubted them at first, especially when they refused to let him hold the papers. "You could have had those printed somewhere in Moscow, and I wouldn't know the difference," he said. Eventually he accepted the news, when they read statements from his parents. The wording sounded like something they would say.[72]

In the moment of realization, he broke down in tears, shocking his captors. "It was just such a relief to know that someone in the world knew I was alive."[73]

Usually facing a five-member team, led at times by a man he later learned to be Roman Andreyevich Rudenko, onetime lead Soviet prosecutor in the Nazi war crime tribunals at Nuremberg, Powers was questioned for nineteen days straight. They discussed the U-2 and his surveillance activities in great detail. The interrogations lasted as long as eleven hours per day, pushing him to the physical and emotional brink. He longed for the opportunity to sleep, to escape the badgering, but rest in his tiny 12'×5' cell, on an uncomfortable cot, featuring what he recalled as "two pieces of cloth with lumps placed on top of a welded iron grid," came fitfully.[74] He tossed and turned, thinking of home, worrying about his wife. He assumed it was only a matter of time before he was lined up against a wall and shot. Or perhaps worse.

"The possibility of torture stayed with me until trial," he said. "I expected them to pull my fingernails or other terrible things. And I think it was the indefiniteness of it all that bothered me the most. Not knowing what or when. If a man knows he is going to be shot at a certain time, then it is settled. . . . They make you uncomfortable and you don't know what is coming."[75]

As Powers embarked on an uncertain road, fearing the worst, he had plenty of time to think about the choices he had made up to this point in his life. He had escaped the dead-end existence of the coal miners but now was learning that following one's dream could come at a high price. Perhaps he reconsidered his decision not to become a doctor.

The pilot could not fully appreciate the impact of his capture.

Eisenhower saw the Paris summit as an opportunity to pursue long-term peace with the Soviets and perhaps achieve some very concrete steps to end the arms race.

"There is no place on this earth to which I would not travel, there is no chore I would not undertake," he said in 1955, before deciding to seek re-election, "if I had the faintest hope that, by so doing, I would promote the general cause of world peace."[76]

The U-2 program had demonstrated the fallacy of the "bomber gap" and was beginning to disprove the "missile gap," despite the hype associated with Sputnik and its successors. The White House had been able to use the intelligence gathered by the spy plane to more wisely allocate finite tax dollars. Now, as Ike began to think about his legacy, he wanted to engage in dialogue to ratchet down the tension.

Khrushchev was driven by a different agenda. American officials believed he was less interested in peace than in finding a way to bully the three Allied powers out of Berlin. Determined to use the U-2 Incident to his advantage—with the hard-liners in his own country who bristled at some of his modernization impulses, as well as the impressionable minds of the third world—the Soviet leader traveled to Paris for the Summit Conference with Eisenhower, French president Charles de Gaulle, and British prime minister Harold Macmillan. He quickly used the opportunity of focused world attention to lambaste the United States; officially rescind the invitation he had extended to Eisenhower to visit the Soviet Union; and demand an apology from the president, who refused. Then he stormed out, ending any hopes of a thaw in the Cold War.

Boarding his plane to Moscow the next morning Khrushchev make sure reporters heard an exchange with Foreign Minister Gromyko, who was headed to New York to denounce the American spying before the

United Nations. "When you get to the United States," he said, "be careful of those imperialists. Be careful to cover your back, don't expose your back to them."[77]

Watching the communist leader seize the moral high ground was a painful experience for American officials.

Khrushchev "used the U-2 as a good excuse for torpedoing both the trip and the conference," Dulles said many years later.[78]

In this Francis Gary Powers emerged as a Cold War pawn.

The KGB interrogators played many different cards to try to pump him for information and break him down, including guilt. Around the time he learned he would be tried for espionage, his captors asked him how it felt to be the cause of scuttling the summit, escalating tensions between the two superpowers.

Up to this point, he had not considered a linkage between his flight and the summit. At least for the moment, the Soviets succeeded in making him feel some level of remorse.

"They told me I had wrecked the summit conference," he said years later.[79] "They put the whole burden on me. It made me feel terrible."

Around nine o'clock on the evening of May 9, a telephone rang at 1650 Pine Valley Road, a spacious, modern-style three-bedroom house on the outskirts of Milledgeville, Georgia.

"Is this Dr. Baugh?"

"It is."

The man on the other end of the line seemed nervous. He requested that James Baugh make a house call to 1626 Marion Street.[80]

Like most small-town doctors of the day, Baugh, known to his friends as Jimmy, was accustomed to phone calls at all hours of the day and night. The beloved general practitioner routinely interrupted family meals and favorite television programs to head out the front door with his bag.

"House calls were part of a doctor's life; Jimmy was very committed to his patients," recalled his wife, Betty George, known around town as BeeGee.

The man was vague about the patient's symptoms, but Baugh dutifully walked out to his car and drove to the address. Two men met him at the curb, including the one who had called him, and escorted him into the house, where they were joined by Mrs. Monteen Brown, who had been his patient for several years. Mrs. Brown was not ill, but she explained that her daughter needed medical attention.

This all struck Baugh as quite odd, until Mrs. Brown led him to one of the bedrooms to meet Barbara Powers.

The doctor kept up with the news and had heard all about the fallen airplane and the captured pilot with connections to Georgia.

Understanding that reporters from all over the country were trying to locate and interview the wife of the man who was suddenly among the most famous individuals in the world, the middle-aged doctor agreed to be discreet.

In addition to her fractured leg, which had been placed in a walking cast by a physician in Turkey, Barbara suffered from a bronchial infection. The other doctor had also prescribed a tranquilizer for nerves. Baugh gave her a thorough examination, administered a shot for pain, and arranged for her to have some tests the next day, including an EKG.

Baugh, who grew up on a farm near Milledgeville and attended the University of Georgia, where he studied political science and history, was profoundly shaped by Pearl Harbor, like many men of his generation. Bright and ambitious, he interrupted his plans—he dreamed of a career in the foreign service—and immediately entered the US Army, becoming a platoon leader of the 82nd Airborne Division, a remarkable unit which proved crucial to the Allied victory. He fought in North Africa, Sicily, Italy, France, Belgium, and Holland, participating in D-day, the Battle of the Bulge, and Operation Market Garden. He watched many of his friends die, so he felt lucky to survive the war.

Baugh returned to the United States no longer so eager to spend his life traveling the world. He had seen liberated Paris and defeated Germany. Now he felt driven to build a regular life, so he enrolled in medical school and eventually moved back to his hometown, becoming a pillar of the community who was so admired, he eventually served eighteen years as mayor. He delivered more than 4,000 babies. Patients often showed up at his house to be treated in a little converted study, and sometimes they paid him in eggs, meat, and vegetables.

"Jimmy was an old-fashioned country doctor, and he worked all the time," Betty said.

Among his close friends was a man from Milledgeville who worked for the CIA. Only a select few people in his life were allowed to know he was employed by the intelligence agency, and no one knew exactly what he did. But after learning that his friend Jimmy was treating Barbara Powers, he telephoned and recruited him for a special mission: Keep a close eye on the troubled wife, with special attention to her "emotional state" and "other related problems."[81] Jimmy was provided a contact and a number to call in Washington. No one knew that the kindly small-town doctor was performing a special service for his government.

"Due to things already known about the weaknesses of Mrs. Powers," Baugh wrote in 1960, in a never-published manuscript concerning his involvement with the case, "[the CIA] believed she could be influenced by the wrong people. … It was implied that she naturally knew a lot about the set-up of the 10-10 Detachment and much of the intelligence program."[82]

Various business related to Barbara wound up on Baugh's desk, including her eagerness to visit Moscow for the trial. At first, the government opposed her attendance, deeming it too risky. However, the CIA changed its mind, apparently influenced by the opinion of Columbia University law professor Dr. John M. Hazard, an expert on Soviet jurisprudence. The CIA asked Baugh to escort her, which required the doctor without a partner to take critical time away from his medical practice.

In the early days after the shoot-down, media outlets were still buying the Company line that Powers worked for Lockheed Aircraft Corporation. Among other things, Baugh was tasked with making sure Barbara did not say anything to the press that betrayed the approved message. When the doctor organized a press conference for the wife on her mother's front lawn, he was able to convince the assembled newsmen to submit their questions in writing.

In a clear attempt to rally support for a trip, Barbara, one of the few people who called her husband Gary, read selected portions from a letter from him urging her to travel to Moscow for the trial. "He is getting plenty of food and has been treated well," said Barbara, who started talking about the tour they gave him of Moscow, including the exhibit of his plane's wreckage.[83]

She talked about her fear that the pilot could spend years in prison or be put to death.

"My husband is not a spy," she insisted.[84]

While he was facing an uncertain fate, his wife was causing much distress for a small circle in Milledgeville. Baugh quickly became disturbed by "the vast amount of evidence pointing to Barbara Powers being a very mentally unpredictable person and judging from some of her recently acquired acquaintances, a very unwise person."[85] She was frequently seen out on the town drinking heavily, in the company of people who were regarded as shady, especially men.

One bizarre incident gave him great pause about her state of mind. About 3 a.m. on June 22, Barbara knocked on someone's front door, demanding some papers and bonds from a man she identified as "Jack Dempsey." When the puzzled lady who answered the door found out who she was, she invited Barbara in, but Barbara "ran down the steps to a waiting car and disappeared in the night."[86]

Baugh's contact in Washington was disturbed but not surprised, "regarding it as consistent with what they had expected."[87]

"It didn't take Jimmy long to figure out Barbara was a mess," Betty said. "She was a very troubled young woman."

After consulting with Washington, he enlisted the help of his friend Eugene Ellis, the Milledgeville chief of police, to closely monitor her activities and interactions.

While the pressure of the ordeal exacerbated Barbara's issues, the family back in rural southwest Virginia was shocked to learn that Francis was involved in spying on the Soviets.

After learning about the shoot-down, Jan Powers Melvin, who was married, with two small children, and was living in the Washington suburb of Falls Church, Virginia, immediately called her sister Jean, who still resided in Pound. Jan knew their mother watched soap operas in the afternoon, and she asked Jean to go over and break the news, so she would not hear it on television.

"We were all just shocked, because we had no idea what Francis was doing over in Turkey," Jan said. "Once the initial shock started to wear off, we were all scared to death what they were going to do to him."

Pulled into the spotlight, Pound and the surrounding area became a magnet for reporters from across the globe, all trying to trace the background of the infamous spy. "You got the impression that some of those people were coming here to find out something embarrassing about Francis or the family," said his sister Joan. "Or they wanted to look down on us country folks."

Oliver happily answered questions about his son, expressing his pride that the boy was doing something important for his country. But the father's frustration was frequently evident. "What can I do?" he once said.[88] "I'm just a little man out here in the coal country and my son's life is at stake."

Several days after his son's capture, Oliver penned a letter to the Soviet leader:

My Dear Mr. Khrushchev:
    I extend to you and Mrs. Khrushchev my regards as one parent to another. Pilot Francis Gary Powers is my only son.

I am asking you to be lenient with him in your dealings with him. He has always been a fine young man and we love him very much.

As one father to another, I plead with you to let him come home as soon as you can find it in your heart to do so that he may be with us a while longer. Please give him this note from his mother enclosed in this letter.

Sincerely yours,

Oliver Powers,

Father of Francis Powers

P.S.—I would appreciate it very much if you would reply as soon as possible.[89]

Khrushchev responded in a telegram, offering to allow Oliver to visit his son but dashing his hopes of an early release. "The law is the law," he wrote, "and I am not in a position to interfere."[90]

When news of the U-2 Incident hit the papers, sixteen-year-old high school junior Rosa Anne Speranza was standing in the kitchen of her house in Richmond, Virginia, near her mother, when her father pointed at the story he had just finished reading on the front page of his morning newspaper.

"If that were my son, I would want to be there," he said.

An Italian immigrant who had built a successful life in Virginia's capital city—developing Richmond's first shopping center and owning a popular nightclub and restaurant—Jimmy Speranza loved his adopted country and appreciated the importance of family. Aware that the pilot's family were Appalachian people of modest means, he worked with three friends to quietly initiate contact and offer to pay the father's way to the upcoming summit in Paris. Oliver wanted to plead his case directly to the Soviet leader, telling reporters he was willing to offer himself in place of his son. When the summit collapsed, Speranza arranged to pay Oliver and Ida's expenses to Moscow for the trial.

"The United States has been good to me so now I want to do something good for this boy who has done his best for his country," he told a reporter when news of the gesture leaked.[91]

Out of the difficult circumstance, a special friendship developed between the Speranzas and the Powerses, who spent several nights at the Speranza home in Richmond. "They were the sweetest, dearest, most down-to-earth people," recalled Rosa Anne. "My mom and dad felt a real connection to them. The situation was awful, but we were blessed to get to know them."

To make matters worse, another American plane fell out of the sky on July 1, 1960. An RB-47 reconnaissance plane was on a secret mission over the Arctic Ocean when it was shot down by the Soviets. Two members of the crew survived and were shipped to Lubyanka, where the KGB began four months of intense interrogations.

If there was one thing that connected the family members to Francis so far away, it was the shared sense of powerlessness.

While his wife and parents worked through various complications with the visa process, Frank was informed that the investigation was finished at the end of June. He had endured sixty-one days of interrogations, while confined to a tiny cell, with only a few censored letters connecting him to the outside world.

When the indictment was announced, he learned that he would be tried for espionage according to Article 2 of the Soviet criminal code. The law provided punishment ranging from seven years' imprisonment to death.

During the summer, a rift developed between Barbara and Frank's parents, starting with their decision to hire separate lawyers. The Virginia Bar Association, believed to be a front for the CIA, stepped forward to fund the legal defense, although Frank would not be allowed to engage an American attorney in his defense.

The real fireworks started when Oliver brokered a deal to sell his exclusive story to *Life* magazine. The figure was never revealed, although speculation ranged from $5,000 to $20,000. Henry Luce, the magazine tycoon who controlled the Time Life empire and happened to be a close friend of Allen Dulles, was well known for such arrangements. For instance, the $500,000 contract he signed with the Mercury Seven astronauts in 1958 was approved by NASA and contributed mightily to the mythology of America's pioneering spacemen.

But the impression that Oliver was eager to profit from his son's tragedy disturbed many, including his daughter-in-law.

"Barbara became infuriated at the commercialization of her husband's ordeal," Baugh wrote. "Oliver dropped a few hints to various people questioning Barbara's fitness in view of the reputation she had acquired from various escapades."[92]

The father suggested that his daughter-in-law was responsible for not giving him any grandchildren—she had experienced a miscarriage the year before—and that his son had only renewed his contract with the overseas assignment so he could continue accommodating Barbara's lavish lifestyle.

The simmering feud eventually reached the media.

"All I can say is that Mrs. Barbara Powers turned down several offers of such a nature," said William P. Dickson, the president of the Virginia Bar Association. "I don't know whether Powers' parents followed the same line of conduct. But I am truly delighted that the wife of a man fighting for his life refused to turn a profit from his plight."[93]

Tensions were so high, Barbara refused to fly to Moscow with Oliver and Ida, so she and her entourage traveled separately from Georgia.

When he was escorted into the ornate Hall of Columns inside the House of Unions on the morning of August 17, which happened to be his thirty-first birthday, Powers was temporarily blinded by the television lights and flashbulbs. This was appropriate symbolism, because the defendant, dressed in a blue pinstripe suit with a white shirt and blue tie, was a made-for-TV villain.

He looked around for his family but could not locate them, which was just as well. Barbara, seated with the rest of the family, broke down in tears at the shock of seeing her husband paraded onto the stage as a criminal.

With a history of hosting classical music performances as well as some of the Stalinist purge trials of the 1930s, the Hall of Columns featured several dozen chandeliers, plush red seats, and a large red-and-gold hammer-and-sickle banner draped above the stage. It looked like a theater, not a courtroom. About 2,000 invited guests, including Khrushchev's daughter, Elena, showed up for the show trial, which for three days focused worldwide attention on what Radio Moscow called "a premeditated and carefully prepared act of aggression against the Soviet Union."[94]

It was clear for all to see that the prosecution was using Powers as a propaganda tool to convict American policy, American leaders, and the American system in the eyes of the world.

Soon after entering the room, Frank struggled with nerves and took a seat when he was expected to stand, causing him to be admonished by the presiding judge, Lieutenant General of Justice V. V. Borisoglebsky, whose Russian pronouncements included an English translation.

Like their son, Oliver and Ida felt very out of place.

Prior to leaving Richmond several days earlier with his party, which included their grown daughter, Jessica Hileman; attorney Carl MacAfee; family friend Sol Curry; and physician Lewis K. Ingram, Oliver told a reporter: "We are doing all we can to help our son and know he will find some comfort from our being in Moscow."[95]

He said he was still willing to trade his life for his son's, if only he could get a chance to appeal to Khrushchev. But the premier would not see him.

Angered by the way many people in his own country were talking about his son, Oliver said he believed the American people had already convicted Francis and "the sentence will be passed by Khrushchev."[96]

While the CIA underwrote the costs of the trip for Barbara, her mother, their attorneys, and Baugh, who provided regular updates concerning the trial and Barbara's activities—his notes scribbled at the end of the day while sitting on the toilet in his hotel room—the rest of the family was essentially cut off from government "direct contact and control."[97] The deal with *Life* angered officials in Washington, who believed they could not trust Oliver.

Despite her health problems, which left her frail, gaunt, and needing help moving in and out of vehicles and seats, the gray-haired Ida—looking very much like the grandmother she was—had been determined to make the trip.

"Talk about culture shock," said their daughter Jan. "They [her parents] didn't know how to act in a country that was so totally different."

During a tour of Moscow, Ida was amazed to see women performing manual labor on the streets.

"It was very nerve-wracking for them to sit there during the trial," Jan said, "especially feeling like the end result was a foregone conclusion."

When the Soviets announced nine days before the trial that Powers had "confessed" to spying, the State Department issued a carefully worded statement noting that the pilot "has been in the exclusive control of the Soviet authorities for 101 days. . . . Despite all efforts of this government, no one other than his jailers and captors had had any access to him, and anything he says should be judged in light of these circumstances and Soviet past practices in matters of this kind."[98]

Even before the trial began, Barbara made news by essentially conceding the argument, which undermined Washington's point. During a press conference, she refused to take issue with the prosecution's charge that her husband had admitted to the central crime in question. "The fact that he pleaded guilty of being the pilot of the plane whose wreckage they found in the Soviet Union—I only feel that it was normal to admit it," she said. "What else could he say?"[99]

Yet she told reporters he should not be held responsible for his actions. "My husband's work and service was all part of a program which required orders from the President," she said. "Therefore, I would term him a reconnaissance scout—not a spy—under orders from his own government."[100]

Handling Barbara during the trip proved to be a tremendous challenge for Baugh.

For weeks, Washington had worried that the Soviets were brainwashing Powers. The CIA asked to examine the letters the pilot had written home, and Barbara complied with the request.

First the correspondence was checked for "evidence of the prisoner's use of the simple code in which he had been instructed during his training."[101] No clue was found.

Further examination of his handwriting led the CIA doctors to believe "more than likely some type or organic psychiatric change"[102] had taken place. The State Department pushed back against the suggestion that Washington should introduce the possibility that he had been brainwashed.

Frank would insist he had not been brainwashed.

At a time when most Americans still relied heavily on daily newspapers, television news remained in its adolescence. The evening newscasts on the three commercial networks lasted a mere fifteen minutes—it would be another three years before Walter Cronkite's broadcast on CBS consumed an entire half hour—and were constricted by various technical barriers. The first communication satellite would not be launched until 1961, which meant that the still-new marvel of video tape represented the cutting edge of broadcast technology. The networks went all out to provide coverage of the trial, including NBC's *The Huntley-Brinkley Report*, which featured the reporting of John Chancellor, on one of his first big overseas assignments.

Radio coverage helped shape public opinion around the world as well. In a report for the BBC, correspondent Ian McDougall painted a vivid picture:

> There stood this crew-cut, diffident, simple, rather polite man, surrounded by the entire apparatus of Soviet law, and knowing himself to be, as he said himself, the cause of a lot of trouble. An astonishingly naïve

person, yet a charming one, a frightened man with his back to the wall, a boy who wanted to own his own service station and instead found himself the cause of the president not being able to come to Russia. . . . [103]

The pilot understood the fine line he was required to walk. He was willing to appear remorseful, which his court-appointed Soviet attorney, Michael I. Grinyov, insisted was necessary to prevent him from being executed. But he was unwilling to cross the line and denounce his own country.

"I've been treated much better than I expected," he told the court while recounting the circumstances of his capture.[104]

Roman A. Rudenko, the Soviet prosecutor general, began his questioning of the defendant by establishing certain basic facts.

Question: When did you receive the order to fly over Soviet territory?
Answer: On the morning of May 1.
Question: Who gave you this order?
Answer: The commanding officer of my detachment.
Question: Who was the commanding officer of the detachment?
Answer: Colonel Shelton.
Question: Where was this detachment stationed?
Answer: Adana in Turkey.
Question: What was the maximum altitude?
Answer: 68,000 feet, plus or minus a few. I don't remember.[105]

For the small task force huddled at the Matomic Building and parsing every word, bracing for the worst, this answer was a signal.

Question: What were you told by Colonel Shelton about the safety of the flight at such an altitude?
Answer: I was told it was absolutely safe and that at such an altitude I would not be shot down.[106]

Often frustrated that his attorney never objected and seemed reluctant to question witnesses, Powers at one point took it upon himself to challenge experts who contended that the fact that his plane contained no official markings suggested it was on a spy mission. Determined to find some way to fight back, even if it was on a technical point, he convinced one expert to concede the possibility that markings could have been removed.

"Why I asked this," Powers said, "is that I have seen all of the planes at Incirlik. This plane was at Incirlik for some months and every plane I saw there had some sort of markings. I cannot agree that there never has been identity markings on the plane."[107]

The prosecution spent significant time trying to establish the poison pin—displayed in the courtroom—as a weapon Powers planned to use against unsuspecting Soviet citizens, along with some other items in his survival pack and his .22-caliber pistol, "intended for silent firing at human beings at short rage."[108]

"On the pistol," he said, "it was given to me and I took it strictly for hunting. Unfortunately, nobody knows that I couldn't kill a person, even to save my own life."[109]

Borisoglebsky interrupted him. "You are aware no doubt that at 68,000 feet it is difficult to hunt for game."[110]

The coverage by state media was predictably dripping with familiar propaganda themes, including one Radio Moscow broadcast, which noted his roots as the son of a Virginia cobbler: "Does an American cobbler, an American farmer, an American worker have any need of war? Can a genuine son of a man of labor voluntarily devote himself to the cause of preparing and unleashing nuclear war? Can he of his own free will, without any compulsion, become an accomplice and hireling of the inveterate spy Allen Dulles? No, you are not the son of a man of labor, Francis Gary Powers. You are the bondsman of the Rockefellers and the Morgans."[111]

Another broadcast spoke of the base in Turkey as a place where "young bloods are trained for the purpose of committing villainous, provocative flights into the skies of foreign countries, and in particular the airspace of the Soviet Union."[112]

Moving toward establishing the crime on the second day of the trial, Rudenko began asking Powers about his May 1 flight.

Question: How did you feel?
Answer: Physically, I was all right. But I was nervous, scared.
Question: Why were you scared?
Answer: Well, just the idea of flying over the Soviet Union. It was not something I would like to do every day.
Question: Do you deny that you violated Soviet air space?
Answer: No, I do not deny it. I had instructions to do this and I did it.

When Rudenko completed his cross-examination, Borisoglebsky asked several questions.

Question: What was the main objective of your flight on May 1?
Answer: As it was told to me, I was to follow the route and turn switches on and off as indicated on the map.
Question: For what reason?
Answer: I would assume it was done for intelligence reasons.
Question: You testified in this court yesterday that Colonel Shelton was particularly interested in rocket-launching sites.
Answer: Yes, he did mention one place on the map where there was a possible rocket-launching site.
Question: Do you think now you did your country an ill or good service?
Answer: I would say a very ill service.
Question: Did it not occur to you that by violating the Soviet frontier you might torpedo the summit conference?
Answer: When I got my instructions, the summit conference was the farthest from my mind. I did not think of it.
Question: Did it occur to you that a flight might provoke military contact?

Answer: The people who sent me should have thought of these things. My job was to carry out orders. I do not think it was my responsibility to make such decisions.

Question: Do you regret making this flight?

Answer: Yes, very much.[113]

In mounting a defense for his client, Grinyov felt compelled to do the bidding of his government, which included a complete refusal to challenge the allegations. He introduced statements that Powers later insisted he never made, including the suggestion that he had been "deceived" by his superiors. After condemning the behavior of the Eisenhower administration in great detail, he told the court, "Ruling reactionary forces of the United States had sent Powers to sure death and wanted him to die."[114]

Powers bristled at such talk, which made him angry at Grinyov. "Since I had refused to denounce the United States," Frank said, "Grinyov was doing it for me."[115] He bit his tongue.

As Grinyov predicted leniency for his client in the final verdict, Radio Moscow softened its tone, telling listeners that the spy pilot had made "a clear distinction between him and those who sent him."[116]

Virtually every night during their twelve-day stay in Moscow, Barbara retreated to her room at the Sovietskaya Hotel and got sloppy drunk. She was often accompanied by journalist Sam Jaffe, who covered the trial for CBS television. Whether Jaffe was merely pumping her for information or engaged in an illicit affair has been debated by certain parties for more than half a century. Baugh suspected they were doing something more than drinking, but Jaffe, a onetime FBI informant who later struggled to combat charges of a collaboration with the KGB, which led him to sue the American government, ultimately winning a federal judgment that cleared his name, told the FBI "at no time was I intimate with her."[117]

By the third day, Frank was visibly tired. He often squinted in the intense lights and no doubt felt the burden of his circumstances, wondering whether he had gone too far down the road to cooperation while trying to save his own neck.

In his closing argument, Rudenko carefully laid out the details of the aircraft, the violation of the Soviet airspace, the mission, and Powers's motivation, as a man who grew up of modest means, having "voluntarily sold his honor and his conscience . . . for dollars."[118]

When the prosecutor asked for fifteen years instead of death, Frank immediately felt relieved.

But Oliver leapt to his feet. "Give me 15 years here! I'd rather get death!"[119]

After Grinyov conceded the facts of the case but asked the court for leniency, Powers was given an opportunity to make a statement:

> The court has heard all the evidence and now must decide my punishment. I realize that I committed a grave crime and that I must be punished for it. I ask the court to weigh all the evidence and to take into consideration not only the fact that I committed the crime, but also the circumstances that led me to do so. I also ask the court to take into consideration that no secret information reached its destination; it all fell into the hands of the Soviet authorities. I realize that the Russian people think of me as an enemy. I understand this, but I would like to stress the fact that I do not feel and have never felt any enmity toward the Russian people. I plead with the court to judge me not as an enemy but as a human being, not a personal enemy of the Russian people, who has never had charges against him in any court, and who is deeply repentant and sincerely sorry for what he has done.[120]

Baugh could understand the pressure the defendant felt, and the way the message sounded back home. It was a humiliating moment for America. Even before his conviction, newspapers had printed banner headlines such as "Powers Pleads Guilty." His carefully worded statement after his conviction hit the papers in the context of three months of swirling doubts. The indignity of a US serviceman apologizing to the Soviets was difficult for many of Powers's fellow citizens to accept.

Writing about the situation, Baugh said, "Clearly there had been some coaching . . . that [this approach] would be the only way to save his life. . . . I'm sure he was sorry to have been responsible for creating the incident that worsened the Cold War . . . [but] he certainly didn't impress us as having defected. He did not criticize or disavow our government."[121]

After a deliberation lasting four hours and forty minutes, the court reconvened and the defendant was ordered to rise. He stood in the dock, his hands holding onto the wooden railings. The three judges began reciting the charges and went further, effectively indicting Powers as complicit in an American scheme to destroy the Paris summit as a means to deepen the Cold War.

In the family section, Ida leaned in and whispered to her husband and daughter. "Don't shed a tear. Don't show any emotion."

When Borisoglebsky announced the sentence of ten years' confinement, including three years in prison, the room erupted in cheers as the defendant tried to keep his cool. He looked for his family but could not see them. He later wrote, "Only as I was being led from the courtroom did the full impact of the sentence hit me."[122]

Escorted into a small room with the assembled members of his family, where a spread of food and wine was laid out on a table, Frank broke down into tears while embracing his wife and mother, father, and sister. A well-armed six-man security team guarded the door. Frank told them he was relieved he did not receive the death penalty but wondered aloud if he had done the right thing by displaying such remorse. It did not take him long to become aware of the friction between Barbara and the rest of the family. This bothered him, and he asked them to try to get along.

Still stinging from Grinyov's harsh words about his country, Powers told his wife he wanted her to make a statement to the press on his behalf. The next day, the two lawyers appointed by the Virginia Bar Association, Andrew W. Parker and Frank W. Rogers, relayed the message to reporters, repudiating much of what Grinyov said.

"I'm an American and I don't want any part of it," Powers told his wife.[123]

The Soviet lawyer had quoted Powers as saying he believed he would be prosecuted if he ever returned to the United States, but not long after word of the verdict reached Washington, President Eisenhower said the government had no intention of prosecuting the pilot, "because it sees nothing in his conduct to warrant such prosecution."[124]

While extending his "sincere sympathy" to members of the pilot's family and pledging to "provide for his wife" while he was confined to a Soviet prison, Eisenhower expressed his disappointment at the way Powers had been used to further Soviet propaganda.

Four days after the trial, as the family prepared to return to the United States, Frank visited with his mother and father one last time, wondering if it would be the last time he would ever see them. Ten years was a long time.

The Soviets allowed Barbara to visit with him alone in a secluded room at the prison, where the husband and wife had intercourse. Afterward, Barbara told her family and other members of the travel party about their intimacy. In case she became pregnant, she wanted people to know.[125]

Chapter Four

REPATRIATED

On the evening of February 7, 1962, two inmates inside Vladimir Prison started their evening walk from the community toilet back to their tiny, 12′×8′ cell.[1] They were in no hurry. Every moment they were allowed to linger beyond the confining gray-and-white walls was precious, like a little whiff of freedom.

Inside the ancient penitentiary built during the reign of Catherine the Great, located about 150 miles east of Moscow, Francis Gary Powers, the world's most famous spy, was just another lost soul who had to piss in a bucket and squat over a big open hole in the floor.

Transferred to Vladimir twenty-one days after his conviction, Powers was introduced to Zigurd Kruminsh shortly after he arrived from Moscow. The American pilot and the Latvian dissident, who said he had been betrayed while hiding out with members of the anti-Soviet underground and given a fifteen-year sentence after a sham trial, quickly became friends. Powers wondered if he was a KGB plant. It all seemed too convenient, especially since the man spoke five languages, including English, and espoused a virulent hatred of the Soviets. No matter. Powers realized his biggest enemy was loneliness and despair. Zigurd gave him someone to talk to. They made each other laugh and took turns looking through the little crack in the cabinet blocking the window, which offered a glimpse into the outside world. Little things. They shared the little things that kept them from going crazy inside. The Latvian taught Frank how to weave small burlap and wool rugs. They also passed the time playing chess.[2]

On the way back from the bathroom, Frank and Zigurd noticed the KGB colonel, who was the most powerful man at the prison, and his interpreter standing outside their cell, number 31, on the second floor of building two.

Stepping into the cell after the two inmates, he approached Powers and said, "How would you like to go to Moscow tomorrow morning?"[3]

Moscow?

He had been confined at Vladimir for seventeen months, so long that he was starting to forget how trees looked.

"Fine," he said, unsure of what was happening.

Then the colonel added one bit of information.

"Without guards."

This could only mean one thing, but he was almost afraid to think it. Several times during those seventeen months, he had gotten his hopes up about an early release, only to be disappointed. Just days earlier, the pilot's wife told reporters in Milledgeville that Soviet officials had told him he had no chance of clemency because of the "seriousness and gravity of his crime."[4]

Unlike any other man in Vladimir, he was truly a political prisoner.

The U-2 Incident was like a grenade tossed into the bitterly contested 1960 presidential election.

Khrushchev believed that releasing Powers before the election would boost the chances of Vice President Nixon against Democrat John F. Kennedy.[5]

Kennedy, who pushed the "missile gap" theme as a way of attacking Eisenhower from the right—relying on estimates that the Soviets would have as many as 500 first-strike-capable ICBMs by 1961, several times the US arsenal—benefited from the U-2 Incident as a potent symbol of the outgoing administration's negligence in the face of a growing Soviet threat. Nixon would always blame Allen Dulles for failing to explain the truth gained by the four-year U-2 program, disproving the gap, although such revelations would have pushed the CIA director into the forbidden realm of domestic politics.

After the Powers shoot-down sent US-Soviet relations careening to a new low, Kennedy told a high-school student, during a rally in Oregon, that he might be willing to apologize to Khrushchev for the overflight. The resulting firestorm made him seem weak and naïve.[6] Ultimately, this gaffe motivated him to become more overtly hawkish.

While Kennedy was an unknown quantity at the Kremlin, Khrushchev was inclined to oppose any continuation of the current American policy. He disliked Nixon, who wore his anti-communism like a beauty-pageant sash.

"Several top Soviets have indicated to me their opposition to you," Ambassador Thompson wrote to the vice president. "I have always taken the line with them that you are a staunch and effective anti-communist just as they are staunch anti-capitalists, but that they made a mistake in assuming that you were opposed to negotiations or agreements with the Soviet Union."[7]

Even with the bad blood stirred up by Powers and by the Kremlin's cozying up to Fidel Castro, the Eisenhower administration quietly pressed for the release of Powers and the RB-47 crew.

But Khrushchev insisted the time was not right, believing any movement on the issue would reflect a tacit endorsement of Eisenhower's handpicked successor. "We would never give Nixon such a present," Khrushchev told his colleagues.[8]

After Kennedy captured the White House with one of the narrowest margins in American history, the Soviet Union released the two surviving members of the RB-47 crew as a goodwill gesture to the new administration. ("You can't sit in a cell for 211 days without it affecting you," Colonel Bruce Olmstead said. "You forgive, and you live with it."[9])

Powers thought for sure he was next. But the news never came.

In June 1961, the two leaders met in Vienna. "You know, Mr. Kennedy," Khrushchev said, "we voted for you."[10] This was apparently meant as a joke, but it was impossible to deny that the U-2 Incident, the scuttling of the summit, and Powers's continued imprisonment inured to Kennedy's benefit. JFK declined to bring up Powers's fate at the summit.

In another instance, Khrushchev said, "Relations deteriorated due to the U-2 and I consider that the American people's vote for Mr. Kennedy was against Nixon, the U-2 and the Cold War policy."[11]

The CIA's attempt to overthrow Castro in April 1961, a covert operation approved by Eisenhower, also worked against Powers's case. The fiasco of the Bay of Pigs demonstrated the CIA's hubris and the ineptitude of the early Kennedy administration, which pulled the plug rather than risk an overt confrontation with the Soviets. It was another very public black eye for an agency that was institutionally averse to sunlight. The axe fell on Allen Dulles and Richard Bissell, leaving the CIA to be managed by a new man, John A. McCone, who was not personally invested in the cause of the U-2 program and Francis Gary Powers.

Four months later, the Soviet-backed East German government began constructing the Berlin Wall. The steady migration of East German citizens to the West—estimated at about 1,000 people per day by the late 1950s—ended overnight, except those souls brave enough to pursue freedom at the risk of a bullet.

The new fortification, which extended for 96 miles, protected by armed guards with orders to shoot to kill, immediately became the ultimate symbol of the Iron Curtain.

By early 1962, it was hard to deny the impact of Powers's ill-fated flight—as if that bright flash of orange light had signaled the dawn of an ominous alternate reality. With the U-2 Incident, US-Soviet relations fell into a dangerous downward spiral.

Given all this disturbing news, Powers remained skeptical of his release—until a guard showed up with a suitcase and told him to start packing. He allowed himself to believe that he was finally going home.

Around six o'clock the next morning, Frank said goodbye to Zigurd and walked out of the prison building and into a waiting car. Within a few minutes, he and the colonel and the interpreter stepped onto a train bound for Moscow. He tried to engage the colonel about the situation, but he refused to discuss it.

When they arrived in Moscow, a car drove them through familiar streets, finally reaching a familiar destination. Powers never thought he would see those iron gates of Lubyanka again. The sight stirred an unsettling feeling.

Once inside, the colonel led him to his old cellblock. This time, however, he was only visiting. The next morning, they were headed to East Germany.

Because his prison account had a balance of about one hundred dollars, but they were only authorized to distribute rubles, which were worthless in the outside world, the colonel asked him what he wanted to do with the money. He thought about it for a moment. Could they transfer the balance to his buddy Zigurd? No. Not allowed.

After some discussion, they allowed him to use the money on some Russian souvenirs, which the interpreter would buy for him, and on a meal brought in from a restaurant.

During his twenty-one months of captivity, he had lost more than twenty pounds, his diet consisting mostly of soup and potatoes. He desperately yearned for some meat and a stiff drink, so the two veal cutlets and the tin cup half-filled with brandy hit the spot.

When they arrived at the airport the next morning, a small plane was waiting, its two propellers already spinning.

"If you had to go from a car into a house or on a plane, you went fast," Powers recalled. "They didn't make you run, but they didn't want you to be in public view very long."[12]

After flying to East Berlin, the American and his two Soviet escorts wound up at a safe house, the sort of cozy, well-appointed place reserved for party big shots. He noticed a very visible security detail outside, which contrasted with his knowledge of CIA safe houses, where the first order of business was to remain invisible. Apparently, the KGB didn't care so much about secrecy once they had their prisoner locked up tight.

When the colonel produced a bottle of brandy and poured the prisoner a drink, he took a sip. "Made me woozy," he recalled with a laugh. The KGB man shook his head.

"No! No!" he said in Russian. "That's not the way we drink in Russia. Chugalug!"[13]

The man proceeded to demonstrate by filling his cup and downing it in one gulp.

Frank nodded and killed his brandy in one swallow.

"If everything goes well," he said, "you will be released tomorrow morning and will have a reason to celebrate."[14]

Before dawn, when they shared a ceremonial brandy and headed out into the cool air, Frank remained in the dark about the specifics of his impending repatriation. In time he would learn that his father deserved part of the credit. At least Oliver was no longer contradicting him on the front page of the *New York Times*.

The week after his conviction, Oliver gave an interview to the *Times* in which he said, "[Francis] said, 'If I had been shot down, there would have been an explosion behind me and an orange flash around me.' He didn't believe he was shot down."[15]

Frank was stunned.

Clearly his father was confused.

He asked for permission to write a letter to the editor of the paper, carefully choosing his words. . .

18 September 1960

Editor
New York Times
New York, N.Y.

Dear sir:

I was given the opportunity to read the article in the August 27th issue of The New York Times in which my father while being interviewed stated that I did not think I had been shot down.

Apparently my father misunderstood the answers I gave to questions put to me during the Trial.

I would like to clear this misunderstanding by saying that even though I did not see what it was that caused the explosion I feel sure that it was not the aircraft itself which exploded. All of my engine instruments were normal up to the time of the explosion which I both felt and heard. I also saw an orange flash or glow when I looked out.

I cannot be sure but I think the explosion was behind and maybe to the right of the aircraft.

I felt no impact of anything against the airplane itself, therefore I think the shock wave from the explosion caused the damage.

I can only guess what happened after that. I am of the opinion that the tail of the aircraft came off first causing the nose to drop sharply resulting in the failure of both wings. The cockpit and what was left of the aircraft tumbled and finally settled into an inverted spin causing "G" forces which made it impossible for me to use the ejection seat. I finally got out of the aircraft at fourteen thousand feet or below. I give this altitude because my parachute opened automatically and it was set to open at fourteen thousand feet. It opened immediately upon my getting free of the aircraft.

I was at maximum altitude as stated in the trial, at the time of the explosion. This altitude was 68,000 feet.

I feel sure that my father misunderstood what was said during the Trial and if so then maybe there are others who also misunderstood. I hope this letter will clear up any misunderstanding on this question.

My father did not misunderstand me when he stated that when this was all over that I was coming home. I do intend to come home and I pray that I will not have to stay in prison for ten years.

Sorry to have bothered you but I felt that an explanation was needed to clear up the question of what actually happened.

Sincerely yours,

Francis G. Powers[16]

From the earliest reports of the incident, American officials began trying to figure out how it had happened. Because many senior officials refused to believe the Soviets had advanced so far in their missile technology to be able to reach a U-2 flying at its operational ceiling, a theory emerged: Powers had descended to a lower altitude, allowing him to be felled by a surface-to-air missile.

No less a figure than Allen Dulles believed this, at least in the summer of 1960. The month after the incident, he privately told C. L. Sulzberger of the *New York Times*, "We think Gary glided down to try and restart his motor. He was then shot down around 30,000–40,000 feet...."[17] Kelly Johnson and President Eisenhower made similar statements.

With the pilot consistently insisting he had not experienced any mechanical problems and had been hit at "maximum altitude"—the definition of which reflected the cat-and-mouse game played by the CIA—such a scenario required an additional leap: He had purposely descended to a lower altitude, which meant he had sabotaged his own mission in order to defect. Even after his show trial and incarceration, the possibility of such an explanation lingered.

In this context, Oliver unwittingly contributed to the swirling doubts concerning his son. The American public was left to draw its own conclusion about the August 27 report, and many no doubt assumed the pilot had spoken in some sort of code to his father, letting him in on a secret. This was a bell that could not be un-rung.

And yet Oliver made the connection that eventually sent him home.

In the years after his unsuccessful defense of the KGB spy Rudolf Abel, James B. Donovan continued to press forward with an appeal. In this the onetime naval commander, OSS official, and associate counsel to the Nuremberg tribunals, who was now consigned to the much-less-glamorous life of a New York lawyer who specialized in insurance cases, believed he was doing his duty. He never doubted his client's guilt. But because he believed in American justice and the message it sent to the rest of the world, Donovan believed Abel—who went by several different aliases and refused to give the government his real name—deserved the most vigorous defense possible, even if such high-mindedness in the age of the Red Scare struck some of his friends as unnecessarily noble.

Anonymous phone calls and letters to his Brooklyn home branded him a "commie lover."[18]

The publicity of the case helped Donovan land the Democratic nomination for the US Senate in 1962, but the baggage of representing a Soviet spy at the height of the Cold War was too much to overcome, especially against popular incumbent Jacob K. Javits, who beat him by more than 1 million votes.

Before the US Supreme Court, Donovan argued that the government violated Abel's Fourth Amendment rights against unreasonable search and seizure when the Immigration and Naturalization Service, armed only with an administrative warrant, detained him and worked in concert with the FBI to search his room at Manhattan's Latham Hotel. Even without the Cold War implications, the case emerged as a closely watched test of Fourth Amendment protections.

Abel, who eventually settled in for a long stay at the Atlanta Federal Penitentiary, once asked his attorney what would happen if his conviction was overturned and he was granted a new trial and an eventual acquittal. By this time the accused and his lawyer had developed a mutual respect, but Abel harbored no illusions about Donovan's sympathies. He understood the representation was all about the larger principle, so he was not surprised by the answer. "If all my work is successful," Donovan said, "I may have to shoot you myself."[19]

On March 28, 1960, the US Supreme Court upheld Abel's conviction. The vote was 5 to 4. "The nature of the case, the fact that it was a prosecution for espionage, has no bearing whatever upon the legal considerations relevant to the admissibility of the evidence," Justice Felix Frankfurter wrote in the majority opinion.[20]

None of the justices could yet understand how the narrow margin would enable a defining moment of the Cold War.

By the time Powers tumbled out of the sky thirty-four days later, and with Abel staring at another twenty-seven years of hard time, Donovan's suggestion of a future spy trade was mostly forgotten.

Somehow Oliver learned about the idea, resurrecting it in a letter to Abel:

June 2, 1960

Dear Colonel Abel,

I am the father of Francis Gary Powers who is connected with the U-2 plane incident of several weeks ago. I am quite sure that you are familiar with this international incident and also the fact that my son is being currently held by the Soviet Union on an espionage charge.

You can readily understand the concern that a father would have for his son and for a strong desire to have my son released and brought home. My present feeling is that I would be more than happy to approach the State Department and the President of the United States for an exchange for the release of my son. By this I mean that I would urge and do everything possible to have my government release you and return you to your country if the powers in your country would release my son and let him return to me. If you are inclined to go along with this arrangement I would appreciate your so advising me and also so advising the powers in your country along these lines.

I would appreciate hearing from you in this regard as soon as possible.

Very truly yours,
Oliver Powers[21]

Such a trade was complicated by various factors, including one rather big problem: Although an East German woman who purported to be his wife was anxious to get him back, the Soviets insisted they had never heard of Abel. But Oliver started the dominos tumbling. One thing led to another ... and twenty-one months later, Washington dispatched Donovan to East Germany to negotiate an exchange, which required several days of back-and-forth with Alexandrovich Schischkin, a high-ranking KGB official; Abel's "wife"; his lawyer; and the East Germany attorney general.

At 8:20 a.m. local time on Saturday, February 10, 1962, the American pilot walked toward the middle of the Glienicker Bridge, which spanned Lake Wannsee, separating Potsdam, part of East Germany, from West Berlin. He was accompanied by two Soviet officials. In his hands he carried the suitcase, containing some clothes, his diary, a rug he made in prison, and the souvenirs purchased on his behalf. It was cold, and he was wearing a heavy coat. Approaching from the opposite direction was an American delegation leading Rudolf Abel.

Joe Murphy took a long look at Powers.

About two weeks earlier, inside the new CIA headquarters in Langley, Virginia, John McMahon, who eventually became deputy director, stopped by Murphy's office. They were getting Powers out, and they needed someone to identify him. "You're it." Murphy arrived in West Berlin via Frankfurt the previous Monday and helped make the preparations, including how and where to hide Abel.

Washington feared the news leaking out. While the bureau of prisons prepared to fly Abel to West Germany, Murphy went to work arranging to keep him overnight at a nearby US Army base while awaiting the exchange. Because the base employed a large number of German civilians, the commander picked up the phone and ordered a subordinate to give all the Germans Friday off. He didn't say why. With the circle closed, the secret held and the small party convened at the bridge without drawing any attention.

Murphy knew Powers well.

"Right away, I knew it was Frank," he said.

Before he could say anything, Powers called him by the wrong name. "Oh, hey, Charley!"

"Nope. Try again."

Recalling the scene, Murphy said, "I knew what he was thinking. The guy who replaced me [as the security officer at Incirlik] was named

Charley. Frank got confused, which was understandable. There was no reaction from the others. They were relying on me, and I had no doubts."

Looking back on the moment, Powers said, "I knew that I knew the man, but I called him by the wrong name."[22]

After going through several security questions—including the name of his dog—the trade was delayed while Donovan waited for a phone call about Frederic Pryor.

Pryor, a twenty-eight-year-old American who was pursuing a doctorate at Yale, spent about two years freely moving between West Berlin and East Berlin while studying economics at the Free University of West Berlin. One day in September 1961, after the wall went up, he crossed into the eastern zone to attend a speech and visit a colleague. He could see the border crossing was becoming too dangerous. Being a foreigner allowed him to move between the zones, but the show of force and the fear of the unknown unnerved him. He decided to tell his friend that they needed to abandon their joint project, which concerned the textile industry.

When he arrived at the woman's house and learned that she had escaped to the West, Pryor was seized by the Stasi, the East Germany secret police. They searched his car, found his dissertation, and were convinced he was a spy. The Stasi spent more than four months interrogating him, threatening him with the death penalty unless he confessed. They never tortured him, but in his cell, he often heard men screaming.

"Once you're arrested, you're always convicted," he recalled many years later. "I expected five or 10 years in prison. I made peace with that."[23]

Pryor's luck turned when Donovan began negotiating the trade of actual spies and was able to convince the East Germans to throw the student in as a goodwill gesture.

He was to be released at the same time at Checkpoint Charlie, in the center of bustling Berlin. But the notification did not arrive at the appointed time, which left the two sides waiting on the bridge.

Powers had already decided, if something happened to prevent the exchange, he would make a run for it. "Even if it meant a bullet, I'm wasn't coming back."[24]

While waiting for word, Powers and Murphy walked to the side of the bridge and casually chatted.

"That's Abel over there," Murphy said, pointing toward the thin man standing near the middle of the bridge. (In contrast to the warm welcome Powers received from Murphy, Donovan, and State Department official Alan Lightner, the Soviets did not seem particularly happy to see their long-lost spy.)

"Who?"

"Rudolf Abel!"

"Oh..."

Until this point, Powers did not know he was released as part of a trade.

Over the course of the previous two days, he had repeatedly asked the Soviets why he was suddenly being released. "They said, 'We just want to show the world how humane the Soviet Union is,'" he recalled. "Right up to the last minute ... even though 10 minutes [later], I would find out [the truth]. This was ... an insight into their psychology."[25]

Soon the two Americans were joined at the edge of the bridge by Schischkin, a tall, friendly man who spoke fluent English.

"Goodbye, Mr. Powers," he said. "Come see us again sometime."

Frank smiled. "Yes sir, I'll come as a tourist."

"Not as a tourist. As a friend."

Several minutes later, a member of the American delegation yelled out that Pryor was safely in the West, signaling the two sides to move across opposite sides of the bridge.

On the drive to the local airport Tempelhof, Frank learned about Donovan's role as the driving force behind the exchange, destined to remain an iconic moment of Cold War intrigue.

While strapped into the back of a military plane for the short flight to the massive Rhein-Main Air Force Base in Frankfurt, where they would board a Lockheed C-121 Super Constellation for the six-hour flight back to the States, Powers was examined by a military doctor. The air was choppy and the doctor had a hard time planting the needle to obtain a blood sample.

One thing bothered Murphy about the first leg of their journey back to the United States: "You would have thought the Air Force guys flying the plane would have been very welcoming to Frank . . . but for whatever reason, they weren't," Murphy said. "They were very cool toward him."

This was a preview of coming attractions.

After twenty-one months of captivity, Frank was happy to be a free man. But the doubts followed him home.

News of the exchange filtered out in time for some of the Saturday-afternoon newspapers back in the United States, including the *Washington Daily News*, where the headline and headshots of Powers and Abel dominated the front page:

U-2 Pilot

Is Freed In

Spy Swap[26]

The release remained top-of-the-fold news across the country the next day, as Americans hungered for details of a real-life spy story with a happy ending.

"Francis Gary Powers is now in the United States and is meeting privately with members of his family," the White House said in a statement. "Mr. Powers appears to be in good physical condition."[27]

The reunion with his parents at the CIA safe house in Maryland was emotional.

"My wife and I were asleep when the big word came," Oliver told reporters before boarding a flight to the secret location.[28] "But it's not very hard to keep awake now. His mother and I thought it would probably be a much longer time—at least four or five years."

Frank had feared he would never see Oliver and Ida again. They had harbored the same anxiety. Getting to see them and hug them and talk with them about the ordeal was an incredibly cathartic experience.

When the early-morning call from the White House reached Milledgeville, Barbara was equally stunned, telling reporters, "I can't sleep. I'm too excited!"[29]

"How can I express my reaction to the happiness I feel when I had no idea I would see him for 10 years?"

The newspapers said Barbara rushed off to her hairdresser so she would look good for her husband. But after flying to Maryland, accompanied by her brother Jack, now a chaplain in the Air Force, she showed up smelling of alcohol. She had put on about thirty pounds. She expressed irritation that she had not been given prior notice of the release, which puzzled her husband. She kept saying she needed a drink but insisted she didn't have a drinking problem.

"Barbara looked terrible, like she had not been taking good care of herself," Murphy said. "I never saw her look so bad."

Even as he enjoyed the long-denied comforts of home—a bed with a full mattress and springs, a toilet with a seat, good food, the freedom to walk around the house and across the large yard—Frank gradually began to feel like a prisoner of the CIA.

During a walk across the snow-covered grounds, he turned to Murphy and asked, "If I wanted to leave right now, could I?"[30]

"Well, I really don't think you could."

When a reporter located the safe house, the CIA moved Powers to another location near Gettysburg, Pennsylvania, where the agency specialists spent the next three weeks questioning him in exacting detail about every aspect of his shoot-down, interrogation, and imprisonment.

After reading the debrief and studying various evidence, Dulles changed his original assessment about Powers descending to a lower altitude. "We are proud of what you have done," he told the pilot during a meeting in his government office.[31]

The new director of the CIA, John A. McCone, remained skeptical. Feeling pressure to assess the failure, McCone appointed a Board of Inquiry chaired by E. Barrett Prettyman, a retired chief judge of the US Court of Appeals' DC circuit.

Among the speculation to hit the media was the question of whether the pilot's employment contract obligated him to destroy the plane if it was downed in Soviet territory.

After eight days of closed-door hearings, the Prettyman commission concluded that Powers was "inherently and by practice a truthful man" who had "complied with his obligations as an American citizen during this period."[32] It ordered his back pay, which amounted to $52,500, to be awarded, and cleared him to return to work at the CIA.

However, the board did not offer a definitive opinion on how the U-2 was felled, which enhanced the murkiness surrounding the incident.

Some within the intelligence community quietly continued to doubt the pilot, including McCone. The agency knew much more about what happened than it was willing to tell, and no one paid a higher price for this silence than Francis Gary Powers.

"In my opinion, Francis Gary Powers handled himself perfectly under the circumstances," argued longtime military and intelligence writer Norman Polmar, who also worked inside the defense establishment. "But the agency could not defend him. The agency did what it should have done at that time. It had the right and responsibility to protect itself. . . . [The CIA] didn't know that they weren't going to have to send another U-2 back over the Soviet Union, and they had to protect those secrets."

During his time in prison, Powers was allowed no access to Western news sources, except for the American socialist publication the *Nation*. So when he returned to the United States and began to be inundated by articles questioning his patriotism, he was shocked.

In one article, John Wickers, a onetime Virginia politician and longtime member of the American Legion, told a reporter, "I view the exchange with astonishment and disgust. Powers was a cowardly American who evidently valued his own skin far more than the welfare of the nation that was paying him so handsomely."[33]

US Senator Stephen Young, a Democrat from Ohio, said, "I wish this pilot . . . had shown only ten percent of the spirit and courage of Nathan Hale."[34]

Immediately after hearing his apology, Philadelphia Mayor Richardson Dilworth blasted the "disgraceful performance" as a "terrible example to the rest of the world."[35]

Each negative article was like a gut punch to a man who had been deprived of his liberty for nearly two years but returned an ambivalent figure, repatriated as something less than a hero.

One of the most devastating blows was delivered by President Kennedy. On March 6, Powers was waiting for a car to take him to the White House for a personal meeting with the president. At the last minute, however, someone from the White House called to say the meeting had been postponed. In fact, it had been canceled. No explanation was ever offered. Previously, the pilot had been told that Attorney General Robert Kennedy favored trying him for treason. "Bobby Kennedy made the initial judgment that the guy was a traitor," said longtime CIA man Kenneth Bradt. Clearly, some within the administration considered him too politically toxic to be seen with the president, in sharp contrast to the RB-47 survivors, who had been welcomed into the Oval Office.

Frank would be haunted by the snub for the rest of his life.

The controversy surrounding him was somewhat analogous to the situation faced by Mercury astronaut Virgil I. "Gus" Grissom, who on July 21, 1961, became the second American in space. After splashing down, explosive bolts fired for some reason, flooding the capsule and eventually sending it to the bottom of the Atlantic Ocean. Grissom was rescued but widely blamed for the mishap. Kennedy shunned him. Long after he died in the January 27, 1967, launch-pad test fire of *Apollo 1* that also claimed the lives of fellow astronauts Ed White and Roger Chaffee, Grissom's memory remained clouded by the mysterious loss of *Liberty Bell 7*.

About two hours after his White House meeting was called off, while testifying in a public hearing of the Senate Armed Services Committee, Powers discussed the fateful day in great detail, telling the senators: "I can remember hearing, feeling, and sensing an explosion. . . . I felt that the explosion was external to the aircraft and behind me." At one point he employed a model of the plane, demonstrating how the right wing "dropped slightly, not very much. I used the controls. The wing came back up level[,] just before or after it got level, the nose started going down, very slowly. So I applied back pressure to the control column and felt no resistance to the movement of the control column[,] and it kept going faster and faster. So I immediately assumed at that time the tail section of the aircraft had come off, because it—a very violent maneuver happened in here. . . ."[36]

After listening to his testimony, Senator Leverett Saltonstall of Massachusetts commended Powers as a "courageous, fine, young American citizen."[37]

Like the CIA panel, the Senate Armed Services Committee and the Foreign Relations Committee determined that Powers acted appropriately. But the details of the reports remained secret, ostensibly for national-security concerns, and therefore exerted virtually no impact on public opinion, which was being shaped to a great degree by negative media reports.

In his prepared remarks to the committee, McCone struck a legalistic tone when explaining one aspect of the Prettyman board's finding:

> Some information from confidential sources was available. Some of it corroborated Powers and some of it was inconsistent, was in part contradictory with itself and subject to various interpretations. . . . Some of this information was the basis for considerable speculation shortly

after the May 1 episode and subsequent stories in the press that Powers' plane had descended gradually from its extreme altitude and have been shot down by a Soviet fighter at medium altitude. On careful analysis, it appears that the information on which these stories were based was erroneous or was susceptible to varying interpretations. . . . [38]

On the same day Powers appeared in a public session with the Armed Services Committee, Senator John J. Williams, a Republican from Delaware, asked McCone, during his executive-session testimony to Foreign Relations: "Don't you think he is being left with just a little bit of a cloud hanging over him? If he did everything he is supposed to do, why leave it hanging?"[39]

When Frank returned to Pound to see the family, the town held a celebration in his honor, including two high-school bands and a large crowd of locals. His father was recognized for starting the ball rolling on the trade. Many welcomed Powers home, willing to accept the shades of gray he was forced to negotiate; but in others, Walton Meade, Powers's brother-in-law, saw the subtle signs of disapproval. "Some people said he was a traitor," he said. "'He didn't do what he should've done. He ought've killed himself.' That's how a lot of people felt."

The Pound was a proud place, teaming with patriotism, full of veterans who had served in both world wars. Francis Gary Powers was their sort of man. Until he got caught up in something they didn't fully understand.

"There's people here, some of 'em would've killed him, if they'd gotten a chance," Meade said.

The talk wounded Powers deeply. Spending all that time in a Soviet prison was a kind of torture, but returning to his own country and having his patriotism questioned was the most hurtful blow of all. The infamy now attached to his name represented a special kind of confinement from which he could never hope to escape.

Why did he not use the poison pin?

Why didn't he destroy the plane?

Is it true he descended to a lower altitude?

What secrets did he reveal to the Soviets?

Why did he say what he said?

The people who were willing to believe Powers betrayed his country hated him for how his failure made them feel.

At the triumphant height of the American Century, when the country was unaccustomed to foreign-policy debacles and unwilling to concede its limitations, the profound humiliation of hearing him apologize to the Soviets was not something they would soon forget.

They needed someone to blame for their shame.

In a world tantalized by James Bond and other fictional spies, the lore of the poison pin captured the public's imagination, playing into preconceived ideas about the shadowy world of espionage. It was easy to believe such a man, shouldering the risk of flying into denied territory for the nefarious purpose of taking photographs of sensitive military sites, would be ordered to prick himself and be done with it—taking one for the team and denying the enemy the opportunity to gain information, leverage, and propaganda points.

At his wedding in the summer of 1962, Joe Murphy could see that some of his friends disapproved of Powers's presence. "Nothing was said to him, but I knew how some felt," he said. "I could never understand that way of thinking."

Even before his parachute tumbled to the ground, the narrative of his life was established in the eyes of many: By allowing himself to be captured alive, Francis Gary Powers was a traitor.

Some didn't know the truth of the poison pin: that it was optional and completely within his discretion. He was under no orders to kill himself.

Some didn't care, believing he should have taken his own life—regardless of what he was obligated to do.

The lack of a definitive public explanation by Washington on this matter and others related to the U-2 Incident enabled various conspiracy theories to swirl, even pulling in the celebrated Ian Fleming, the creator of James Bond, who said:

> I don't for a moment believe that Powers was shot down at 68,000 feet by Russian rockets. I believe it was sabotage at the Turkish base— delayed action bombs in the tail section. . . . [40]

Like many others, Fleming believed Washington should have disavowed Powers—"throwing [him] cold-bloodedly to the dogs"—and that the pilot should have accepted the consequences of his job, which warranted such a handsome salary primarily because it was fraught with such risks. "He was expendable. Expend him!"

Of course, his family and friends and various others thought differently. They saw him as a good man who did his best under trying circumstances and loved his country but was not required to sacrifice his life to prove his patriotism.

"I knew my brother was no traitor," Joan said. "He did his duty. Some people just didn't understand."

Some of the people in the office at Langley enjoyed teasing Jeannie Popovich. Young and impressionable, the wide-eyed eighteen-year-old had recently migrated from a coal-mining community in western Pennsylvania to take a job as a clerk-typist at the agency. Sometimes the others told her outlandish stories just to test her level of gullibility, invariably sealing the ritual with an admission of the lie and a good-natured laugh shared by all. She took it all in stride and never considered it mean-spirited. But she was determined not to believe the next tall tale.

One day in the spring of 1962, about three months after she joined the CIA, Popovich heard a knock at the department door. Their office did not have a receptionist, but since her desk was located nearest the door, she got up and answered the knock. The man said he was there to see the gentleman in charge of the section. "My name is Powers," he said.

When Jeannie ushered the man into her boss's office and returned to her desk, one of her coworkers approached and said, "Do you know who that was?"

"The man said his name was Powers."

"That was Francis Gary Powers. Do you know who Francis Gary Powers is?"

Of course she knew.

But she assumed her colleague was trying to tell her another whopper, and she wasn't going to fall for it.

Soon others joined in, trying to convince her. One even went to the office safe and retrieved a file, which showed that the famous spy was scheduled to start work in their office that very day.

"Read this!"

She began to believe it might be true.

A while later, when the boss opened his door and began introducing Powers to the staff, Popovich accepted a different kind of grief from her friends, negotiating an important milestone in her evolution to skeptical CIA veteran.

Soon after the shoot-down, the agency recognized a glaring vulnerability by creating a program to train pilots to deal with being captured and interrogated. Simulated prison experiences, which benefited from knowledge gained about Soviet and Chinese methods, taught pilots how to recognize and deal with their own vulnerabilities while maneuvering in an environment without Geneva Convention protections.

"Our people would have a cover story, flimsy as it may be . . . and they can't simply clam up and refuse to say anything," said Kenneth Bradt, one of the psychologists who administered the program. "What can you say and what do you need to protect? That was a big part of the training."

Unable to put Powers back in the air, and not knowing what else to do with him, the CIA leadership assigned him to the training program, where his experience became a closely examined case study.

Studying Powers's incarceration, Bradt admired the way the pilot handled the situation. "Considering what he had [to deal with], the guy did a remarkable job," Bradt said. "His whole focus was on not revealing secret information. And he did a good job of that . . . not realizing the main focus of the Soviets was to use him for propaganda."

"The pressure on him was twofold," Bradt said. "In addition to waking up every morning and wondering if this is the day they're going to take him out and shoot him, he had to deal with . . . what was going on with his wife. The Soviets were most happy to let all the letters through . . . to let him know his wife was becoming an alcoholic and sleeping with other men."

Even as he dealt with the complications of his ambivalent repatriation, Powers learned in greater detail about his wife's activities while he was away.

Increasingly out of control, Barbara was seen at all hours of the day and night at the bars in Milledgeville, where she often caused a scene. She made no attempt to conceal romantic liaisons with several different married men around town.

One night she caused a stir in the parking lot of a drinking establishment while partying with her African American maid in the front seat of Powers's Mercedes. Authorities were dispatched to the scene. "The Ku Klux Klan got into the act," Baugh said, "and it was only the timely intervention of Chief of Police, Eugene Ellis, that [prevented] every newspaper in the country [from writing] about the wife of the U-2 pilot . . . being placed in jail for violating the race mixing laws."[41]

During a trip to Jacksonville, Florida, accompanied by the wife of another pilot, a drunk Barbara drove off from her beachside hotel and ran a car into someone's yard. She was arrested and spent the night in jail, cursing and threatening the officers, revealing her identity as the wife of the world-famous pilot. The FBI and CIA smoothed things over, and her mother bailed her out of jail. Nothing ever wound up in the papers.

"All of these incidents simply pointed to the completely amoral state that Mrs. Barbara Powers had descended," Baugh wrote.[42] "Surely no sane person would endanger her husband with such irresponsibility and disgraceful conduct."

Especially while Frank was in prison, the Powers clan in Pound saw how whiskey ruled Barbara's life. It was an eye-opening experience for a bunch of teetotalers.

"She'd come in here, swear she'd never drink another drop, and by ten o'clock the next morning, she wouldn't know where she was," Jack Goff recalled.

When she ran out of liquor while staying at Goff's house, his brother-in-law Walton reluctantly replenished her supply.

"She would get it one way or another," Goff said. "It was sad."

When she left, they found empty bottles hidden throughout the back bedroom.

"It was very awkward for the family to deal with," Jan said. "She was clearly a very troubled girl, and none of us really knew how to handle it. She didn't seem to like the family, which made it even worse."

Barbara often directed her anger at her mother, who also drank heavily.

On Christmas night in 1960, Baugh's home telephone rang. On the line was Mrs. Brown's maid, who breathlessly said, "Something terrible [is] about to happen."

When Baugh arrived at the Brown home, he discovered both the mother and the daughter in a state of inebriation and the house strewn with furniture and belongings. Barbara, bruised and with her clothes torn, came out of the bathroom, where she had taken refuge, and told the doctor that she had been beaten with a broomstick by her mother. Monteen, who was employed at the Milledgeville State Hospital, Georgia's primary facility for mentally disturbed patients, insisted that she would not take any more of her daughter's insults and curses. Barbara began relating how her mother had fallen asleep drunk while smoking and set her mattress afire—awakened just in time by the Powers's dog, Eck.[43]

"Tragedy with a sensational overtone could be clearly seen in this most difficult family conflict," Baugh wrote.[44] "Publicity of the antics of this household could prove as a reflection on us nationally and provide the Soviets with excellent propaganda."

In the spring and summer of 1961, the issue reached a boiling point, as Baugh confronted Barbara about her behavior; one of her boyfriends threatened the doctor for meddling into their private affairs; and the wife experienced two run-ins with the law. On June 10, she was in the passenger seat when a male companion was charged with drunken driving near Dublin, Georgia. On June 22, Milledgeville police arrested her for drunk driving.

In September, with the backing of Monteen as well as Barbara's sister, Mrs. Neil Findley, and brother, Baugh successfully petitioned the court to involuntarily commit Mrs. Powers at the University Hospital Psychiatric Center in Augusta, Georgia.

"Her brother and her sister really worked with Jimmy to try to get some help for Barbara," Betty Baugh said.

While being treated by Dr. Corbett H. Thigpen—the acclaimed psychiatrist known for the multiple-personalities case that spawned the motion picture *Three Faces of Eve*—she told of hearing voices, including the dulcet tones of the singer Tennessee Ernie Ford.

In a letter to Powers, Baugh tried to put the best spin on the situation:

November 25, 1961

Francis G. Powers
Box 5 110/1 OD-1
Moscow, U.S.S.R.

Dear Francis:

I have at long last had an opportunity to sit down and write an answer to your letter dated October 27.

I am happy that you knew it was possible for me to make the trip to Moscow at the time of your trial. I feel that I was able in some small way to contribute to the comfort and assistance to your wife and her mother, Mrs. Brown. I too regret that it was not possible for me to have seen you for I have heard many kind and complimentary remarks by all who knew you. We of course are looking forward to the day that you may be released so you can again be with your family.

It is quite natural for you to be concerned about your wife when you learn that she was sent to a clinic for treatment. You may rest assured that her physical and mental condition have not been so serious as you have been led to believe. Well-meaning people sometimes tend to exaggerate the facts, especially where illnesses are concerned. Barbara did become highly emotional from the stress and strain of the past few months but at no time did I feel she was in serious condition which could result in insanity. I feel that she deserved the best care medical science could offer so when I was presented with the case by her mother I immediately got in touch with the Augusta Clinic where she remained for only a few weeks. She has returned home and, as far as I know, been doing well. I have advised the family to have her seen by the group at Augusta. I don't know which of the group connected with the University Hospital has the case at the moment. I hope to go to Augusta within a few days and find if those physicians need information from you. I feel, however, since she has responded to treatment and has now been returned home, the case needs no further study.

I appreciated your letter and interest. Your wife has received and will continue to receive the best medical science has to offer in whatever problem may arise.

Please feel free to write to me about any problems you may have. I want to take this opportunity to wish you as merry and happy a Christmas as conditions and circumstances will warrant.

Sincerely,

James E. Baugh, M.D.[45]

After returning from captivity, Frank wanted to believe he could save his marriage.

When he was assigned to CIA headquarters, Jan took Barbara shopping for groceries for their new apartment in Alexandria. "She was drinking quite heavily," Jan recalled.

As proof that she was able to control her drinking, Barbara left a full vodka bottle in the kitchen. Eventually Frank discovered it had been emptied and filled up with water.

In August, Powers took a trip to Pound alone to see the family and contemplate his future, feeling only pity for the women he had once loved. "In continuing the marriage I was only holding onto the shell of what was and what might have been," he said.[46]

Frank filed for divorce, which was granted in January 1963 and made national news. The court ordered him to pay Barbara a settlement of $5,000 and $500 in attorney's fees.

"I found [Francis] to be a very nice man who deserved better," Betty Baugh said. "It was a shame he had to deal with all this mess when he got back from such a traumatic experience."

Even as the marriage was breaking up, it was affecting CIA policy. With new pilots being recruited for the A-12 Oxcart program—eventually to evolve into the Air Force's SR-71 Blackbird—the CIA began placing much greater emphasis on a pilot's family situation. The agency overruled any candidate whose wife appeared unstable or otherwise potentially problematic. "We didn't want to inherit another Barbara," Bradt said.

The next chapter of Powers's life began with a spilled cup of coffee.

The pretty young woman who bumped into him at CIA headquarters, causing him to splatter her with the hot liquid, worked for Ken Bradt as a secretary/office manager. Her duties as a psychometrist included administering psychological tests to those agents who came back from abroad so that the CIA doctors could check the answers against their profiles.

Claudia Edwards Downey, known to one and all as Sue, had been married to a CIA operative who was stationed in Greece. She arrived home one day to find the husband in a compromising position with the Greek maid, which ended the marriage.

"Sue was a great gal," Bradt recalled. "She was very personable and outgoing, and everybody liked her."

Especially Frank.

The romance began quickly, while the pilot waited for his divorce to become final.

When he returned from the Soviet Union, Powers expected to be able to return to the Air Force. This was part of the deal he struck in 1955. But his commission was blocked, for reasons that were never fully explained to him. A decade later, he lamented to a reporter, "I guess they didn't want to have a known spy in the Air Force." [47]

With no flying available to him in the CIA, he began looking around for an opportunity to get back in the air, which led to an interview with Lockheed's Kelly Johnson in October.

While he was in California, the world learned that the Soviets had stationed offensive nuclear weapons in Cuba.

The U-2 Incident.

The Berlin Crisis.

The Bay of Pigs.

The Cuban Missile Crisis.

It all connected.

The hope invested in the Paris summit had devolved into the missiles of October, pushing the superpowers to the brink of thermonuclear war.

Photographic intelligence gleaned by U-2 flights confirmed the presence of the missiles, which President Kennedy and his United Nations ambassador, Adlai Stevenson, were able to use to great effect in proving the case to the world.

When US Air Force Major Rudolf Anderson Jr. returned for his sixth mission over the island nation and was blasted out of the sky by an

SA-2 missile, some in the White House and the Pentagon saw the hostile action as the first shot of a war. But Kennedy kept his cool and eventually forced the Soviets to withdraw the missiles.

For those in Washington who continued to insist that the Soviets did not possess the capability to reach a U-2 at maximum altitude, the Anderson mission was definitive proof that they did, and it supported Powers's claim that he had not descended to a lower altitude over Sverdlovsk.

When she heard about the U-2 going down over Cuba, Sue Downey immediately thought that it must have been piloted by Powers, thinking the trip to the West Coast was just another agency cover story. But Frank really was in California.

He was back in the air, far from danger.

After landing a job as a U-2 test pilot at Lockheed, Frank began a long-distance relationship with Sue. They both thought it felt right, but since they had each failed the first time they were married, they wanted to take the time to be sure.

The wedding took place in a little chapel in Catlett, Virginia, on October 26, 1963. Frank quickly began the process of adopting Sue's daughter, Dee. The family lived for a while in the pilot's penthouse bachelor apartment before moving to a house near the Burbank airport and eventually to the San Fernando Valley town of Sherman Oaks.

In contrast to his relationship with Barbara, which was always full of doubts and suspicions, Frank found true happiness with Sue. They argued like any couple, usually when Sue had too much to drink. But Frank never doubted his second wife's devotion.

"Our mother was smart, kind, and sassy, with a fabulous personality," said Dee, who turned six the month after the wedding, "and she loved our father beyond belief."

When they found out they were going to have a child of their own, Frank and Sue started saving their loose change, so they could afford a private hospital room.

During her pregnancy, Sue experienced a particularly memorable dream: Seeing their baby on a bear-skin rug. Determined to make his wife's dream come true, Frank bought her a bear-skin rug.

This is where I, Francis Gary Powers Jr., enter the story.

According to Mom and Dad, not long after I came into the world at Burbank's St. Joseph's Hospital on June 5, 1965, one month premature, they took me home and placed me on the rug for a memorable picture.

By this time, my father was feeling increasingly alienated from the CIA. In April 1963, every U-2 pilot was presented with the prestigious Intelligence Star—except the man who spent twenty-one months in a Soviet prison. Not until two years later—when John McCone was on his way out—would the slight be rectified. It was not the last time some high-ranking officials of the agency found it more convenient to pretend Francis Gary Powers had never existed.

Not everyone felt conflicted. Frank was attending a function for Lockheed employees at the posh Beverly Hilton in 1964 when Allen Dulles took the opportunity to praise him from the podium. It was unexpected and incredibly gratifying. "Embarrassed the devil out of me," he later recalled.[48]

Happy to be back in the air, Powers struck a "quiet, introspective" vibe at social gatherings, according to Mary Finch, then the wife of fellow Lockheed test pilot Bob Gilliland.

"Frank was a warm, kind, decent man," said Jeannie Popovich, Sue's friend from the agency, who saved up her money to make several visits to California.

During her first trip west, in 1965, Popovich was on the freeway with Sue, heading out to do some shopping, when they heard an announcement on the radio that a U-2 had crashed in the California desert.

"Sue nearly wrecked the car," she recalled. "Awful thoughts were going through my head. What if Frank had been hurt, or worse, killed?"

They were all relieved to soon learn that my father was fine, but they were saddened by the death of another U-2 pilot, Buster Edens. They had even considered naming me in his honor.

I enjoyed a special connection with Jeannie. As a four- or five-year-old, I often sat in her lap with my arms around her neck, soaking up every ounce of her attention.

"I love you, Jeannie Popovich! Will you please wait for me until I grow up so I can marry you?"

The man I knew growing up was not mad at the world. He was a good and loving father and husband who enjoyed his life and was determined to move on and make the best of the cards he had been dealt.

But the echoes of 1960 haunted him.

Too many people believed what they wanted to believe.

"I still feel like a scapegoat," he told one reporter.[49]

It hurt him to think anyone could actually believe he would betray his country.

Dad and I were very close. As a little boy of three or four, I sometimes visited him at the Burbank Airport, his home base as a Lockheed test pilot, and I would carefully walk on the wings of his U-2 as he held my hand.

"His dad always had a smile on his face," recalled my childhood friend Joe Patterson.

Chris Conrad, the son of actor Robert Conrad and one of my closest friends, envied the father-son connection he witnessed between us.

"My father was famous and all that, but he was a guy who was mostly not around for me growing up," the younger Conrad said. "It was completely different for Gary. Mr. Powers was really about Gary and spending time with Gary. He really loved his son. They had a relationship that I didn't have with my dad."

I guess I didn't know how lucky I was to have a dad who wanted to spend time with me and involve me in things. I looked up to him. He was my role model.

My mother was a widely liked figure among my circle of friends, who appreciated her Southern hospitality. "She was very charming and welcoming," Patterson said.

Several years after the CIA denied his request to write a book about the U-2 Incident, Dad moved forward with the project, working with author Curt Gentry on *Operation Overflight*, which was published in 1970. It was a cathartic experience. For the first time, he felt a measure of power over his own story.

However, soon after the book was submitted to the CIA for review, Lockheed dismissed him, and he became convinced that the order came down from Washington.

Around this time, Dee was sitting in her fifth-grade history class when the teacher began talking about the U-2 Incident, telling the class that Francis Gary Powers should have killed himself to avoid capture by the Soviets. His little girl was stunned. Her father? Her father was a bad man because he hadn't killed himself?

"I was crying when I got home that afternoon, and Mom wanted to know why," she said.

Mom promptly drove to the school and got in the face of the teacher and the principal.

"It was a very traumatic moment for me," Dee said.

After leaving Lockheed, Dad landed a job flying a Cessna 170 traffic airplane for Los Angeles radio station KGIL. When I became old enough, I sometimes flew with him during the summer, soaking up the experience as Dad patrolled high above the freeways.

In the beginning, the onetime U-2 pilot conceded a certain amount of "stage fright,"[50] but in a short amount of time, he became a radio veteran, typically reporting four times each hour while flying at an altitude of 1,000 to 3,000 feet.

Even though it was not quite the same as the thrill of flying off into the stratosphere, Dad enjoyed the job because it allowed him to make a living in the sky. Trying to explain the special feeling that had captivated him for nearly his entire life, all the way back to that day at the fair in West Virginia, he told a reporter, "The higher you get, the greater the sense of detachment. It's indescribable, but it's the detachment."[51]

Many of my most powerful memories occurred at my father's side.

Over the course of writing the book about his life, my father became good friends with Curt Gentry. Not long after their book was published, Curt arrived in Los Angeles. He was already at work on his next non-fiction work, the blockbuster *Helter Skelter*, about the Tate-LaBianca murders, which rocked America in the summer of 1969. One day in 1970, I rode along as Dad picked up Curt at the downtown courthouse where Charles Manson and his gang were being prosecuted. While being transported away from the courthouse, the three young female followers of Manson who would soon be convicted of the gruesome crimes saw me, an innocent child amid the circus atmosphere.

"Look, Daddy," I said. "They're waving at me and blowing me kisses."

"Well, wave back," he said.

So I did.

I was about five, unable to fully appreciate my momentary brush with history.

The closeness between father and son was forever evident, as I grew big enough to follow in my dad's footsteps. We played golf, rode bikes, bowled, and played in the snow during family trips to the California mountains. On a vacation in Hawaii, Dad taught me to body surf. He also got me excited about solving puzzles and other logic problems and collecting coins.

One time, when I was about eight or nine, I got up way before dawn and we headed off for a deep-sea fishing adventure off the Pacific Coast. I became very sick and spent much of the day throwing up at the side of the boat. I don't think I'll ever forget that smell. But at least I caught a fish.

Several family trips to "the Pound," as we called it, formed powerful memories of a world very different than our suburban California life, including one holiday in the summer of 1976.

I will always remember helping my father paint the big heating-oil container out behind the house and running a string tied to a bunch of tin cans between two trees in the backyard.

Getting to shoot his .22 rifle was a great thrill. What a rush to pull the trigger and hear the distant ping of the bullet penetrating tin!

The man everyone back there still called Francis regaled me with stories of his childhood hunting, fishing, and spelunking in the surrounding country-side. One particular tale made a big impression. When they were young boys, he and Jack Goff were climbing through a nearby cave. At one point, while crawling through a very tight passage in the pitch dark, Francis got stuck. Jack was ahead of him and could not turn around. Francis was on his own.

After several tense moments, when he thought he might not make it out, he finally realized that his belt had gotten twisted up on a rock, and he started moving back and forth, side to side . . . until he finally worked his way free. Imagine the feeling of relief. The two friends then continued their exploration, only to realize they had gotten confused and lost their way out. After more than an hour of going around in circles, Francis finally noticed a candy-bar wrapper that had fallen out of his pocket on the way in. This little piece of litter showed them the way home.

"When you get in a tough spot like that, son," Dad told me, "always remain calm. If you can keep from panicking, you can work the problem and solve it."

It was impossible for me to know at that point, before my world shattered, but such moments would loom large in my life. I would cherish every thread of a recollection, remembering my father through the stories he told me; the advice he offered; the little rituals we shared.

In 1976, NBC aired the two-hour TV movie *Francis Gary Powers: The True Story of the U-2 Spy Incident*. Starring Lee Majors, it was based largely on Dad's book, which gave him yet another opportunity to tell his side of the story.

I was cast in the small part of a young Russian boy being warned not to touch a poisonous coin.

I thought it was cool to be in a movie with the Six Million Dollar Man, but I didn't know until many years later that the scene had never happened in real life. It was pure Hollywood.

In a small, seemingly innocuous way, I was drawn into the mythology surrounding my father's real-life drama, which set me on the circuitous road to someday understanding how fact and fiction could be melded in ways that undermined true history. Sometimes a stubborn fact is no match for a juicy lie.

In a city filled with movie stars and other celebrities, Francis Gary Powers was a rather-unique figure in Los Angeles in the 1970s, especially as he settled into his high-profile job as a traffic helicopter pilot for Channel 4.

Dad and Mom were included in many things and given various opportunities because of the fame forever attached to his name. Still, wherever he went, he was shadowed by those pervasive doubts. Everyone who encountered him wondered what really happened over there. This was his particular burden, and he was never able to escape it. Even his friends invariably felt compelled to ask.

After their sons' sixth-grade graduation, Dad and Robert Conrad headed for the bar at the Van Nuys Airport, sidling into a booth while the boys played in the parking lot. Eventually the conversation turned to a familiar topic.

"Did they want you to kill yourself?" Conrad asked.

Dad shook his head. "No. They never told me to do that." Then he smiled and pointed toward his son in the distance. "If I'd done that, I wouldn't have Gary, wouldn't have this life."

Recalling the scene, Conrad said, "He was used to the question, and he knew I didn't buy any of that stuff about him being a traitor."

All those years after the wide-eyed young man earned his Air Force wings, Dad remained a flag-waving patriot. But he was struggling with a certain amount of creeping cynicism and resentment concerning the CIA.

In 1975, the whole country started getting an education about the agency, thanks to the efforts of Senator Frank Church, who chaired a select committee charged with investigating alleged abuses of power by the CIA. Like the U-2 Incident, the very public hearings drew unwanted attention to a part of the government unaccustomed to the spotlight.

The Church Committee exposed many of the agency's darkest secrets, including various assassinations and coups. Dad watched the proceedings with great interest and took the opportunity to compose letters to Church and his colleagues, trying to plead his case. Complaining of the agency's impact on his dismissal from Lockheed, he said, "I am a living example of that misuse of power."[52] He added, "In retrospect, my two years in a Russian prison was easy when compared to my treatment by the CIA."

This must have been a very difficult thing for my father to do, but, ultimately, he was making the same sort of distinction that permeated the Church Committee report. He believed it was his patriotic duty to challenge the CIA's behavior—taking issue with the weaknesses of an organization that had grown increasingly powerful and unaccountable.

The Church Committee decided not to investigate his case, but two years later, another congressional committee invited him to speak. The hearing was scheduled for September 1977, and he was planning to take me with him. He believed it was time for his son to start learning about his complicated history.

On July 31, Dad called his sister Jan to wish her a happy birthday. Because Jan worked for the National Park Service, he asked if she could arrange a private tour of the White House for their upcoming trip. She said she would work on it the next day.

"I'm going to reopen my case, and they're either going to brand me a traitor or clear me," he told his sister.

Chapter Five

LOST IN A CROWD

I t was early afternoon when Chris Conrad picked up the ringing telephone.

"Is your mom there?"

Chris did not recognize the woman's voice and realized his mother didn't want to be disturbed.

Because of Robert Conrad's celebrity, the family was accustomed to crank calls and bizarre people showing up at the front door. Some insisted the tough guy take them up on his offer to knock the battery off his shoulder, echoing a well-known television commercial. For such nuts, Joan was always prepared, carrying a loaded .38-caliber pistol in her pocket.

Through the years, arriving at all hours of the day and night, unannounced, I learned to approach the Encino house with caution. Knowing Joan was packing, I always waved my arms in the air and yelled: "Don't shoot! Don't shoot! It's Gary!"

The reply from the sweet-sounding voice was a confirmation that the human alarm system had been temporarily disabled. "Oh, Gary! Is that you, Gary?"

Mrs. Conrad spent most of her time locked in her room watching television, rarely cooking, and leaving the son and his friends with virtual free rein in his part of the house, which became the group's clubhouse. When we were older, she sometimes bought us kegs of beer after extracting a promise that we would not drink and drive.

In this case, his mother happened to be standing nearby when the phone rang.

But Chris knew enough to lie when someone asked if his mother was available.

"Not really."

He could hear a woman sobbing in the background.

"Uh . . . can we drop Gary off over there?"

"Oh, I don't know. . . ."

When Chris put his mother on the phone, he watched the anguish quickly rise across her face. She liked Frank and Sue very much. They were kind people. When she learned that Frank had died, along with cameraman George Spears, after his Channel 4 Telecopter crashed just a few miles from the Conrads' home, Joan immediately felt compelled to do whatever she could to help.

Devastated, my mom struggled to deal with the situation. When word reached Dee, who was in the Air Force Reserve, our mother asked her to fly home—even though she was stationed at Norton Air Force base in San Bernardino, just a 75-mile freeway drive from Sherman Oaks. "Mom wasn't making much sense, which was completely understandable," Dee recalled.

Marvine Neff, one of Mom's closest friends and part of the Rand McNally and Libby fruit family, decided she needed to remove twelve-year-old me from the scene for a while, so she could get a grip. Mrs. Neff dropped me off at the Conrads', where Joan gave me a big hug. This is when I realized something was wrong, and I fought to hold back tears so that Chris would not see me cry.

"My mom took Gary and me to a toy store and bought us a bunch of toys," Chris said. "That was her way of trying to deal with the situation. We just sat and played with trains and stuff."

I remember the events of August 1, 1977, through a fog.

It was brush fire season in Southern California. In addition to his patrol of the freeways, which often included police chases, my father had been dispatched to the Santa Barbara area, north of Los Angeles, to capture footage of flames streaking ominously toward the sky.

"The helicopter was a real game changer for us in those days," recalled longtime Channel 4 reporter Frank Cruz, who often worked with my father. "It made for some exciting television when you had something dramatic to shoot."

Typically, the local news break during NBC's *Today* program included a broad mix of news, sports, and weather. But on this morning, local anchor Cruz quickly tossed immediately to Dad, who offered a detailed report featuring some very captivating video, while hovering near the action. "It was all about the fire that day, and Frank did a great job of reporting, as he always did," Cruz said.

A representative from KNBC told the media the pilot had checked in via radio around 12:25 p.m., reporting that he was flying to the Van Nuys Airport to gas up his Jet Bell Ranger and head back out on his next assignment. The copter crashed about 12:40, near a velodrome and a Little League baseball field at Balboa Park in Encino. One witness saw the tail rotor fly off as it plunged to the ground, though this was never confirmed. Dad died of blunt force trauma to the chest.

Police speculated that the pilot may have tried to put the aircraft down in the vacant lot to avoid the nearby playground. "Just south of there are single-family residences, to the west large apartments, and to the northeast there were kids playing ball," reported Lieutenant Mel Melton of the Los Angeles Police. "I don't know what was in his mind, but he didn't hit any of them."[1]

Investigators determined that the helicopter ran out of fuel—impacted by a malfunctioning gauge that had been repaired. This fell into the realm of pilot error.

As grief enveloped the Channel 4 news team, where my father had been employed for ten months, a former colleague at radio station KGIL spoke of her sadness at the loss of the "sweetest, gentlest man I've ever met."[2]

"This station is devastated up and down the halls," said Joann Larson, a controller at KGIL.[3]

Some members of the family back in Virginia suspected foul play, reflecting the level of distrust and bitterness many harbored for the government. The difficult-to-accept truth was colored by an overwhelming irony: A man who had once survived a violent crash in the stratosphere followed by twenty-one months in a Soviet prison died because he ran out of gas less than five miles from his Sherman Oaks home.

Family friend Gregg Anderson arrived to help my mother work through various decisions she needed to make, including scheduling the memorial service at First Christian Church in North Hollywood.

Mom relied on Gregg very heavily because she was going squirrely.

Moving through the list, Anderson asked Sue where she wanted Frank to be buried.

"Arlington."

To Mom, the decision was simple. Her husband had risked his life for his country and deserved to be buried among heroes.

The widow was walking around the house, with Gregg following closely behind, pressing the subject.

"Yes, I understand," Anderson said, "but what if we can't get him into Arlington?"

Sue was adamant. "Gregg, there's no alternate plan. Frank will be buried in Arlington."

Even at the most heart-wrenching moment of her life, she was focused on securing her husband's legacy.

This was something my father and mother argued about when he was still alive. Dad told her, "They [the government] don't want me at Arlington. Don't waste your time. It will never happen."

But Mom was stubborn. Understanding that the country was divided into two camps about her husband, she was determined to achieve the public validation that burial at Arlington National Cemetery conferred.

While working the problem, Gregg was provided with a telephone number to reach a certain figure at the CIA. He called the number and was greeted by silence. He would have to start speaking without any acknowledgment from the other party, which offered the real-estate developer—who built Westlake Village in the San Fernando Valley and other high-end properties—a window into that mysterious world. Gregg later told me it was the weirdest thing he'd ever done.

The family and several friends in the government, including Air Force General Leo Geary, successfully maneuvered through the system and secured Dad's burial rights at Arlington, which ultimately required the authorization of President Jimmy Carter.

Before boarding the jet at Los Angeles International Airport, Mom insisted on visiting the cargo bay, where she lifted the lid on the casket to make sure it was indeed her beloved Frank. (In DC, she became embroiled in an argument with some of his sisters, who wanted him to have an open casket at the ceremony. "No fucking way!" she said. Aware that the event would attract press photographers, she was determined to deny them a picture of his cold, dead body.)

On the morning of the interment, with various members of the family gathered at my mom's parents' home in Fairfax, Virginia, Mom was standing at the kitchen sink when suddenly something outside the window caught her eye.

"There's Daddy!"

Dee was startled. "What are you talking about?"

Sue pointed to a white dove fluttering beyond the glass, which she took as some sort of sign.

"A great calm came over her at that point," Dee recalled.

Before the limousine pulled up to Section 11, Lot 685-2 of the massive graveyard, Mom handed me half of a sedative to steady my nerves. It was hot and humid, and I fidgeted in my suit. I was seated between my mother and grandmother Ida, who looked very frail as they lowered her boy into the ground with a twenty-one-gun salute.

Surrounded by a sea of simple white markers stretching into the horizon, commemorating thousands of others who had served their country honorably, a gathering of friends, including many spooks, shielded our family from the media and anyone else who might want to intrude on our privacy.

"A lot of people were concerned Barbara might show up and cause a scene," Joe Murphy recalled.

At the church services, three days after the crash, Barbara had made an appearance. Everyone felt uncomfortable. This was the only time I was ever to catch a glimpse of my father's first wife.

At the burial, Barbara stood in the distance, silently paying her respects. She had remarried and apparently had transcended her troubled past, which gave Murphy a good feeling on a sad day.

When the enormity of my father's passing began to sink in, I welled up with emotion. My very masculine father had always taught me that big boys don't cry. And my mother had made me aware of all the photographers who were waiting like vultures to capture the family's weakness in a time of stress. So I fought against the emotion of the moment, determined to honor both my father and my mother, at one point biting my lower lip. I was not going to give anyone the satisfaction of seeing me cry.

Like many people, my mother drank alcohol to unwind. She and Dad typically shared a cocktail or two when he arrived home from a stressful day of flying. They laughed and talked and enjoyed each other's company while gathering a little buzz. Drinking was part of the context of Mom's daily life. She loved to tell the story about how she and her beloved Frank spent the hours before the cameras rolled on a pivotal, late-night scene of NBC's movie about the U-2 pilot on location in Long Beach: Sipping martinis with Lee Majors in his trailer. As a result, Majors was drunk when they shot the scene of him walking across the bridge.

Sometimes, she stumbled over the line.

"Every single year, my dad would take my mom out to dinner on her birthday, and every single year they would get into a fight," Dee said. "I'm sure it was her drinking. She was not a good drinker. She could get really nasty when she drank."

op, left: Ida and Oliver Powers found themselves in the spotlight when their son's plane as shot down. (Powers Family Collection)

op, right: As a First Lieutenant in the US Air Force, Powers trained to drop nuclear bombs. *owers Family Collection)*

ottom: The only boy in the family, with his sisters. (Powers Family Collection)

Top: Young Francis with his father, Oliver and grandfather, James. (Powers Family Collection)

Bottom: As a young US Air Force pilot, Francis prepares for a mission. (Powers Family Collection)

Top: Heading to the edge of space required a specially designed pressure suit. (Powers Family Collection)

Middle: Pilots from the CIA's air force, circa 1956, including Powers *(back row, far left)*. (Powers Family Collection)

Bottom: Powers with Lockheed's Kelly Johnson, who designed the U-2. (Powers Family Collection)

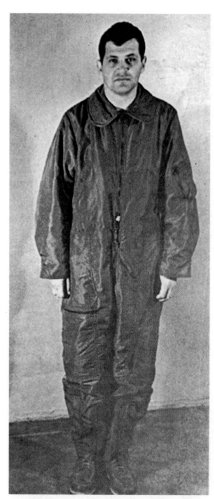

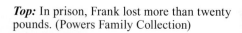

Top: In prison, Frank lost more than twenty pounds. (Powers Family Collection)

Bottom left: Replica of the US silver dollar and poison-tipped pin U-2 pilots were given the option of carrying and using in the event of torture. (Powers Family Collection)

Bottom right: Standing in the cell his father once occupied, Gary Powers felt the weight of history. (Powers Family Collection)

9 November 61
#32

Dearest Barbara,

I received your letter number 29 on the fifth of this month. I would have answered sooner but since Monday, Tuesday and Wednesday are holidays here I could not mail my letter until the ninth. Your letter was posted on the 26th in Milledgeville and I received it on the 5th which was only ten days. That is the fastest I have received one of your letters. Of course you wrote it on the 15th and it wasn't mailed until ten days later so that makes a long time.

You mentioned in your letter that you were in the University hospital at Augusta and had been since the 21st of September. I always knew this before you condescended to tell me but I can't say that I blame you very much. You must be a little ashamed of yourself or you would have told me earlier. You only mentioned "tension" as the reason for your being there but I happen to know that it was much more drinking than tension and I must admit that I am not very proud of you. (I thought you got to the Hospital on the 22nd)

I remember the last time I saw you in August of 60, I distinctly remember telling you at that time to be careful and also not to drink too much. I didn't ask you not to drink at all only not to drink too much. You apparently paid only as much attention to what I said then as you have paid to everything I have said or have ask you to do, that is very little at all. Well, Barbara, I know the time has come for me to put my foot down. As you know I have always wanted children and a home but I will never want to have children if their mother cannot take care of them and an alcoholic isn't known to be the best of mothers or fathers. You can see what kind of position your actions have placed me in.

You said you didn't know when you would be released from the hospital. Well, I have heard that you are already out now as I write this letter. Barbara the thing I don't like about this is that you did not recognize your condition and seek admittance yourself. Instead you had to be legally committed. That, to me, only shows that you had no desire to change your way of living and would not have undergone treatment unless it was forced upon you. This is not good at all because you will have to have the desire to be cured or you will not be cured. I am sure the time you spent in the hospital helped some even if only for the rest and balanced diet you got there. (Now I know why you had the vitamine deficiency you wrote me about many months ago.)

Barbara, all I can do is tell you exactly how I feel about all this and let you make up your own mind as to what you will do after you know my feelings. As I said before I am not proud of you at all. I knew something was wrong for a long time but I didn't expect you to reach extents that legal commission to a hospital would become necessary. But it has happened and therefore I can only say that I am extremely disappointed in you. Now maybe you realize why I said that I didn't have the confidence in our marriage that I had before. Can you blame me?

first page of a letter from Powers to Barbara, November 1, 1961. Letters were numbered to help Powers know which letters he sent and received. (Powers Family Collection)

In the early part of October 1960 my cell mate ask me why I did not keep a diary. I had been thinking about doing this but his question decided me to start. I I bought this book specifically for this purpose. It was ordered in October but I didn't receive it until early November.

I think it would be best to try to recall as much as possible of everything that has happened to me since the morning of the first of May and until the present time and then keep a daily recording of my thought, impression and daily experience.

May 1, 1960

It is very hard to recall all that happened on this day. It is definitely a day that I will never forget. I came closer to death on this day than any day that I can remember.

At about three o'clock in the morning, local time in Pakistan, I was awakened. The night before I had been told that I might have to fly the next day so I had gone to bed early. Upon arising I washed up and ate a good breakfast (it is a good thing I ate before I found out what my assignment was to be or I am sure I would have been too nervous to eat). At about four thirty I prepared myself for pre-breathing. While pre-breathing I received my assignment. The take off was to be at six thirty, and I was to fly from Pakistan to Norway across the Soviet union. I thought that having mechanical failure of the aircraft that it was safe to make this flight. Even though I thought it was safe it looked a very long way on the map and that meant that a lot of

Top: Prison journal entry. (Photo by Eric Long, Smithsonian National Air and Space Museum [NASM], Washington, DC, February 3, 2011)

Bottom: Powers's prison journal. (Photo by Eric Long, Smithsonian National Air and Space Museum [NASM], Washington, DC, February 3, 2011)

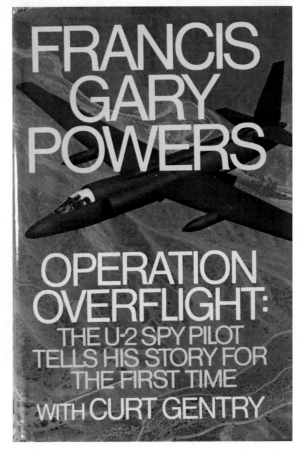

Top: Finally free after
twenty-one months, Powers
reunited with his mother, Ida.
(Powers Family Collection)

Bottom: Powers's autobiography,
published in 1970.

FRANCIS
GARY
POWERS

OPERATION
OVERFLIGHT:
THE U-2 SPY PILOT
TELLS HIS STORY FOR
THE FIRST TIME
WITH CURT GENTRY

The original tapes for use in *Operation Overflight*. (Powers Family Collection)

Top: Digitized version of one of the interview tapes for *Operation Overflight* and the original tape. (Powers Family Collection)

Bottom: Francis Gary Powers Jr. holding one of three Latvian-style rugs that his father wove in Vladimir Prison. A similar rug is on display at the Smithsonian National Air and Space Museum. (Dan Currier)

The Powers family circa 1970: Frank, Sue, Dee, and Gary. (Powers Family Collection)

Inset: Frank and Sue's wedding. *(Left to right)* matron of honor Edith Costello, Sue, Frank, and best man Joe Giraudo.

POW Medal, Silver Star, CIA Director's Medal, and Award Citations. (Photo Courtesy of SAC and Aerospace Museum)

as they turned from one prearranged frequency to the other. Then one of the ████████ operators decided to tune in the guard frequency where the Morse transmission was strongest. He was able to discern a break in the letters, making the message read ████████ The detachment chief, Col. William Shelton, who had been waiting anxiously inside the radio van for a "Go" or "No Go" message, leaped from the van and ran across the field to give the signal for takeoff to Powers, who was sitting in the U-2C at the end of the runway.

Powers started his takeoff roll at 0159Z on 1 May 1960. Once airborne, Powers guided his aircraft toward Afghanistan. Following standard operating procedure, Powers clicked his radio switch when he reached penetration altitude of 66,000 feet, which signaled the operations unit at ████████ that everything aboard the aircraft was working and the mission would proceed as planned. Aside from this simple signal, Powers and all U-2 pilots maintained strict radio silence during penetration missions.

Powers' first target was the Tyuratam Missile Test Range after which he headed for Chelyabinsk, just south of Sverdlovsk. The planned route would take him over Kyshtym, Sverdlovsk, northwest to Kirov, north over Yur'ya and Plesetsk, then to Severodvinsk, northwest to Kandalaksha, north to Murmansk, and, finally, ████████.

May Day turned out to be a bad time to overfly the Soviet Union. On this major holiday, there was much less Soviet military air traffic than usual, so Soviet radars could easily identify and track Powers' U-2. In addition, the Soviets responded to the intrusion by ordering a ban on civilian air traffic in a large portion of the Soviet Union. Soviet radar began tracking the U-2 when it was still 15 miles south of the Soviet-Afghan border and continued to do so as the aircraft flew across the Central Asian republics. When Powers reached the Tashkent area, as many as 13 Soviet interceptor aircraft scrambled in an unsuccessful attempt to intercept his plane.

Powers never made it past Sverdlovsk. Four and a half hours into the mission, an SA-2 surface-to-air missile detonated close to and just behind his aircraft and disabled it 70,500 feet above the Sverdlovsk

(Winter 1983):29 (S). ████████ Message Received—Unfortunately," Studies in Intelligence 27

over and content portion of CIA report that cleared Powers, confirming that he was at his assigned altitude when he was shot down. (Powers Family Collection)

The CIA and the U-2 Program, 1954-1974

Center for the Study of Intelligence

area. The plane began spiraling down toward the ground and Powers looked for a way out. Unable to use the ejection seat because centrifugal force had thrown him against the canopy, he released the canopy and prepared to bail out, waiting to arm the destruction device at the last minute, so that it would not go off while he was still in the plane. When he released his seatbelt, however, he was immediately sucked out of the aircraft and found himself dangling by his oxygen hose, unable to reach the destruction switches. Finally, the hose broke and he flew away from the falling aircraft. After he fell several thousand feet, his parachute opened automatically, and he drifted to earth where he was quickly surrounded by farmers and then by Soviet officials. His aircraft had not been destroyed by the crash, and the Soviets were able to identify much of its equipment when they put it on display 10 days later. Even if Powers had been able to activate the destruction device, however, it would not have destroyed the aircraft. The small explosive charge was only designed to wreck the camera.

How had the Soviets succeeded in downing the U-2? Although some CIA project officials initially wondered if Powers had been flying too low through an error or mechanical malfunction, he maintained that he had been flying at his assigned altitude and had been brought down by a near miss of a Soviet surface-to-air missile. This turned out to be the case, for in March 1963, the US air attache in Moscow learned that the Sverdlovsk SA-2 battery had fired a three-missile salvo that, in addition to disabling Powers' plane, also scored a direct hit on a Soviet fighter aircraft sent aloft to intercept the U-2. Mission planners had not known about this SAM site before the mission because they always laid out flight plans to avoid known SAM sites.

THE AFTERMATH OF THE U-2 DOWNING

The first indication that something was wrong with Powers' mission came even before he was overdue at ████████ The CIA Operations Center learned on 1 May at 0330 hours Washington time

Powers, Operation Overflight, pp. 82-84; Beschloss, Mayday, pp. 26-28; Transcript of Debriefing Tapes of Francis Gary Powers, 13 February 1962; Board of Inquiry on the Conduct of Francis Gary Powers, Operations ████████ files, OSA records, ████████ (S).

Cunningham interview, 4 October 1983 (TS Codeword); OSA History, chap. 14, p. 55 (TS Codeword).

The US Air Force chief of staff, General Norton Schwartz, presents Francis Gary Powers's posthumously awarded Silver Star to his grandchildren: Francis Gary Powers III, known as Trey, and Lindsey Barry. (US Air Force)

Joe Patterson, Jon Teperson, Gary Powers Jr., Chris Conrad, and Bob Kallos at the Silver Star ceremony. (Powers Family Collection)

Movie poster from *Bridge of Spies*, directed by Steven Spielberg. (Glendale, CA: DreamWorks, 2015)

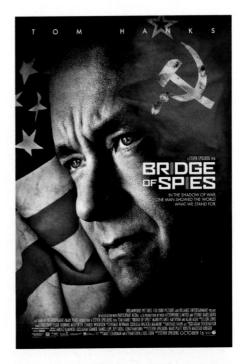

...ary Powers *(left)* helped Spielberg and actor Austin Stowell, who played Francis Gary ...owers, with technical details. (Courtesy of Storyteller Distribution Co., LLC)

On the set of *Bridge of Spies*, director Steven Spielberg toasts Francis Gary Powers. (Courtesy Francis Gary Powers Jr.)

The Powers family circa 2015 in the Senate chamber of the Czech Republic while in Pragu for a European press screening of *Bridge of Spies*. (Powers Family Collection)

ancis Gary Powers Jr. pays his respects at the memorial of Russian pilot Sergei Safronov, e MiG pilot who was shot down by friendly fire in his pursuit of Powers on May 1, 1960. fronov's wife communicated to Gary Powers that she did not blame his father for her hus- nd's death nor bear any ill will toward him and his family, making this moment a symbol healing between the East and the West. (Powers Family Collection)

For the Cold War generation, Powers became synonymous with the U-2.
(Powers Family Collection)

When Mom got drunk and abusive during a party at the Andersons' house, Dad politely said his goodbyes and led me out the front door. We walked home more than two miles through darkened streets, leaving Mom to sleep it off.

When Dad died, Mom's drinking became much worse.

"She crawled inside a bottle, and that's where she lived her life till she died," Dee said.

One night, when she was falling down drunk in the house, I had to help her to bed.

You never forget that.

After watching her spiral into a dark place, I made a call to an alcoholic support group. I wanted to get my mother some help and learn how to deal with her problem. But I wound up not attending any meetings, because I was sure they would want to know my name.

This was a conversation I didn't want to have—not at an age when I just wanted to fade into the wallpaper.

I knew I couldn't go there. My own anxiety trapped me into not doing anything.

Left without a father at the most critical time of any young man's development, and forced to deal with a mother who abused alcohol as a way of coping, I headed into my teens riddled by insecurity.

My closest friends witnessed my struggle.

"Gary's life was turned upside down overnight," Chris Conrad said. "His dad had been the center of his universe, his hero, his role model. Boom. He's gone. And his mom is dealing with her own pain. So Gary sort of felt like he was on his own, which must have been a pretty lonely feeling."

The summer after Dad died, I flew to Virginia by myself to visit my family. It was the same farm where I had once delighted in shooting targets and handling chores with my father. But something was different. Separated from the fast pace of Los Angeles, I quickly grew bored. At one point, I placed a long-distance call to a friend back in California, whining about how much I disliked the Pound.

I was miserable and couldn't wait to go home. Without my father, it felt like a totally different place. Without my father, I felt lost.

Even though Dad's passing left us in a much more difficult financial situation, Mom somehow managed to keep sending me to Montclair Prep, a prestigious private school in the San Fernando Valley, where I was surrounded by the sons and daughters of the rich and famous. Sometimes, in that rarified air, I felt invisible. Earning spending money by working at a pizza place and a video arcade after school and on weekends, I eventually drove to school in a Chevy Citation, which I parked alongside the Mercedes, BMWs, and Porches that filled the school parking lot.

I felt very out of place. I was trying to figure out who I was without my dad, and being in a school where I never felt like I fit in made it worse.

I tried to convince Mom to let me enroll in a nearby public school. She would not hear of it. We often argued about the subject, cutting straight to the heart of my struggle for identity and a sense of belonging.

Joe Patterson, who has been my friend since second grade, saw me begin to withdraw into a shell. "You could tell he was struggling with the situation," Patterson said. "He was devastated by his dad's death, which made the usual teenage problems much worse."

Jon Teperson, who became my friend in the seventh grade, recalled: "Word got around that the morose giant kid's father had just died. That's all. Just a kid with a dead father. Nothing more. Nothing less. Just a kid going through hell. And he looked it. No one knew his dad was a star in the first few weeks of seventh grade. No one knew his dad was also a villain. Gary would walk around the school with a blank expression. Looking distant."

When I was fifteen, after my mother went to bed, I started running the streets of the San Fernando Valley with my friends, including Conrad, Patterson, Teperson, and Bob Kallos. We rode bikes through the darkness; slipped into bars with fake IDs—produced by printers we bribed, sealed with the lamination machine in Conrad's room—so we could drink and party; drag-raced on Mulholland Drive, often using cars from the fleet of Robert Conrad's production company; and played gorilla golf with balls dipped in a glow-in-the-dark substance ... until somebody invariably heard the commotion and called the cops. We usually made it home around 4 or 5 a.m., time enough to grab a couple hours' sleep before heading off to school, where we fought the power structure by testing the strict dress code, sometimes sporting Hawaiian shirts and prescription sunglasses to stand out from the crowd.

We were not out to cause any harm. We were just out having fun—pushing the edge, when our parents thought we were asleep.

Late one night, after they discovered the pillows I had carefully arranged to make it appear that I was sleeping under the covers, Mom and her boyfriend went looking for me. Finally, she saw me walking out of an arcade and began embarrassing me in front of several buddies.

"What are you doing here? We were so worried! You come with me! You are grounded!"

Eventually Mom realized she was powerless to prevent me from sneaking out.

One night after playing a round of gorilla golf, we got hungry. With no restaurants open, we broke into a Mediterranean place on Sunset Boulevard and cooked our own breakfast. After doing the dishes, we left a wad of money on the counter and walked off into the darkness.

"We were just bunch of drunk guys who got hungry after playing some golf," Conrad recalled. "The way we looked at it, no harm, no foul."

Many times during high school, a bunch of us guys would drive off to the California mountain resort of Mammoth Lakes on a Thursday night—which required skipping school Friday, protected by a series of carefully crafted lies. After skiing and partying all weekend, we drove home Sunday night, arriving back all bleary-eyed in time for the first bell at Montclair on Monday morning. "The teachers kept trying to catch us but never did," said Conrad, who often pulled up to school with snow still covering parts of his car.

During those days, I started experimenting with marijuana, often joining fellow employees from the pizza place to share a joint in a nearby park. One of the first times I smoked pot at a friend's house, Mom and my sister arrived to pick me up.

Trying to hide the smell, the friend sprayed me with disinfectant. When I got into the car, they started teasing me about the overpowering smell of disinfectant, and as I tried to make light of it, attributing the odor to horseplay, I was overwhelmed with a powerful thought: "Can they tell I'm stoned?"

Dee suspected it, but she didn't give me away.

Some of my friends worried when I appeared to be using more and more illicit drugs.

They were right to be concerned. I was looking for a way to escape. Smoking pot was just another way to avoid the depressing and complicated realities of my life. It was just another way for me to test the boundaries. Looking back on those days from the vantage point of a middle-aged man, I can see where the teenage me was heading in a dangerous direction and could have ended up in jail or, worse, dead.

Always one of the biggest guys in my age group, I slowly matured into a good athlete. At my mother's suggestion, I joined the Blizzard Ski Club and became a very good skier, winning a long list of competitions and having a pipe dream of someday participating in the Olympic trials. Eventually I blew out my knee, but the success I enjoyed on the slopes gave me a jolt of self-esteem.

I yearned for a positive male role model, someone to show me how to be a man.

Would I have rebelled less—or more—with a dominant former military man looking over my shoulder? I don't know the answer to this question. I know I needed guidance that I wasn't getting.

When I was in the seventh grade, Robert Conrad showed up at Montclair and announced he was going to coach the school's flag football team. He was a big star, so no one argued. Soon his friend Red West, onetime bodyguard to Elvis and a co-star on Conrad's TV show *Baa Baa Black Sheep*, joined the effort.

Instilling a sense of discipline, toughness, and ambition, and teaching sound techniques, Conrad and West pushed the guys relentlessly. The first year, we posted a winning season. The second year, we were undefeated.

"Mr. Conrad was the epitome of macho, this very dominant male figure," Joe Patterson said. "He was a great influence on all of us—an inspirational figure. Those two guys were out there teaching us how to be men."

It mattered not that Conrad had been largely absent in his son's life, which caused resentment to bubble up on the practice field when Chris suddenly found himself interacting with his father as a coach, or that he often walked the sidelines drinking a beer. Sometimes, he would hand me an empty beer can during the middle of drills and tell me to dispose of it in "the wall," our code for a hole in the concrete wall adjacent to the athletic field.

Out of that experience I learned a lot about teamwork and competition. It also helped me get my mind off Dad. It was a good distraction at a time when, as Teperson said, I was like "a guy in a giant whirlpool grabbing at little pieces of flotation devices."

"Gary was still lost all through high school," Jon added. "He didn't know what he was searching for. He couldn't articulate it."

A couple of years after Dad died, Mom started to date a man named Bob, who worked on black ops programs at Area 51. Many times, she corrected and disciplined me in front of Bob, but he never got involved. Nobody was ever going to take my father's place, and Mom never allowed Bob or anyone else to cross that line.

It might have been different if she had decided to remarry. But she never did. As much as she grieved for my father, I always got the impression that Mom never wanted to stop being Mrs. Francis Gary Powers. This was a role that was deeply imbedded in her identity ... even as I viewed my name with mounting ambivalence.

Often, while hanging out in the basement, my friends would ask questions about my father. "Everybody now forgets that no one knew what happened back then," Teperson said, recalling our late-night conversations, usually while Mom was passed out upstairs. "Did he not pull the ejection because he thought it was wired to blow? Was he supposed to use the poison pin and didn't? Gary grew up surrounded by this, smothered by this."

This extended conversation was the beginning of something. I could not imagine what. Not just yet.

Mom didn't realize it at the time, but one of the ways her son dealt with the loss of his father was by becoming a spy.

As part of my fascination with puzzles and ciphers, I taught myself how to pick locks. It started out with me wanting to get into Mom's drawer or Dad's desk, just to prove I could. I became pretty good with a paper clip.

It eventually evolved beyond picking locks. Bored and irritated by what I thought was unfair grading by some of my teachers, I developed a routine of writing tiny crib notes on a pen, which I repeatedly clicked to reveal answers during tests.

"We had a signal," Conrad said. "I'd say, 'Ah, my pen ran out of ink . . . and he'd say, 'Oh, I have a pen' and throw it to me."

Increasingly frustrated by his inability to score well in his Spanish class despite working hard, Conrad started bellyaching about the situation one day, as the final approached. "Well," I said, "I can get the test."

The planning resembled a CIA covert operation.

For several days, I arrived at school early and stationed myself in a distant area of the parking lot. Armed with binoculars, I closely watched the teacher, who approached the front door and keyed in the security code. "By this time, we knew which four numbers it was; we could tell by the condition of the keys," Conrad recalled. "But Gary had to figure out the sequence."

Having the security code allowed the small team of burglars, dressed in black and wielding penlights, to penetrate the building.

During class, I had closely studied the movements of my teacher and knew exactly which folder contained the test, and which drawer.

Using my lock-picking skills, I quickly opened the file cabinet. We retrieved the test and rushed to a nearby post office, where we utilized a copy machine located in the 24-hour lobby. Soon we returned the test to the appropriate folder and exited the premises without detection.

The school featured several security cameras, and, obsessed with every possible detail, I suggested we paste a still picture of the appropriate scene onto the camera lens. But the other guys decided this was unnecessary. The day before, we went around the school slightly adjusting the aim of the cameras. No one noticed. No evidence was captured.

To prevent suspicion, we all agreed to purposely miss a few questions.

Emboldened by the experience, during our senior year, we acquired the final exam for every one of our classes. After learning that one of our teachers kept the all-important document in his briefcase and took it home, we bribed the son. A wad of cash did the trick. We all scored well and gained admission to good colleges. No one outside our tight little circle ever knew.

Am I proud of that all these years later? No, I'm not. I'm also not ashamed, but did I learn from it? Yes, I did. Fortunately, we never got caught.

If the cloak-and-dagger operations satisfied some powerful desire for me to feel closer to my father, I remained dubious about probing too deep into an existential question.

Ever since Mr. Conrad tried to buck me up by telling me to be proud of my father "no matter what you might hear," I had been haunted by the mystery swirling around his memory. This idea was deeply engrained in my teenage insecurity. It filled me with doubts about who my father was and how this might affect me.

But this was one secret I was not quite ready to unlock.

Chapter Six

SEARCHING FOR THE TRUTH

In the summer of 1983, while approaching my freshman year at California State University at Northridge, I showed up for a rush party at the Sigma Alpha Epsilon fraternity house. It immediately reminded me of one of my favorite movies, *Animal House*. After making my way across the overgrown lawn, past two stone lions draped with flowered leis, I walked through the front door amid the sound of blaring rock music.

The place was packed, and I was only a few feet past the door when somebody pointed me to the nearest beer keg. The mastermind of the great final exam heist at Montclair was no stranger to alcohol and loud music, but my introverted nature still made it hard for me to meet new people—I was more comfortable reading science fiction books in my room and solving logic problems than chatting up pretty girls. Nevertheless, I started walking around the house, introducing myself and striking up conversations with perfect strangers.

Moving into one room, I walked up to a member of the fraternity and extended my hand. "Hi! Gary Powers. Nice to meet you!"

His name was Jay Rose. Immediately, a bell rang. "Any relation to the U-2 pilot?"

I felt a wave of anxiety.

"Well, yeah," I said reluctantly. "That's my dad."

As we started talking, I was overwhelmed with a rather ominous feeling: I can't go anywhere without someone knowing who my dad was.

Jay Rose knew all about my father. In fact, he appeared to know more about all that history than I did, which left me with an uneasy feeling.

I was very guarded, didn't trust people easily, and was very uncomfortable with people who knew about my dad when I didn't know anything about them.

Growing up, my mother made me a little paranoid about people I didn't know or what would happen if I was caught during a youthful indiscretion. After all, what if the son of Francis Gary Powers was arrested? It would be on the front page. While mom's warnings did not stop me from living on the edge in high school, I was much more discreet in college. Mom taught me to be very careful with girls, pounding into my brain that some only want to trap a guy by getting pregnant—especially if he happens to be the son of a legendary spy. She taught me to be skeptical of whatever someone told me—especially the government—and to read between the lines of what was written in the press.

I didn't really understand it at the time, but even though my father was dead, he was exerting a certain amount of control over my life.

When Jay made the connection between me and my world-famous father, my trained inclination was to politely retreat and find another fraternity. For various reasons, I didn't want to be defined as "the son of . . ."—including the simplest of all: I didn't know the whole truth about what had happened all those years before. No one did.

Of course, I was aware of the U-2 from an early age. The memory of walking on the plane's wings was deeply embedded in my psyche. Among the autographed pictures decorating my childhood room—alongside football icon O. J. Simpson, actor Robert Conrad, and five-star General Omar Bradley—was one from Kelly Johnson, the designer of the U-2 and Dad's onetime boss.

When I was in the fifth grade, my teacher was talking about the Cold War when she asked, "Does anybody know what CIA stands for?" Growing up, I had heard my father refer to the CIA many times, although he usually called it "The Agency." I had a vague understanding of what it was, and that my father had somehow been involved with it, but I didn't know what the letters stood for, so I didn't try to answer the question. One of my classmates raised his hand and was able to fill in the blanks: Central Intelligence Agency.

I remember thinking, "Oh, I never knew it stood for anything."

Hanging out on the set of the TV movie helped me understand more about the story, but I was still too young and sheltered to get beyond the basics. I guess I thought everyone's dad had been shot down over the Soviet Union and had been exchanged for a Soviet spy.

In addition to the more universal impact of my father's death upon my development, I was deprived of reaching the point of maturity where I could ask him pointed questions about his ordeal, which exacerbated my insecurity and introversion.

Only later would I recognize meeting Jay Rose as a turning point in my life.

The truth is, I almost decided not to join Sigma Alpha Epsilon, after meeting Jay, because I didn't want to be known as Dad's son.

Ultimately, I resisted the urge to run away, realizing that the same thing might happen if I joined another fraternity.

By pledging SAE, I took a small step toward conquering my fear.

One day during my sophomore year, with my curiosity mounting—and determined to be armed with the right answers when people asked me about my father—I stopped by the library and decided to look him up in the card catalogue. I didn't know what I would find. Sure enough, there he was, firmly entrenched in the Dewey Decimal system. After some searching, I found a May 1960 issue of *Time* magazine featuring a picture of Dad on the cover. This was one of the many things I never knew.

What a strange moment it was, holding that magazine in my hands.

By this time, I had become very active in my fraternity. I partied, made new friends, and assumed a leadership role, eventually becoming the Eminent Archon, the SAE equivalent of chapter president, which included significant responsibilities in managing events and people. Slowly gaining confidence, I began to shed some of my emotional baggage. I learned that I could be myself. I started to feel comfortable in my own skin.

In time, I became more at ease around girls, and more conscious of my appearance, which could be seen as I started combing my hair back, wearing nicer clothes, and taking fewer risks. I began to walk a little taller than the young man who always felt out of place at Montclair.

"Gary struck me right away as someone who was very levelheaded and had a great sense of humor," said Chris Means, who was two years behind me in the fraternity and who would become one of my closest friends. "He was the kind of guy who was very concerned with being fair to everybody [and would] always introduce you to everybody."

Chris and the other guys could see in me an awakening sense of mission and purpose.

"I remember when I first got to know Gary and started hearing about the controversy about his father ... talking to some of my [older relatives] about it," Means said. "They had no sense that [his father] had done anything wrong. But I think Gary took the idea of the controversy to heart. He wanted to know the truth. He wanted other people to know the truth."

The past sometimes assaulted me in unexpected ways.

One night I was out to dinner with my college girlfriend, her parents, and the headmaster of a prestigious prep school at the Jonathan Club in Santa Monica. Someone asked an intriguing question: What would you have for your last meal?

Apparently I said the wrong thing.

"A salad."

At this, the headmaster snapped: "You, my friend, are a liar!"

Caught completely off guard, and still uncomfortable with talking back to an adult, I said nothing in response. I just let it go.

But privately I seethed at how a nice, friendly conversation had taken such a nasty turn and thought to myself, "And you, my friend, are a bad judge of character."

That moment affected me more than I realized at the time. The guy didn't even know me, and he was calling me a liar? The only thing I could figure was that he thought my dad had lied. So, naturally, I must be a liar? That really got under my skin. It was part of this resolve bubbling up inside me, to find out the truth about my dad.

Of course, in this, my most powerful ally was my mother. Mom always believed Dad got a raw deal out of the U-2 Incident. Her bitterness on the subject profoundly influenced me, planting the seeds for me to see my father as a victim of an injustice, which motivated my effort to learn all I could about him and his controversial flight into the history books. She encouraged me to dig and learn, even as I began to confront her over her excessive drinking.

During one family Thanksgiving at Dee's house in Minnesota, I told mom, "You've turned into what Dad hated most: Barbara!"

This was a hard thing for me to say, and hard for Mom to hear.

She was stunned and hurt, and she stopped drinking for a week or two. Eventually, however, she started again. I felt powerless.

Whenever I called her on the phone—no matter the time of the day or night—I could always hear the ice cubes clinking in her glass. This was a sound I grew to dread.

Yet, even as her alcohol problem emerged as a point of tension, the search for truth and justice kept us close.

As my curiosity began to bubble up, while visiting Mom in 1986, I flashed back to the night of Dad's wake: to a conversation with General Leo Geary while we stood next to a little bookcase in the living room.

Geary, the Air Force's liaison officer on the U-2 project, spoke admiringly of Francis Gary Powers's service to his country and revealed that he had been awarded the Distinguished Flying Cross in 1959, along with the other CIA U-2 pilots—but that it had not been released, because of the clandestine nature of their work. "I'll make sure we get it to you," the general said.

For some reason, nine years later, I wondered: "Whatever happened to that medal?"

No use wondering, Mom insisted. "Call Leo," she said.

After finding his number, I placed a fateful telephone call to the retired general's Colorado home.

"Oh," Geary said, before I could bring up the question of the medal. "You're calling about the U-2 unveiling tomorrow night!"

U-2 unveiling? What U-2 unveiling?

Mom was sitting nearby, listening to my side of the conversation, learning that an exhibit of the U-2 was being dedicated at the Smithsonian National Air and Space Museum in Washington, DC the following night. No one from the family of the most famous of all the U-2 pilots had been invited or even advised of the special event.

Mom was hurt, but more than anything else, she was pissed. She felt it was par for the course. It was yet another case of the Powers family being snubbed because of preconceived ideas about what Dad did or didn't do.

After hastily making travel arrangements, Dee and I caught a flight to the East Coast several hours later, around midnight. Mom was determined for us to crash the party. It was early morning when we arrived in Washington and checked into one of the nicest hotels in DC, the Mayflower, after catching a ride from family friend Jeannie Popovich Walls.

Walking up the stairs at the Air and Space Museum that evening, I recognized Kelly Johnson, the aging icon now confined to a wheelchair. I noticed representatives from all of the government entities and contractors who played a role in the U-2, including Lockheed, the CIA, Pratt & Whitney, and Kodak. I chatted with my parents' friends Edith "Eddie" Costello and Joe Giraudo, longtime agency spooks who served as the matron of honor and best man, respectively, for Frank and Sue's wedding.

Someone came up to me and asked where my mother was. "She couldn't make it on such short notice," I said.

A few minutes later, Dee leaned in to me. "Good job with what you said. You weren't rude to them, but you gave them an idea of what happened. . . ."

Like my mother, I saw the situation as yet another slap at my father's memory. No one was willing to accept responsibility. Lockheed blamed the CIA for not inviting us; the CIA blamed the Smithsonian; the Smithsonian blamed Lockheed. I was thinking, *Yeah, right.* It left a bitter taste in my mouth.

While shaking hands with other U-2 pilots, fighter pilots, spies, and government officials, I proudly, if tentatively, embraced my role as "son of…" This was an important passage, the start of something I did not fully understand.

I would hate to think how this story might have turned out if not for that unlikely sequence of events.

All I wanted was to procure Dad's Distinguished Flying Cross medal. I didn't know this trip would become the catalyst to a much broader and more ambitious quest, which would consume the better part of my life.

With new urgency, I began to follow my mounting curiosity, pestering my mother and other relatives with questions, reading whatever I could find about the U-2 Incident, and confronting a provocative question: Did Francis Gary Powers betray his country?

At the start, I didn't know what I would find. I really didn't. I didn't start out trying to vindicate my father. I wanted to find out the truth of what took place so I would be able to answer the questions I was being asked, as candidly as possible. I saw it as a mystery to be solved.

Even as I tried to remain objective, determined not to let my personal feelings color any facts, it was impossible to completely neutralize the familial connection that filled my journey with such urgency. After all, I was trying to make sense of a man who shared my name, a man who had always been my hero.

What if my father really was a traitor? How would this alter the way I viewed him? How would it change me?

During my fourth year at Northridge, my grade point average plummeted. The truth is, I was focusing most of my energy on the fraternity and the Thursday-to-Sunday construction job that helped me pay the bills. School was the last thing on my mind, and I flunked out.

After receiving a letter from the dean advising me to take some time off and figure out what I was going to do with my life, I organized a gala commemorating the SAE chapter's twentieth anniversary. Among the alumni I met that night was Vance T. Meyer, one of the fraternity's first Eminent Archons, who was now vice president of Los Angeles–based Pardee Construction. One thing led to another and I landed a job in the human resources department at the company headquarters in Westwood.

Happy to have a job in corporate America, while living in a tiny cinderblock basement apartment in the Hollywood Hills—where the only separation between the bathroom and the adjoining room was a dilapidated swinging door, reminiscent of a Western saloon—I began to think I could work my way up the company ladder. I figured I didn't need a college degree.

About eighteen months later, after proving myself in human resources, I applied for a job in land acquisition, which seemed like a perfect fit for a guy who aspired to become a real-estate developer. The interview went well—until the very end. "I can't hire you," the man said, "because you don't have a college degree."

I was stunned.

Disappointed but starting to feel the tug of ambition, I gave my two weeks' notice and enrolled at nearby Cal State–Los Angeles, determining that I could combine my Northridge transcript to obtain a philosophy degree in about a year. By then, I knew it didn't matter what the degree was in. I just needed to acquire that all-important sheepskin, so I decided to go for the easiest route. To reduce the financial burden, I moved back in with Mom, who was supportive of my finishing college but demanded I follow her rules, which caused tension.

Soon I was enrolled in a speech class, which required me to craft and deliver lectures about various topics.

There was a time when I would have recoiled at the thought of making a speech about my dad. It was not that I was ever ashamed of him or wanted to deny being his son. But I wanted to be my own person and didn't want to deal with all that baggage, especially since I felt so inadequate concerning what happened to him. But as I started to learn more about him and felt more comfortable about the facts and controversies, my reticence started to recede. At the age of twenty-four, I was ready to take a big step in my personal development.

I talked to my teacher, who knew who Dad was, and she helped me put together a speech. I didn't know how to give one. And she understood that this was a pretty unusual presentation I wanted to deliver.

Ignoring my butterflies, I began talking about a man who grew up in Virginia, joined the Air Force, and eventually was recruited by the CIA to fly a special aircraft. I talked about the day the plane crashed. The trial. The imprisonment. The exchange.

Bringing it in for a landing, I paused and looked out into the audience of students. "What I haven't said about this individual yet is that this pilot is my father."

My classmates clapped enthusiastically as I felt the greatest satisfaction of my young life. It was as if a lead weight had been lifted off of me.

Several months later, one night in November 1989, in a world being rapidly reshaped by the fall of the Berlin Wall, I happened to be watching a KNBC newscast featuring a broadcaster on loan from a Soviet news agency, named Svetlana Starodomskaya. Brainstorm.

With Glasnost and Perestroika in full swing, I called family friend Jess Marlow and arranged to meet with the Soviet reporter to pitch my idea: Wouldn't it be great for me to travel to the Soviet Union to commemorate the thirtieth anniversary of the U-2 Incident on May 1, 1990? Starodomskaya loved it and immediately began pushing the visit with government officials in Moscow, while I placed a telephone call to family friend Gregg Anderson, the man who had spearheaded the effort to bury my father at Arlington.

"There's this opportunity for me to go to Moscow . . . and I'd like to invite you to go with me."

For a moment, silence filled the line.

"Oh, wow," Anderson said. "Let me call you back."

In 1990, travel between the United States and the Soviet Union remained relatively rare. Visas were still difficult to procure. But things were changing.

About five minutes later, Anderson called me back. He had thought it over.

"Gary, I'll be delighted to go with you," he said. "And I'll pay for the trip."

"Now, Gregg, I wasn't asking for you to pay—"

"Gary," he said, interrupting me in midsentence. "Stop. I'm hosting you. It's the least I can do."

After spending a night in London—where I was interviewed for the first time about my father, and the lingering impact of May 1, 1960, by a British newspaperman—I joined Gregg on an Aeroflot flight to Moscow, noticing how the Soviet flight attendants felt no need to secure the overhead compartments or announce safety procedures.

It was surreal. I remember thinking: *Wow, I'm flying the same airspace my dad flew in. I'm retracing his footsteps.* It was a soul-searching moment for me.

While going through customs, I witnessed a memorable scene. I presented my passport to the Soviet attendant, who carefully looked it over and shared it with a colleague. They looked at me. They looked at the passport. They looked at each other. Then they looked back at me.

I didn't need to speak Russian to see what was going through the minds of these young guys. It's not every day that the namesake of an American spy comes walking through customs.

The man who picked us up at the airport drove a BMW, which looked out of place amid the vast army of Soviet-made sedans filling the streets.

It was a sign of the changing times. The car did not have any hubcaps; the driver explained that they kept getting stolen.

After settling into a high-end Soviet-era hotel and sitting for a series of interviews, I went off to dinner with my sponsor and our Soviet interpreter, enjoying a nice meal at one of Moscow's newly privatized restaurants. Eventually the interpreter pulled me out onto the dance floor. We all had fun.

Still, I could not help wondering if my room was bugged.

The next night, bored and feeling the need to connect to some ordinary Soviet citizens, I took a bottle of vodka someone had given me down to the lobby and began drinking shots with the bellmen. They didn't speak much English, and I didn't speak any Russian, but we tried to communicate through the language barrier. One of the bellhops eventually boiled some hot dogs, and we finished off the bottle before I stumbled back upstairs to my bed.

The next thing I knew, someone was banging on my door.

It was morning and Gregg had been knocking vigorously for a good ten minutes until he finally woke me from a deep sleep.

My head was pounding from a severe hangover. I was young and while I could hold my own drinking beer at an SAE party, I wasn't used to drinking vodka like that.

Gregg shook his head, seeing that I was in bad shape, and told me he would stall the people downstairs until I could hurry up and get ready for our big day.

While being driven to a dacha far from the city, I was seated in the back seat next to Gregg. I felt horrible. At one point I whispered, "I'm not going to make it." Fearing an international incident if we needed to pull over for the son of the famous spy to get sick on the side of a Moscow street, Gregg said, "Gary, got to maintain." Eventually we ate some food, which helped the hangover, and we enjoyed a nice day in the countryside before returning to Moscow.

I desperately wanted to see the wreckage from my father's plane. But no one seemed to know where it was. I wanted to see the Hall of

Columns, but the closest we got was having someone point it out from inside a moving car.

It was an interesting time to visit Moscow. Mikhail Gorbachev was opening things up, and everyone was friendly, but I got the impression that they didn't quite know what to do with me or how to deal with my desire to learn about what happened to my father.

I especially wanted to watch the May Day parade, to experience the Communist celebration in Red Square, where Khrushchev had once learned of my father's shoot-down. But our handlers insisted that this was impossible. Only later would we learn that Soviet officials were determined to keep us Americans as far as possible from the parade, because they were expecting a crowd of protesters, reflecting the revolution just starting to gather strength. We had our first insight that the Soviet Union would disintegrate—as happened nineteen months later—and I remember Gregg making this prediction on the plane ride home.

On the way home, we visited Berlin, where I chipped off a piece of the quickly disappearing wall. The separate nations of West Germany and East Germany were starting to talk about reunification, which many thought they would never see.

There was this euphoria on the streets, a festive atmosphere. But what I remember most is the conversation I had with a bartender, who told me about how all of their lives, he and his peers in East Germany had been told what to do. Now that the wall was down, there was no one telling them what to do. A lot of the younger generation was lost. They didn't quite know how to handle freedom. It was going to take time for them to transition out of that communist mind-set.

While retracing my father's footsteps across the Glienicker Bridge, I was interviewed by a camera crew from NBC News, which was placing one of the landmark events of the Cold War into context as the epic struggle between East and West ended without a shot.

I tried to imagine how Dad must have felt walking across that bridge, to finally be free.

When my grandmother Ida passed away in 1991, I caught a plane to Virginia for the funeral.

After graduating from Cal State–LA the previous year, I had moved to Mammoth Lakes, California, with a friend, taking a construction job and then transitioning into a night auditing position at the Mammoth Mountain Inn, adjacent to the ski slopes. I was able to ski more than one hundred days that season, while figuring out what I wanted to do with my life. I used that time to get my head on straight.

Once back in Pound, I experienced a rather-unsettling realization: My Virginia relatives felt like strangers.

If I was going to get to know all about my father and try to understand him, I needed to spend more time with my family.

Since I was already thinking about graduate school, I eventually enrolled at George Mason University in Fairfax, Virginia, which allowed me to visit my relatives. I got to know Aunt Jan, who lived in suburban DC, and frequently made the six-hour drive to Pound, where the Powers clan was surprised by my sudden interest.

"We didn't know what to think of him at first," recalled Aunt Joan with a laugh. "He wasn't accustomed to us or our ways."

The road to my past always reminded me of a rollercoaster. Carefully steering my way along the narrow, curvy, bumpy country road in southwestern Virginia, plotting a course for the isolated hollow where my father's story began, I was headed for a place of shadows and ghosts. My father's. And my own.

Sometimes I flashed back to that miserable trip to the Pound in 1978. I remembered how empty the place felt without my father. But time slowly changed me, allowing me to put that painful memory in perspective.

By the early 1990s, my trips to the old hometown no longer felt obligatory. Each time I arrived to a warm welcome and set up camp in Joan and Walton's or Jack and Jean's spare bedroom, I felt a bit closer to my father and the world that shaped him.

"It didn't take us long to figure out what a fine young man Gary is," Joan said. "He was making a real serious effort to get to know all about his daddy and the family. We told him all the stories we could remember. He always wanted to know more."

I wanted to know all about the pivotal day when my father took his first flight; the jobs he held; how Oliver felt when his son decided not to go to medical school; and the day those government men showed up in the shoe-repair shop to tell Oliver his son had been "lost" while flying a routine weather-reconnaissance mission.

They told me about the day when the pilot came home after returning from the Soviet Union and helped a newsman get his car out of the mud. "Francis was trying to keep his distance from the press, but what was he going to do?" Walton recalled. "It had rained a bunch and the road got muddy. The man needed help. Naturally, Francis got out there and helped him push his car out of the mud. That's the kind of guy he was."

I learned that Dad used to run track and liked to compete with his hands sticking straight out, as opposed to in a fist; that he sometimes hopped the rails to get back to Pound; and that he had been inducted into the local Masonic lodge, convinced by his childhood friend Jack Goff that it would be good for career advancement.

Walton told me about the day when he and Francis drove a truck off a mountain road on a hairpin turn, an accident which very nearly ended in disaster. He took me to the scene and walked me through the mishap.

"Gary wanted to know all there was to know . . . like it was all one big mystery," Goff said.

One of the memories I held close from my childhood was how Dad and I always stopped for milkshakes at Robo's, a little drive-in with a walk-up window and picnic tables on the road between Pound and the home place. I was happy to see the little restaurant still open in the early '90s. Pulling over for a shake or perhaps a chilidog would remain one of my regular rituals every time I returned, well into the twenty-first century.

At a meeting concerning POW/MIA affairs inside a hotel at Pentagon City in 1995, I stood up from my seat in the audience and introduced myself. Murmurs rumbled across the room. *Is that really HIS son?*

Fighting through nervousness, I told the crowd I was trying to find out all I could about my father and that I would appreciate any help. This led to a series of introductions, which enabled me to start maneuvering through the bureaucracy to learn the still-hidden truths.

Around this time, I heard about an upcoming conference concerning the U-2 in Bodo, Norway, where Dad was supposed to land on May 1, 1960. Not having much money, I bartered my way into the event, agreeing to set up an exhibit of U-2 artifacts, including a piece of the plane, fragments of the crashed helicopter, and a rug Dad had woven in prison, in exchange for having my airfare and hotel accommodations covered. The exhibit remained in Norway for six months and later was displayed at the National Reconnaissance Office, Central Intelligence Agency, and Defense Intelligence Agency headquarters. It has been traveling the world for more than two decades (and is currently on long-term display at the Strategic Air Command and Aerospace Museum near Omaha, Nebraska).

One part of the trip was especially memorable: Meeting Sergei Khrushchev, son of the late Soviet leader.

In September 1991, the younger Khrushchev started a one-year contract as a visiting professor at Brown University's Institute for International Studies. Three months later, when the Soviet Union disintegrated, his permanent position back home disappeared. He decided to stay in the United States, eventually becoming a proud American citizen. Nothing reflected the end of the Cold War quite as powerfully as Khrushchev's son happily pursuing his own version of the American dream as an instructor at an Ivy League university, as well as a lecturer at the Naval War College.

Invited to the Bodo conference to speak about his father and the Soviet side of the Cold War, Sergei was introduced to a young man who looked familiar. "I thought he looked Bulgarian," Khrushchev recalled. "My father never liked Bulgarians."

In time, I would learn many of the hidden details of the Soviet side on the day my father was shot down, some of it directly from the premier's son. "Everybody knew our missile technology was getting better, including the Americans," said Sergei, who was employed as a high-ranking missile engineer at the time. "Of course the CIA knew it was only a matter of time."

On May 1, 1960, Sergei heard the news of the latest incursion from his father at the breakfast table. They lived in the same house. "I was very upset and asked my father what would happen next," he recalled. "He thought this a stupid question. 'Of course we will try to shoot it down. . . .'"

He later learned from this father that some of the people who greeted the American pilot when he tumbled from the sky asked him if he was Bulgarian. "So when I see this young man who looks Bulgarian, I was not surprised to hear he was Gary Powers," Sergei said. "He looked a lot like his father."

At first, Sergei was skeptical of me. But Khrushchev was quickly disarmed by the son of his onetime Cold War adversary. He could see I was sincere and only wanted to know the truth.

"I found that he was a good and honest person who was strongly interested in preserving the memory of his father," he said. "I appreciate and respect such people."

That day was the start of a wonderful friendship between a young American and an aging Russian.

After speaking about my father's ill-fated flight, I invited questions from the audience at the Bodo conference. A Norwegian man stood up and started heckling me, telling me how a Norwegian spy had planted a bomb in the tail section of the U-2 before Dad took off from Pakistan. This was one of the many conspiracy theories that colored the incident in the sort of hazy mythology so often associated with the Kennedy assassination.

Politely but forcefully, I began to refute the charge.

The man did not think much of my answer. He kept insisting that I was engaged in some sort of cover-up.

"You can't always believe everything you read in the press!" I finally said.

And the room exploded in applause.

A feeling of deep satisfaction swept over me. It was an important milepost in my journey to combat the misinformation about my father.

As part of my process of discovery, I developed a deep interest in the Cold War, which began to fade into the history books as the old Soviet Union splintered into fourteen different independent countries, leaving a much smaller and less powerful Russia, and the nations of the old Eastern bloc embraced freedom for the first time in more than four decades.

In 1996, John C. Welch and I founded The Cold War Museum. At first it was little more than an idea and my traveling U-2 Incident exhibit, as I began working through various roadblocks, including fund-raising, artifact collection, and the search for a permanent physical location.

"In a way, I am honoring my father," I told reporters as the project began to gather momentum. "But I want the museum to honor all of the men and women who died for American freedom during the Cold War."[1]

One of the first people I recruited to help with the effort was Sergei Khrushchev, who joined the advisory board of directors and helped make sure it reflected both sides of the conflict.

"It is important that we remember," Khrushchev said.

Sergei and I often spoke on the same panel. One time, Mom was in the audience, and she turned to my friends Jon Teperson and Bob Kallos during the program. "His daddy put Gary's daddy in jail."

While pursuing a career in public administration—including serving as the executive director of several different nonprofit organizations and chambers of commerce—and eventually marrying and starting a family,

I remained committed to learning the truth about my father. I filed Freedom of Information Act requests and began lecturing about the U-2 Incident across the country and beyond, emerging as an expert on the subject and a vigorous defender of my father's memory.

My search for knowledge led to a memorable trip to a free and capitalist Russia in June 1997. As part of a so-called spy tour, organized by former intelligence officials on both sides, with a group of other Americans, I drove by Lubyanka Prison and the KGB headquarters and visited safe houses, drop sites, and other once-clandestine points of interest around Moscow.

The various once-unimagined changes roiling the onetime evil empire, now abuzz with capitalist activity, could be seen in something very personal: The KGB museum exhibit featuring artifacts from Dad's fateful mission, including his .22-caliber pistol with silencer and the poison-tipped pin Dad took on his mission. I learned that other items from the U-2 were being displayed at the Border Guard Museum, including items from his survival kit: a book of matches, a saw, a canteen, a compass, and a shaving kit. The display included a large stack of rubles, which had been sewn into Dad's jacket all those years ago, and a pack of Kent cigarettes. (In Soviet lore, Kent became "the cigarette of spies," because the pack was found on the spy pilot.)

Especially excited to see wreckage from the plane, I was intrigued to see a plaque claiming, in Russian, that the ejection seat was rigged with an explosive that would have killed the pilot. I knew that there was an explosive charge under the seat—it's what was used to blast it out. But to kill the pilot? This sounded like Soviet propaganda to me.

Still, as I began to learn about every detail of the aircraft, I would always remember a private conversation with high-altitude specialist Tom Bowen. After the pilot was shown the charge and told it was set to explode seventy seconds after the buttons were pushed, Bowen said, "he would have no way of knowing if it had been reset to zero."

I would always wonder if Dad had decided not to use the ejection seat because he was concerned it would explode instantaneously, or because he would have severed his legs had he used the ejection seat. This was yet another mystery I would never be able to solve.

With the help of Jim Connell, whom I met during the POW/MIA meeting, I wrangled my way into Vladimir Prison, which required a three-hour drive from Moscow.

Walking into the still-open penitentiary, the commandant greeted me graciously and escorted me to the cell my father had once occupied. We exchanged gifts. I stepped into the small space, which had been freshly painted for my visit, and smiled as Connell snapped a photograph.

I asked for a few minutes alone, and carefully studied the walls, trying to imagine how it felt for Dad to look out from behind those bars and wonder if he would ever get to go home. It was hard to believe I was actually standing there.

Something stirred in me that day, while standing in my father's footsteps. It was a moment I would never forget.

In 1997, after a decade of learning everything I could about my father's story—and the peculiarities of the federal government's bureaucracy—I began to seek for him a measure of vindication.

The effort started with a letter:

August 7, 1997

Secretary of the Air Force (SAF/MRC)
DoD Civilian/Military Service Review Board
Washington, DC 20330-1000

Dear Members of the Service Review Board,

I am writing to request a determination by the Service Review Board for my father's eligibility to be awarded the POW Medal posthumously. Subsection 1128 (a) of Title 10 states that, "The Secretary shall issue a prisoner-of-war medal to any person who, while serving in any capacity with the armed forces, was taken prisoner and held captive"—It is also my understanding that the Secretary can make a special determination when circumstances permit.

Francis Gary Powers, my father, was in the USAF from 1950 to 1956. In 1956, he began working for the CIA flying U-2 reconnaissance aircraft. He was stationed at Incirlik Air Force Base in Adana, Turkey, and reported to USAF military personnel. On May 1, 1960, he was shot down over the Soviet Union and held prisoner for three months by the KGB in Lubyanka Prison. On August 17 he was put on trial by the Soviet Union and sentenced to ten years in prison. He served 18 months in Vladimir Prison before he returned to the United States after being exchanged for Soviet spy, Col. Rudolf I. Abel.

I believe that my father was classified as a civilian working for the government during his involvement with the U-2 program and during his subsequent imprisonment. He had DoD and NASA identification and it was understood that U-2 pilots upon fulfillment of their CIA contracts could return to the military at a rank comparable with their peers. Many of the other U-2 pilots did return to the military at a comparable rank, but my father after returning home from Vladimir Prison decided he could best serve his country by working for Lockheed Aircraft Corporation as a U-2 test pilot.

I look forward to hearing from you with a favorable determination. If you should have any questions or need additional information, please do not hesitate to call.

Very truly yours,

Francis G. Powers, Jr.

Chairman, The Cold War Museum[2]

Several weeks later, a reply arrived from James D. Johnston, executive secretary of the Military Service Review Board, stating that DoD Directive 1348 limits the issue of the POW Medal to "those taken prisoner by foreign armed forces that are hostile to the United States, under circumstances which the Secretary concerned finds to have been comparable to those under which persons have generally been held captive by enemy armed forces during periods of armed conflict."[3]

"The Cold War is not one of the periods noted in the directive," Johnston wrote.

Johnston left open the possibility of an exception, but I began to understand the unique circumstances weighing against my father. Not only was his clandestine service treated differently, but combatants in the Cold War, the most important conflict of the previous four decades, were being denied the honors reserved for "shooting" wars such as Korea and Vietnam, which many historians considered battles of the larger Cold War.

I traded several letters with the Air Force pushing my father's case, but it took a flurry of once-secret documents to move the ball.

For all I had learned about my father's brush with history, several questions remained unanswered.

My father always said he had been hit at maximum altitude, but I knew that several key figures in Washington doubted his story, including CIA director John McCone. My father felt so betrayed by McCone that when he was finally awarded the Intelligence Star, his initial inclination was to tell the CIA boss to "shove it."

Mom was able to calm him down, and he eventually made the trip and graciously accepted the medal.

Caught between my admiration for my father and my determination to consider all of the evidence, I was left unable to offer any definitive evidence to refute the notion that he had descended to a lower altitude.

Until 1998.

With the Cold War fading in the rear-view mirror, my mother and I attended a declassification conference at Fort McNair, home of the National War College in Washington, DC. At this event, thousands of pages of once-classified secrets concerning the Cold War were finally exposed to the public. For us, it was a moment fraught with excitement.

Flipping through a book containing various letters and files, there it was: a document definitively stating that Francis Gary Powers's U-2 was disabled at 70,500 feet.[4]

That proved that Dad had been telling the truth all along.

Other evidence pointed to the likelihood that as many as eight different surface-to-air missiles exploded in the vicinity of the aircraft, none of them landing a direct hit.

Nearly four decades after the U-2 Incident, it was clear that Washington knew the aircraft was more vulnerable to Soviet missiles than it was willing to acknowledge at the time. By refusing to definitively refute the potential of a flame-out or an intentional descent, Washington protected its secrets at the expense of the man who spent twenty-one months locked up by the KGB.

Reading through the large cache of released documents, I located other pages showing the U-2 was a joint operation of the CIA and the Air Force, which was just the evidence we needed to push the Pentagon on the question of whether or not to award my father a POW Medal.

Equally troubling to the family was the way the government had allowed the misinformation to linger concerning the poison pin. Only after the Cold War ended were many of my dad's former colleagues free to discuss the device. I sought out a long list of pilots and CIA officials, who shared my frustration that Dad had been branded a traitor by some.

"That pin was only there if you thought you couldn't take what they were doing to you," said Tony Bevacqua, his onetime roommate. "No way was he expected to use it. Frank had a hard time when he got back, and one of the reasons was because too many people thought it was his duty to kill himself. And that's baloney."

Even with demonstrable evidence that he was never under any orders to commit suicide, I often dealt with people who believed he should have sacrificed his life to deprive the Soviets of a Cold War trophy.

While appearing on Oliver North's Fox News Channel broadcast, I was confronted by a caller who insisted Dad was a traitor because he didn't use the pin.

"Well, I'm glad he didn't, because I wouldn't be here if he had," I said with a chuckle, before calmly explaining the facts.

Armed with the declassified documents, I kept flooding the Pentagon with paperwork, including a letter supporting the award from retired General John A. Shaud, the executive director of the Air Force Association. Shaud, who had successfully petitioned for the POW Medals to be bestowed on Colonels John McKone and Bruce Olmstead, the only survivors of the RB-47 shoot-down, who were imprisoned at Lubyanka at the same as my father, urged the Air Force to look beyond the U-2 pilot's CIA employment and treat him as a member of the armed forces.

Like the Berlin Wall, the American government's official antipathy toward Francis Gary Powers began to crumble.

In announcing the Air Force's decision in a letter dated November 22, 1999, Staff Judge Advocate Colonel R. Philip Deavel said, "We believe there is substantial evidence in the record to support the applicant's request that the AFBCMR [Air Force Board of Correction of Military Records] characterize his father's service with the CIA as 'military' service."[5] This determination cleared the way for my dad to receive the POW Medal.

Forty-five years after President Eisenhower insisted the overflights be conducted exclusively by civilian pilots, the distinction was understood as a necessary conceit to avoid violations of airspace that might be interpreted as overt acts of war. Only in the most technical terms could the military establishment argue that my father was not a prisoner of war, especially given his previous Air Force service and the Air Force's decision to posthumously promote him to captain—although no one in the Powers family knew about this until his military record was officially updated in 2000.

Once the decision to award my father the POW Medal was made and the wheels were set in motion, I began talking with one of my new friends, Colonel Buz Carpenter, a former wing commander at Beale Air Force Base, to see if it was possible for me to get a ride in a U-2. Carpenter sold the flight to the brass at the Pentagon, including General Mike Ryan, the Air Force Chief of Staff. "[Ryan] thought it was a great idea . . . [to] gather some good national press coverage," Carpenter recalled.

On May 1, 2000, the fortieth anniversary of my father's shoot-down, I strapped on a yellow pressure suit and stepped into the back seat of a U-2 trainer piloted by Colonel Brian Anderson, who quickly headed for the edge of space. Reaching an altitude of 72,123 feet on a beautiful, blue-sky day, we flew for more than three hours, high above San Francisco, Los Angeles, and Sacramento.

I was able to see the curvature of the earth and the pitch-black sky above. It was exhilarating, awesome, wonderful. And after a while, it was a little boring.

No one was firing missiles at us.

It was yet another way for me to try to understand my father's journey on a very personal level.

After we touched down and taxied to the reviewing stand, a contingent of officials recognized my father with the POW Medal as well as the Distinguished Flying Cross, the National Defense Service Medal, and the CIA Director's Medal.

It was a wonderful show of support, with the Air Force and the agency publicly acknowledging my father's role in helping win the Cold War. I would never forget the look of satisfaction on my mother's face.

When Dad was inducted into the 2000 class of the Kentucky Aviation Hall of Fame, the emcee said, "Our next enshrine endured much in the service of his country, not the least of which was the misunderstanding of the American people."[6]

Friend Bob Gilliland, who nominated him, called Powers one of "the most famous pilot ever to go aloft."[7]

The honor gratified Mom and me, but we still chafed at the periodic insults to his memory.

Despite the lingering bitterness caused by the Smithsonian Institution's snub of the Powers family in 1986, we donated a large number of Dad's items to the National Air and Space Museum in 1995. When the Smithsonian's Udvar-Hazy Center opened in 2003, adjacent to Dulles International Airport, displaying several of those items, the Powers family was once again excluded. Two different officials, including the director, General Jack Dailey, told me that tickets to the grand opening were limited to financial donors, and there were no seats available for the family of an iconic aviator.

Not to be denied, I worked the phones and found a way into the event, as an aide to Congressman Tom Davis, a Republican from Virginia.

Once the festivities began, and a long list of artifact donors and the family members of prominent pilots were recognized—everyone, it seemed, except the Powers family—I was surrounded, in the back of the hangar, by a sea of empty seats.

It was yet another painful blow. It was hard not to see it as a direct insult not only to my father but also to the Powers family.

After I traded letters with the director of the National Air and Space Museum, my mom fired off her own message to Dailey. "I am again hurt by the lack of respect afforded my husband and his family . . . especially after our family's artifact donations that you so proudly display at both facilities," she said.[8]

Out of this unfortunate experience, we eventually developed a good working relationship with the Smithsonian. It makes me proud to see Dad honored among all those important figures in the history of aviation.

Chapter Seven

VOICE FROM THE GRAVE

When my mother died in June 2004, I took possession of a large collection of reel-to-reel audio tapes, featuring my father talking about all aspects of his life, which he recorded in 1969, while working with coauthor Curt Gentry on *Operation Overflight*. After converting the tapes to compact discs, I began methodically listening to the audio. Sometimes I played a CD while negotiating traffic. Other times I set aside time to go through a track in my office, slipping on headphones to make it easier to hear Dad's words forming sentences and paragraphs. The details they contained proved very helpful in my journey of discovery, while producing a rather-powerful listening experience.

Oh, that's how Dad sounded, I remembered thinking at one point. Time had stolen something that the tapes restored: I had forgotten the sound of my own father's voice.

One reel was especially emotional. While listening to Dad discuss an aspect of his captivity, I was startled to hear the broken English of a small child's voice injecting himself into the conversation.

"Hello, Daddy!"

It was my own voice.

"Hello, Gary," Dad replied. "Your face is dirty!"[1]

It was a heartwarming moment for the son to hear his four-year-old self, interacting with his father and then his mother, who talked about their upcoming dinner.

I played the passage over and over again, all the while wiping back bittersweet tears.

As the custodian of such things, I also took great care to preserve and transcribe the personal journal my father kept while incarcerated at Vladimir Prison, as well as a large cache of family letters, including dozens Frank wrote and received while in the Soviet Union.

One batch of letters was presumed lost for good. Fortunately, a couple from Georgia salvaged Dad's prison correspondence to Barbara from a storage facility after the rent went unpaid in the 1960s. After hearing about my efforts to learn about my father, they sought me out. We rendezvoused while I was on the road, between speeches, and they returned the letters while sharing a meal.

I was very surprised and so grateful for their kindness.

Thus the very personal exchanges between a husband and his wife, trapped on opposite sides of the Iron Curtain during a very trying time, were safeguarded for posterity.

After filing several different Freedom of Information Act requests, and being flooded with paperwork that was mostly useless, I finally acquired the transcript of the lengthy debriefing of my father by CIA officials in February 1962.

Together, these four surviving media instruments offered me a remarkably intimate glimpse into the most difficult period of my father's life.

It was almost like Dad was speaking to me from the grave.

Not long after arriving at Vladimir, Dad's new cellmate encouraged him to start keeping a diary. In this Zigurd Kruminsh contributed significantly to his friend's enduring record. (I repeatedly tried to track down Kruminsh's family, without success, but eventually concluded that he was a KGB plant.)

Writing about the day of the U-2 Incident several months later, Dad recorded:

May 1, 1960. It is very hard to recall all that happened on this day. It is definitely a day I will never forget. I came closer to death on this day than any day I can remember. . . .

Before and during the flight I continually thought of all the small things that could happen to cause trouble to the plane. One little screw could come loose or one little wire break and I would have to land on Soviet territory. . . . I was not worried at all about being shot down. I firmly believed that there was nothing that could reach my altitude and as long as I maintained my altitude and had no engine trouble I would be safe. . . .[2]

Exactly what constituted his "maximum altitude" was to be debated for years, contributing significantly to the swirl of misinformation. CIA debriefers addressed the subject two years later:

US Interrogator: Alright. Let's discuss altitude, ah, to the best of your recollections, Frank.

Powers: Starting at the beginning of the flight?

US Interrogator: Well, yeah, as to what your programmed altitudes were and, ah, what your recollections were.

Powers: Now briefing on that was to climb according to, ah, the regular schedule we had to carry in the climb which I did and, ah, climb to 70,000 feet—level—stay at 70,000 feet the entire flight. But the airplane will not with a full fuel load would not climb to, ah, 70,000 feet immediately. It takes normal[ly] a half hour or so, or I don't know exactly how much time—I can't recall. But I was at 70,000 feet I think shortly after crossing the Russian border. I don't remember exactly where I got the, ah, altitude, but I remained at 70 the entire flight until this happened.

US Interrogator: You would say then that you were at 70,000 on this when this occurred?

Powers: When, ah, that's what my altimeter, ah, showed, and the altimeter was set on a, a sea level, ah, well, ah, I even forgot the term. But 29.92, ah ah, was set in my altimeters at sea-level pressure.

US Interrogator: Barometric pressure?

Powers: Yes, ah huh. And it was indicating 70,000 feet. So any error that it might have had would be the only—

US Interrogator: Well now, was that the ceiling of the plane?

Powers: No, no. I could have possibly got up to, when the plane was hit, I say hit when the accident happened, the explosion occurred, ah, I could possibly get it up above 72,000 feet because I had retarded the power so I could remain at 70,000 as instructed to....

US Interrogator: What was the ultimate, ah, ceiling of the plane and with, ah, minimum fuel?

Powers: Minimum fuel, I could have gotten up to approximately— minimum fuel approximately 75,000 feet. But with the load I had at the time, I'd say maybe about 72. And that time. Maybe even 73, but somewhere in between those two was my estimate then....

US Interrogator: You were reported and said you were at 68,000 at that time I think. Was this . . . this I believe was a lesser altitude, wasn't it, than you had?

Powers: Yes. That was. . . . I tried to save as much altitude as I could. I mean, not to let them know what the altitude was.

US Interrogator: But you had . . . oh, I see. Were you actually at 70?

Powers: I was at 70. . . . My scheduled plan was to climb until I reached 70 and maintain 70 for the duration of the flight.[3]

This exchange demonstrated the game my father played with his KGB interrogators. By claiming that he was flying at 68,000 at the time of the incident, he believed he was preventing the Soviets from knowing the limit of the U-2's capability, which he believed might protect future pilots, while also communicating to the CIA that he was attempting to withhold key secrets. This was his way of saying, "Hey, guys, I'm not telling the full truth."

By the time I secured the interrogation transcript, I had already confirmed that the government eventually concluded he had been shot down at an altitude of 70,500 feet.

I found it interesting that the CIA debriefers repeatedly came back to their question about how high Dad was flying and whether he was sure he did not have a flame-out or descend to a lower altitude before being shot down.

They pressed on this matter because of the classified National Security Agency report on the shoot-down. Only later would Washington learn that a Soviet fighter sent to try to ram the U-2 had been felled by one of the SA-2 missiles and was falling out of the sky at the same time, contributing to the murky situation, which key CIA officials eventually concluded that the NSA misinterpreted.

In 2010, I obtained a previously classified internal CIA interview with John McMahon, the deputy director of special projects during the U-2 Incident. McMahon left no doubt about the hostility some harbored toward Dad, especially McCone.

McCone—influenced by the National Security Agency report, which argued that the pilot "descended to a lower altitude and turned back in a broad curve toward Sverdlovsk before being downed"[4]—ordered the Prettyman board to reconvene to consider the additional evidence. However, the commission found the evidence inconclusive. The difference in opinion among the American intelligence establishment was hidden from the public but apparently played a role in the CIA's unwillingness to offer a full-throated defense of him.

McCone was trying to save face. He had put his reputation on the line when he suggested Dad was complicit in his capture, and he was going to do everything he could to show he was right, at the expense of Dad's reputation.

After McMahon determined, based on certain secret information, which was never revealed during the trial, that Dad had "followed our directions to the letter," an argument broke out "between myself and [James] Angleton on what would happen with Powers. I urged an exchange and I wrote a paper that General Cabell approved. Then I attended meetings where we tried to figure out, as a community, where to go next. Those meetings were usually at State. President Kennedy approved that we try and get Powers out. Our friends in the CI [Central Intelligence] Staff did everything they could to torpedo that exchange. I can remember several officials in State speaking against the exchange. I pointed out that President Kennedy authorized the exchange, and I wanted the names of those that were against it. The objections disappeared. John McCone, who was the head of the ABC when Powers was shot down, proclaimed then that he defected. So, as Director, he wasn't too happy eating those words."[5]

Air Force Major Harry Cordes, who began working with Detachment B at Groom Lake and eventually deployed with the unit to Turkey, released a written history that also proved enlightening. By the time of the shoot-down, he had been reassigned to SAC as an intelligence officer, but he received all of the intelligence reports concerning the U-2 Incident. While Cordes defended my father, his immediate superior, Colonel Keegan, "considered Powers a traitor for talking to the Soviets, not destroying the U-2 with the destruction switches, and especially for not taking his life with the lethal needle concealed in a coin."[6] Cordes wound up as one of the men who debriefed Dad for the CIA.

The agency men went to great lengths to rule out every possible alternative to a shoot-down.

> US Interrogator: That orange glow yeh—a—a—would that sort of phenomenon occur possibly in connection with a flame-out? Could it?
> Powers: Well let's see. I've had several just ordinary flame-outs in this airplane and there's nothing like that, a, in fact, flame-out[s] earlier in the program were, a, very, a, frequent and, a, it couldn't have been associated with a flame-out in any way. Now, I thought maybe that if say the, I, I remember hearing one time that after an engine change, inspection and so forth, working on a[n] airplane that they were running it up on a, a test stand and the whole tail pipe—jet exhaust pipe—there blew out. Now something like that might have caused it, but I'm sure I would feel that definitely in the airplane if this thing was going through—and not only that, the paint on the tail section would be, I'm sure, would be burnt completely off.

US Interrogator: Now—now one other question. Have you given any consideration to the possibility that there are, a, that this, a, that there could have been sabotage to the plane?

Powers: I've done a lot of thinking about this, and I don't see how there could be. I don't really see how there could be, because we had tight security and the plane was flown from [REDACTED] moved into a hangar and all of our people who I would trust anywhere worked on it. The plane was taken out—no one else got around it—and then I felt it, so it—it had several hours on it before this time, and no one knew whether the plane would go the next day or not, so they couldn't—say—set a bomb of some kind in it because they wouldn't know.

US Interrogator: Could a bomb be set in it that would go by altitude? Or by time?

Powers: Well, no, because—well, timing would be it but—see—there was a thirty-minute delay on my flight, and we didn't even known that the fight would go the next day. It might be canceled and go— go back to Turkey.

US Interrogator: Then—professionally—with your reasoning, you can't think of any way that this thing could be sabotaged?

Powers: I don't see how it could possibly be sabotaged. . . .[7]

Several years after I acquired the interrogation document, I received in the mail an unmarked envelope with a transcript of the once-classified interviews conducted by the Prettyman commission. The members also spent significant time investigating the possibility someone could have gotten to the plane in Pakistan or provided intelligence about its takeoff to the Soviets.

An official whose name was redacted told the commission: "From the time that the Detachment left [REDACTED] until the time that it arrived back at [REDACTED] . . . [we] were on guard for any unusual activity or personnel that might be involved. There was a limited number of contacts with base people, and I personally did the majority of these.

The other people of my Detachment stayed within the small hangar area. So if there had been any unusual personalities within that general area, then we would have discovered this, I feel sure of this, from a security standpoint. . . ."[8]

The agency people also investigated the possibility of mechanical problems.

US Interrogator: I was wondering whether the autopilot had given you any trouble.

Powers: It gave me some trouble for several minutes there and finally I just discarded it altogether. I could have made a decision to turn around and come back, which would have been a very good decision to make I think, but since I was—by looking at the maps— approximately halfway, the weather was bad behind and perfectly clear ahead, and I had some short-cuts I could take ahead—I thought I'd go along. . . . [9]

The controversy caused by Oliver's apparent confusion on the cause of the crash caused Frank significant distress.

After trying to clear up the matter with his letter to the *New York Times*—which so served Soviet purposes that they made sure it also ran in Pravda—Frank wrote directly to his parents:

6 September 1960

Dear Mom & Dad,

I guess you will be surprised to get this letter so soon after the other one. I would have waited until I received an answer to my last letter but I have been shown an article in the August 27th issue of the New York Times and I thought I had better clear up an apparent misunderstanding. In that article you stated that I said I didn't think I was shot down. I do not remember talking about this at all except during the trial.

There I stated that I did not see what it was that hit me. I felt and heard an explosion and saw an orange colored flash. My engine was working good up to this time. My only conclusion is that something exploded near the airplane. What it was I do not know because I did not see it. I did not feel an impact therefore I think it was the shock wave from the explosion that caused failure of my plane. I think the tail came off first because the aircraft nosed down. Then I think the wings came off and I started spinning in an inverted position.

The thing that I want to stress is the fact that I did not say I didn't think I was shot down. In fact I think it was for the reasons stated above. The flight had been normal up to this time. Everything was working good except the automatic pilot which I had disengaged several minutes before the explosion because the pitch control was not working good. The air was smooth and the plane was flying good and there was no reason for any explosion except an external one not connected with the airplane. I was flying at maximum altitude as I stated during the trial. I asked you when I saw you to be careful what you said. I wanted everything to die down as soon as it could. Maybe you did not say these things and the newspaper misunderstood, or if you did then you misunderstood when I said here.

I have been told that there are people in the States who think I landed the plane here to give it to the Russians. This is not true. My intensions [*sic*] were to carry out my assignment as near as I could and if I had not been shot down I think it would have been successful. Anyone who saw the remains of the plane would know it would not [have] landed normally but in many pieces.

I ask you once again to be careful what you say to reporters. I said nothing to you that could be used as news so I ask you not to quote me. You can say anything you want about your experiences here and what you think. But please don't say what you think I may be thinking or look for any hidden meaning in what I said to you or what I write to you. I am very sorry to be writing to you like this but that article in the newspaper upset me and I wanted to straighten it out.

I love all of you very much and I know you would not do anything to hurt me in anyway if you can possibly help it. You might think it is worth it to be in prison if my pay continues. It might be to someone else but there is not enough money in the US and USSR put together to make me want to stay in prison. I would gladly give everything I have now and anything I would have in the future to get out today. Since the only way I can get out is to serve my term or be exchanged or pardoned then I will just have to wait and see what happens. It isn't pleasant but there is no alternative.

Well that is about all for now except that I hope all of you and Barbara are getting along together. Please, for my sake, don't let the hard feelings continue. My trouble is enough for several families without you people making it worse.

I would appreciate it if you all kept in contact and learned to be closer together. I hoped and prayed that my misfortune would keep you close rather than cause trouble.

Well, bye for now.[10]

Love,

Francis

In a reply from his parents dated September 17, 1960, Ida expressed remorse for the controversy, telling her son: "I was so sorry the newspapers misquoted the news. Daddy only stated what you said at the trial. . . . I told Daddy not to say anything to the reporters. . . . I hope nothing has hurt you any."[11]

After he returned home, Francis told the CIA debriefers: "When I read [the *New York Times*] article, it made me very angry with my father. . . . I personally wanted you people to know that I thought I had been shot down."[12]

With all the time in the world to let his mind wander, my father understood that the question of what happened to cause his crash reflected a fundamental issue that cut to the heart of the most closely guarded secrets on both sides.

"I got the impression," he said in his tapes, "that someone was going out of their way to stress the fact that there was a malfunction in the airplane or something to hush-hush the fact that [the Soviets] did have a defensive weapon that was capable of [shooting the U-2 out of the sky]. . . . All I could see was a friend of mine coming over and getting shot down himself. I wanted it known that they had this capability. Someone apparently was trying to cover up the fact that they had this capability."[13]

Especially in light of the U-2 that was shot down over Cuba in 1962, I understood my father's frustration. All of the sudden, Washington officials were faced with the political dilemma of having to admit that the Soviets were more advanced than they realized. Instead of clearing this up, the government allowed the misinformation to continue to circulate.

When I first started to transcribe my father's journal, while in graduate school at George Mason, I took great care to methodically type the words. It became something I usually did after arriving home at night, hunched over my computer for an hour or two at a time. I always felt like I learned something. It was part of the puzzle slowly being revealed to me, including the early portions when Dad described the moments after he lost control of the plane.

"My first reaction was to reach toward the destruction switches," he wrote. "I knew that after activating them I would have seventy seconds in which to leave the plane before the explosion. I then thought I had better see if I could get into the position to use the ejection seat before activating the switches. It was a good thing I did this because I spent several minutes I suppose (I don't know how long I was in the spinning plane), trying to get my feet in the proper place and trying to get far enough back into the seat so that I could eject without tearing my legs off on the canopy rail as I shot out of the cabin. I could not get into the proper position. I was not sitting at all but hanging by the seat belt and it was impossible to shorten the belt with all the forces against it. . . ."[14]

This sequence became an important part of the debriefing.

US Interrogator: As you moved down in your seat in that odd inverted position, the plane was not flaming or smoking or anything, was it, as far as you could recall it?

Powers: I would say there was no fire connected with . . .

US Interrogator: No fire connected with it. In other words, . . . it wasn't billowing smoke or . . .

Powers: If it was, I knew nothing about it.

US Interrogator: And, and then, then . . .

Powers: I feel sure that the engine stopped at this, ah, was stopping as this, ah, maneuver started to take place. Because I can remember somewhere along this that the, ah, RPM gauge was going down. But I can't remember exactly when I noticed that. There was some—when the nose dropped there was some very violent maneuvers. I've never experienced anything quite like it. I don't know exactly what happened there. And it didn't take long. But it ended up in that inverted position going around, and I think it was going around clockwise . . . .

After deciding to bail out and eventually parachuting to the ground, Dad wrote about his feelings concerning his impending fate: "I knew I was as good as dead and I also knew in my own mind that my death would not be a fast one but one of slow torture. . . ."

US Interrogator: When you got to the ground . . . you didn't try to escape?

Powers: No, there was . . . while I was still lying there on the ground with the parachute dragging me, one man was helping me out of the parachute and the other was trying to help me up, and by the time I got on my feet and took the helmet off, there was a large group around.

US Interrogator: There was just no opportunity to even think of escaping?

Powers: I think I couldn't have gotten through this group if none of them were armed. . . . I don't think any of them were, but it was just a large press of people and I could not have gotten through anyway.

US Interrogator: Yeah, now then . . .

Powers: And they had also taken this .22 pistol away from me before I had an opportunity to even think about it.

US Interrogator: You didn't resist in any way?

Powers: No, I gave no active resistance.

US Interrogator: Why didn't you resist?

Powers: Just too many people.

US Interrogator: Uh-huh. It just would have been foolhardy, in other
words?

Powers: That's what it seemed to me. It just seemed that ... well, I'm
alive right now. I could try to escape, which I wanted to do. I
was pretty much in shock at the time also, I don't suppose I was
thinking too clearly, but I was looking around, trying to see some
way to escape or something to do, and all these people milling
around. . . . It was just impossible to do anything, in my opinion.[15]

After concluding the interrogation, Harry Cordes and his colleague
John Hughes, who represented the Defense Intelligence Agency, flew to
Washington to brief a series of high-ranking officials, including Secretary of Defense Robert McNamara, who criticized the pilot's decision to
proceed after his autopilot malfunctioned. Cordes emerged as an important advocate for my father against the forces who doubted his story,
especially John McCone.

Confronting the NSA report suggesting the pilot had descended
below 30,000 feet before being shot down, Cordes shot holes in the theory
by citing inaccurate data produced during similar incidents, including the
loss of the RB-47. "I had knowledge of the same intelligence information," he said, "but I believed Powers."[16]

While reading and transcribing my father's journal entries concerning
the KGB interrogations, it was difficult for me to maintain any sort of
detachment. I could feel my father's desperation, the emotional rollercoaster ride he was experiencing, not knowing whether he would ever get
to go home.

Writing about the experience several months after the fact, Frank said:

> I felt that there was no hope for me. I thought I would be tortured and later shot—probably without anyone outside the Soviet Union ever knowing what had happened to me. I did not realize or even think of the political importance of the incident and how it would be used. If I had been able to think clearly I might have come to the conclusion that the incident and therefore myself were too important to keep secret and not used to the utmost to sway world public opinion away from the US and to the USSR. . . .
>
> During the interrogation on the third of May I was asked about the radio communication equipment on board the U-2, and if I informed my base of what happened to me. I refused to answer these questions and told them that I personally felt it was to my advantage not to answer them. . . .
>
> My thinking at the time was that my mother, with her bad heart, might be killed by the news of my probable death, not to mention how it might affect my father and wife. I thought that the Soviet Union, not knowing whether or not I had communicated with my base would be more likely to release the news that I was alive than they would be if I told them I did not communicate the details of the accident to them. I assumed that if they thought that I did call my base and told them that there had been an explosion and that I was bailing out that they would go ahead and release the news of my being alive. . . .
>
> Now that I think back I am sure they would have released the news anyway because the incident was too important to the Soviet Union politically to be hushed up and put aside.[17]

How he interacted with his captors was a subject that loomed large in his CIA debriefings.

US Interrogator: Almost immediately you had to . . . arrive at some decision in your mind as to how you were going to deal with these people, that is . . . you could decide to tell them to go to hell, you weren't going to talk, or you were going to cooperate with them to a certain extent, or you were not going to cooperate with them. How did you . . . what decision did you arrive at in this regard and how did you arrive at it?

Powers: And when?

US Interrogator: Yeah.

Powers: At Sverdlovsk when I saw that my story that I had made up was no good whatsoever, I decided then . . . I remember then hearing this briefing that I had that there would be torture, that may as well, in an event like this when there was capture, may as well tell them everything because they would get it out of you anyway, and just make it last as long as possible because . . . the longer they thought you knew something, the longer you would live, and I decided then that I would cooperate with them to a certain extent. There [were] some thing, things, that I was never going to tell them.

US Interrogator: Now this was briefings that you got from [REDACTED] prior to going or over a period of time?

Powers: I think . . . I'm pretty sure they were all from [REDACTED] and not just prior to this flight but over a period of time before this flight. One probably was when we . . . when this pin was given to us and we were told what it would do, and we were told we could take it if we wanted to and so forth. . . . I think he briefed us some there, and I'm not positive whether this particular question about telling everything came up before my flight while we were studying the maps, or maybe before someone else's operation that I was in on. But I do remember hearing it and I do remember that it came to my mind at that time.

US Interrogator: But finding yourself in this situation you had the background of briefing of that type?

Powers: Yes, and that decided my course. I don't know what I would have done if I had not thought of that. I have no idea; but, you've got to realize that I was in a pretty good state of shock at the time. I . . . probably wasn't thinking too clearly, although it seems to me that I was, but I was nervous, my heart was . . . pulse rate very fast, and, felt horrible. I don't remember how long I'd been up at that time, but I was completely exhausted seemed like. But anyway, this entered my mind and when I saw that my cover story did not hold up or the one that I made up would not hold up, I knew there was . . . I wanted to keep as much information from them as possible . . . and I knew there were some things that . . . that it would be very embarrassing for a lot of people [to] find out about it, and I was going to do my best to keep that type of information from these people; but I also decided at that time and between that . . . that time and also on the airplane to Moscow, which took a few hours, I don't remember how long . . . that in order to . . . to withhold this information that I thought was very important, I had to convince these people that I was telling them the truth. And doing that, I had to anticipate what would be released in the press, which I had no idea what would be. And maybe my imagination ran away with me in some of these instances because the press seems to have a pretty good intelligence system of their own. . . . There was a lot of thoughts like this running through my mind, but I definitely made up my mind that some things couldn't be revealed. Other things that might appear in the press, they would know that I was telling the truth in everything. And I think it worked fairly good in several cases. . . .[18]

On this matter, the Prettyman inquiry interviewed at least one senior official who worked with my father.

[NAME REDACTED]: We followed a practice—at least I did—of telling the pilots that if they were captured that they were of course to attempt not to reveal any information at all, if possible—and this usually degenerated into a fairly general discussion of ways and means. We would discuss Air Force experience with PW's [prisoners of war], and the fact that eventually almost anyone could be broken down and compelled to talk—and that the tactics should be to delay—not an out-and-out lie if you're going to get caught in it, but delay your interrogators as much as possible—give him a limited amount of information and specifics ... [especially with regard to] altitude and performance of the aircraft. ... [19]

The CIA debriefers eventually moved on to finding out what the Soviets learned about his mission.

US Interrogator: Did they ask you questions concerning what you were after in the remaining portion of the flight?

Powers: See, there were a few notations [at this point, he was gesturing to a map similar to one captured by the Soviets]. I think, up here, we had a few airfields annotated. The main thing they wanted to know was how I knew or how I got the information that there would be an airfield there. See, it wasn't on the map, we had put it there ourselves, and I just told them that someone gave it to me to put it on. Where he got it I don't know. They wanted to know what I was looking for, and I told them, "I don't know." And actually I don't know.

US Interrogator: Did they try to pump you with any suggestions?

Powers: Well, I don't know whether they mentioned rocket-launching sites or if that's the thing that came into my mind when they asked this question, but I know it was in my mind anyway—these rocket-launching sites.

US Interrogator: Did they at any time at all threaten you with any physical harm during your interrogations?

Powers: No, but they did just the opposite, told me that I would not be tortured. Of course, I didn't believe them. They at no time— well, at Sverdlovsk, one time, I had some ear trouble, I guess from past descent, and I reached up two or three times to—well, I don't know, habit, I guess—to try to clear the ear and one time, I guess, a man grabbed my hand and threw it down, and that is the roughest treatment I got. They never hand-cuffed me. Those people at that first place looked fairly angry and mean, but the only thing was this throwing my hand down.

US Interrogator: Did they, on the other hand, try to coerce you by bribery of any kind? Did they promise you something?

Powers: Now, this is something I don't know. I tried to find out, now this was where [Roman Andreyevich] Rudenko was attorney general, or whatever he is, came in at one of the meetings with him. I was feeling fairly despondent and I said, "I'll never get out of here." And he said, "Oh, there are ways." And I said, "What kind of ways?" He said, "Oh, there are just ways." "Well, what kind of ways?" "Well, I think you should think about it." And I went to the cell and thought about it, and I kept waiting for him to bring it up again because I was interested in what they were talking about, and they never did bring it up. So I mentioned it to the interpreter. I asked what kind of ways did he mean, and he said, "What do you think?" And I said, "Well, I have no idea." And that is all that was mentioned. And it seemed at one time they might have had some sort of plan to maybe try to talk me into doing something and giving me my release as pay for something, I don't know. That was just my impression of this little incident. I never did know what was meant by what he said.[20]

The KGB pushed him hard on the question of previous overflights. "They harped on it so much . . . every day," he said on his tapes. "When I got angry, I said, 'If I'd taken a thousand flights, do you think I'd tell you? They stopped [asking] shortly after that."[21]

The CIA wanted to know about the condition of his wreckage.

US Interrogator: Frank, could you describe your visit to the Gorky Park to see the remains of the aircraft—the circumstances of that?

Powers: I think it was around the middle of May. I don't remember whether they told me the night before or not. I think they did at the last interrogation on the day before that at a certain time—I think it was about nine o'clock in the morning that they were going to take me to review the remains of the aircraft. I don't know that it was Gorky Park, but it seems like I've heard it mentioned here and that's why I called it Gorky Park, but it was definitely a park. Took me out in an automobile and there was another automobile or two following. Got there. You know, they had ropes around, had all this roped off. There was one or two places they let me get in behind the rope to see something close, but most of the time I had to stay out in front of the ropes. Could get close to the stuff that was there. And they took me around, asking me about each of these individual pieces of equipment and so forth.

US Interrogator: What specifically did they ask you to identify, certain—?

Powers: Yes, it seemed to me they wanted me to identify some of this stuff, and some of it I couldn't identify. I told them I didn't know what it was. I couldn't have identified it if I'd known what it was before, most of it. Some of it was in bad shape—you could see some of it, instruments banged up, but you could tell what they were.

US Interrogator: Were they interested in parts of it more so than others?

Powers: Well, they wanted to get some photographs of me standing in this area where they had the cameras and special equipment. They seemed to ask more questions about the special equipment than about the regular flight instruments and so forth.

US Interrogator: Was this a closed section of the park or were there others there?

Powers: There were a bunch of people there but they were all associated with KGB and guards and so forth.

US Interrogator: Not the general public?

Powers: No, not the general public. In fact we remained there a little longer, I guess, than they anticipated because when we came outside there was a group of people apparently waiting to get in blocked off out of the way. And they whisked me right into the car and out. I suppose they opened it up to the public then—I don't remember how long it took or what time this was—I know it was in the morning—I think nine o'clock.

US Interrogator: Frank, was the aircraft, as you evaluated it, in condition generally consistent with what you might expect knowing you didn't see it go down? Was there anything inconsistent or illogical in what you saw there?

Powers: Well, I don't know. I know from some of the fighter planes that go down there's very little left, but they probably go down much faster. It seemed to me to be in a little better shape than—well, it was in much better shape that I had hoped it would be, but I thought there would be a little more damage than it appeared. I was very glad that [much] of this stuff was mashed up so it couldn't, I don't believe it could be taken apart—looked like to me, but I guess they could. I was surprised that the—Oh, they showed me a photograph this morning that the tail section—it was from the side that I didn't see—I only saw the other side—and this photograph looked much more damaged than the one that I remembered seeing of the tail section. In fact, I thought the horizontal stabilizers were on, but in this photograph one was missing. But since I only saw one side—I'm sure one side was on—it must have been.

US Interrogator: All of the stuff you saw at Gorky Park was—the best you could tell—was part of the U-2? Didn't look like there was anything added?

Powers: Yes, it looked like everything I saw there was part of it.[22]

Completely shut off from the outside world, and unaware what his family had been told about the incident, the pilot was eager to contact his parents and his wife. Several days after visiting the wreckage, he was allowed to begin writing letters. The first was to his wife.

26 May 1960

My Dearest Barbara,

I want you to know that I love you and miss you very much. I did not realize how much until I found myself in this situation. Not knowing, when, if ever, I will see you again, has made me realize how much you mean to me. I have had plenty of time to think since I have been here and plenty of time to regret past mistakes.

I am sincerely sorry to cause you the suffering you must have had before you found out that I am still alive. I am also sorry to be the cause of any suffering or pain that you may be having because of the situation that I am presently in.

I hope with all my heart that you are well and everything is all right with you. I hope your trip back to the States was a good one. It looks like we will not get to take the boat trip back that we were planning on.

It is very hard to write this letter even though I have been wanting to write ever since I have been here. I don't know what to say or how to say it.

I have been told that there is a lot of publicity in the U.S. papers about me. I was also told that you had returned to the States and that you are presently with your mother.

Barbara tell me how my mother and father are taking this. Is my mother all right? I was afraid that it might be too much of a shock to her. I am going to write to them as soon as I finish this letter but if my mother is ill they might not let me know like they did once before. I am depending on you for this information.

Well to get back to me, I am getting along as good as can be expected. I get more than I can eat and plenty of sleep. I have also been reading a lot. I have been treated much better than expected. For the first week or so I had no appetite at all but I am doing fine now.

When I had to bail out of the plane I skinned my right shin a little and carried a black left eye for two weeks. A lady doctor treated them both and they are well now.

That was my first experience with a parachute and I hope I will never have another. I could not use the ejection seat because of the G forces and had to climb out. My chute opened immediately how I don't know, I don't remember pulling anything. The people here tell me I am lucky to be alive but only time will tell me whether or not I was lucky.

Things happened pretty fast after that. Before dark that night I was in Moscow. I have been in the same cell since then. It gets pretty lonely here by myself but they have given me books to read and it helps to pass the time. I also get to walk in the fresh air every day that it doesn't rain. One day I even took a sun bath. It has been a little too cold to do that every day.

On May 2nd I was taken on a tour of Moscow which I enjoyed very much. These people are real proud of their Capitol city and it is a beautiful city. Another time I was taken to a park to review the remains of my plane. Those are the only two times I have been out of this building.

Just now a guard asked me if I wanted to walk but I prefer to finish this letter so I said no.

Barbara, I don't know what is going to happen to me. The investigation and interrogation is still going on. When that is over there will be a trial. I will be tried in accordance with Article 2 of their criminal code for espionage. The article states that the punishment is 7 to 15 years imprisonment and death in some cases. Where I fit in I don't know. I don't know when the trial will be or anything. I only know that I don't like the situation I am in or the situation I have placed you in. I will try my best to make the most of it and I hope you will do the same.

I was told today that I could write letters to you and my parents. That was good news. I was also told that there appeared in one of the U.S. papers a statement that my father had made that he would like to come here and see me. I was told that if the U.S. government would let any of you come that you would be allowed to see me. I would rather you waited until the trial or after so that I could tell you what the results were. But I will leave the decision of when to come up to you.

I did take a walk after all. I just came back from it. It was getting pretty smoky in here and I needed the fresh air. I am still smoking too much. By the way these cigarettes here are pretty good.

I want to assure you Barbara that I am getting along fine. I am being treated very good and as I said before, much better than I expected. You probably have the idea that I had before that the treatment would be bad. Well it isn't. It isn't like home but a person can not expect to be treated at home in any prison. I don't like to be locked up but under the circumstances I don't expect anything else.

Darling I wish I had good news to give you. I know you worry about me but I don't know what is going to happen. I will let you know of any new developments if I am allowed to.

Darling you are in charge of everything now. You have those Powers of Attorneys so use them as you see fit. Everything is in your hands and I trust to your judgment. I don't want to hear anything about what you do with the money you and I saved, use your own judgment and do what you think is best but don't bother me with your decisions. You are on your own now and I do not know for how long. Just be careful and maybe we can still buy a house some day. It is a pleasant thought, owning our own home, especially as I sit here in my cell thinking about it.

Well Darling, it is dark outside now and I guess I had better go to bed. I have written a lot more than I thought I could. At first I didn't seem to think of what to write but it kept coming out.

Barbara, once again I say I am very sorry for everything. I hope that you are all right and I want you to know that I love you very much. I am sending you, with this letter,

All my love, Gary[23]

As the production and consumption of correspondence quickly became a central part of his existence, my father wrote steadily to his wife and parents, including this second letter to Oliver and Ida:

21 June 1960

Dear Mom and Dad,

I received your answer to my letter yesterday and was very glad to hear that all of you are well. Several days ago I received your note that you sent in care of the American Embassy. I did not answer it but waited for an answer to my letter.

I have not heard a word as yet from Barbara. Do you know if there is anything wrong that she hasn't written? I was told that it was written in the newspapers that she had received my letter. I should have had an answer by now. I guess it is on the way. Maybe I will get it tomorrow.

You stated in your letter that you would be leaving for the USSR in about fifteen days or when you received my answer to your letter. By this I take it that permission has been granted for you to visit me. I would like to see you very much but I still think it would be best for you to wait until the trial or after it when we could know what my fate is to be. I have no idea when the trial will take place but I could let you know when I find out.

If you come now the only thing you could find out is that I am getting along fine and am healthy. I don't know how long you could stay but I am sure with your work back there that it couldn't be long. You would then have to return not knowing any more about what is to happen to me than you did when you came. If you come after the trial than you could see me and know the results too.

Maybe you think that you will be able to help me in some way. I wish that you could but I see no way that you can. Your presence here could not alter the outcome of my trial.

I would give anything I possess if this had not happened. Not only because of the position that I find myself in but because of the worry and trouble I have caused you, not to mention an increase of tension in the world.

One can always look back and say that I wish I had not done that, but no amount of wishing or hindsight can change the results of something already done.

I hope that one of these days I will be able to do something that will make up for all the pain and sorrow I have caused you. If God is willing I will do my best. I know you are disappointed in your son and I know that I have not always been the dutiful son that you desired. For this I am very sorry. I want you to know that no one could have had better parents than I have had.

How I wish I could be there telling you this in person instead of writing it from a prison cell in Moscow. There are so many things I would like to tell you, things that I can't seem to find words to express but things that I feel very strongly in my heart.

I am still getting along all right. I am being treated good and I have read numerous books. I am now studying or attempting to study Russian.

The weather here is warm now. Not quite as warm as it is there now but it is very nice. It rains a little more often here I think than it does there at this time of year.

I have been taking a walk and getting some sun every day. They still bring me too much food and I cannot eat it all. I have learned to like their yogurt very much. When I need cigarettes all I have to do is ask and they give them to me.

The people here have been much nicer to me than I expected them to be and I appreciate it very much. I think the Russians and American people would like each other if they knew each other better.

Well I guess I will stop for now. Please tell all my sisters and their families that I think of them often and wish them the best of everything. Please take care of yourselves and remember that I love all of you very much.

Your son
Francis[24]

After one especially long and exhausting interrogation, he was taken back to his cell and fell into a deep sleep. He dreamed about being back on the farm in Virginia, with all of his family around. They were walking along a road toward the house when suddenly, he began to experience a severe pain in his leg, which caused him to fall behind. "They kept getting farther ahead of me and I tried to call to them to slow down," he noted in his journal, "but for some reason could not do so. . . . I sat down beside the road watching all my family walking away from me, seeming not to know or to care that I was not with them. . . ."[25]

Dad's feelings of abandonment and isolation were easy to understand. He was especially concerned that he had heard nothing from Barbara.

When he finally received a reply from his wife, he quickly put pen to paper:

28 June 1960

My Dearest Barbara,

I cannot find words to describe what it meant to me to receive your letter. I have been very worried about you and could not understand why I had not heard from you. Knowing that you are okay has made me feel much better.

There is very little I can say about myself. Nothing has changed since I last wrote you. I still do not know any more than I did then about what is to happen to me or when my trial will be.

I am still taking daily walks and am getting a suntan. I still have plenty to eat and books to read. I have no complaints for the treatment I am receiving. My only complaint is that I am not there with you.

There is no need for you to try to send anything to me at the present time. There is nothing I need. If in the future I need anything and I am allowed to have it I will let you know.

Darling I am very sorry for the mess I have made out of our lives. All our plans and all our hopes seem to have been in vain. Needless to say my life would be much different if I had it to live over again. What's done is done and there is nothing I can do about it now.

Stateside life apparently agrees with Eck. I can remember how we tried to get him to gain weight before. I suppose he gets better food there. Take good care of him Barbara for he is a fine dog.

I hope your mother is getting along all right. Tell her to take care of herself and not to work too hard.

Barbara try to keep my mother from worrying too much, and I would appreciate it very much if you would get in touch with her doctor and find out how her health is and let me know. I have been afraid that my being here might cause her to have another heart attack. I could never forgive myself if I were responsible for that.

I remember how you used to try to get me to write home more often.

I always kept putting it off even though I know they wanted to hear from me. They desired a better son than they had. Maybe I can make up for it someway in the future.

Darling I can't tell you how much I miss you or how sorry I am that all this has happened. You also deserved better than this. It seems I have done nothing but hurt the people I love most in the world. I hope that I will have the opportunity to do better in the future, but the future doesn't look very bright.

Barbara I can't find words to express what I feel for you. You mean everything to me and I love you very much. Please take care of yourself Darling and don't worry about me. You have your life and future to think of.

Well Darling I will stop for now. Remember that I love you very much and miss you more than I can say.

All my love,
Gary[26]

Not until I began listening to the tapes did I realize how much care the Soviets took to censor his letters while he was at Lubyanka. They often would make him rewrite a letter, with words changed and paragraphs moved.

In time, CIA officials wondered why he had not tried to communicate by inserting coded messages into his letters, which the government men pressed him on after his repatriation:

US Interrogator: Did you at any time, in any of your letters, attempt to make use of the Air Force communications system?

Powers: At first it was impossible—before the trial when I really wanted to do this it was impossible because it takes a little preparation work to do this and at first I had no paper and pencil. They gave me some a little later, but they kept track of the number of sheets of paper they gave me and counted them and there was—I could tell that someone was in my cell occasionally when I was out—apparently nosing around through things—and some of the letters I even had to write in the presence of someone. They weren't particularly watching what I was writing, but they were sitting around somewhere in the room so it was impossible at that time. Later on I attempted to write twice. That was after the trial. After I'd been transferred to another prison and—well—my cell-mate I think was all right, but I thought I couldn't trust him. One day he was asleep and I started doing this and he woke up and I immediately stuck the stuff in my pocket. Another time he had gone to a dentist or something—I don't remember what—and I started to do this, but he came back too soon and other than that we were constantly together all the time and it was impossible to do it without someone knowing you were doing something.

US Interrogator: In other words, this required certain deliberate arrangements of your writing in such a manner that you just couldn't sit down—?

Powers: Well, I don't know whether it would require all people to do this, but for me. I had to sit down and figure out this particular code and so forth on paper where I could watch it and continuously refer to it while I was writing and count up letters and words, etc. If there was some little simple arrangement, but if it is simple, then it might be caught too easily.

US Interrogator: In other words you found that it was just a little too complicated, the system itself was a little too complicated to apply under the condition that you were living in?

Powers: Yes. Now I thought that what I had heard about work camps—I thought that if I was transferred to one of those I would have ample opportunity to do this whenever I needed to say anything.

US Interrogator: Were you asked—?

Powers: Pardon?

US Interrogator: Were you asked something like this: "Are you trying to communicate in any code?" Or were you told—don't try any codes?

Powers: No, they didn't ask, was I trying to communicate, but they had asked me earlier if I knew any—any codes and I knew no codes. I told them, yes, I knew Morse code and that we used a little bit, but I probably couldn't use it. International Morse Code. Well, they didn't ask me code. They asked me cryptographic. Did I know any crypto—something, and I said, what is that, code? And he said, yes; and I said, I know only the Morse code and I never did know that too well so even though I'm sure they checked those letters very closely they seemed to believe that I didn't have any way to communicate.[27]

Unaware that officials back in Washington had worked with Barbara to evaluate evidence of brainwashing, the pilot dealt with the issue in his journal:

Most all the people I came into contact with were kind and considerate. I was forced to do nothing. They gave me books to read to occupy my time and they were not political books. They showed no desire what-so-ever to convert me to their beliefs. . . . All of the publicity about brain washing is pure nonsense, and I personally think a figment of some-one's imagination who cannot believe that it is normal for someone to have a belief that is different from his own.[28]

Seven years after his release, once he was able to look back on the period, Dad displayed a more nuanced view on his tapes:

I didn't have to read anything. Didn't have to listen. If I had wanted to ask a question, they would have been more than happy. But they didn't press things on me. They didn't sit me down and lecture me about the Soviet Union or customs or how bad I was and how good they were. But I could see where when a person has only one source of information . . . 99 percent of any news I got was [from a] Russian source. Best source I had was the British *Daily Worker*. . . . These things, all major events there, slanted to the communist viewpoint. . . . Could see how you could start questioning things that you didn't question before. After a year or so of reading nothing but one side you begin to lose track of the other side. I can see how a person if he was in prison, given nothing but communist literature for ten years, that he would probably be a communist when he got out. Unless he had something to compare it to.[29]

Without access to Western news sources, the letters he regularly received from his family helped cut through the veil of propaganda.

After the KGB completed its interrogation and the date of his trial was set, Frank composed his third letter to his wife:

19 July 1960

My Dearest Barbara,

Apparently you wrote your last letter before you received mine. I suppose you have received it by this time. The only reason that my parents received a letter before you did is because I received theirs before I received yours and I answered them.

While speaking of letters, there is no need for you to send them other than by regular air mail, they will reach me just as fast.

Since I last wrote you I have received one letter from home and one from my sister Joan. I have answered both of them and also, as my father requested, sent him a cable gram telling him he could come to visit me when it was convenient to him. He said his bag was already packed and apparently he plans to come soon.

The only reason I requested you to wait until the trial before visiting me was because I didn't know how long it would be. I know that you would be very lonely here if you had to wait a long time. More lonely than you would be there with your Mother. I was told that you would be allowed to see me after the trial but I don't know how often.

The trial date has been set for the seventeenth of August. I sure didn't expect a trial for my birthday. Now you can make plans for your trip. I don't want you to have to stay here in Moscow alone for a long period of time. You know how it is to be alone in a strange city.

You know that I would like to see you more than I can tell. You are always in my thoughts and it is impossible to tell you how much I miss you.

Please tell all the people that have offered their help to me that I appreciate it very much. If I knew of any way they could be of assistance I would let you know, but I know of no way. If they know of any way and want to help me I could never thank them enough for I am charged with a very serious charge, one of the few that carry the death penalty.

I have a Russian defense counsel appointed to defend me. I have talked to him several times and feel sure he will do his best and that is all I can ask of anyone.

Darling, I hope you can forgive me for making a mess of our lives like I have. I wouldn't feel too bad if only I were involved. When I think of the pain I have caused you and my parents, I realize that no individual has the right to do things that affect others so much without their consent.

I would give all that I possess to be there with you again. Just to have the chance to start all over again and make you happy is something that I pray for. You mean too much to me, and because you do it hurts me very much to know that all the pain you are having now and may have in the future was caused by me, who would do anything to keep you from suffering. The old saying to the effect that you always hurt the one you love is too true.

I am still taking walks every day and am getting a fairly good suntan. I would much rather be getting my suntan on a beach somewhere with you. It's the same sun but it looks much better before all this happened.

In Joan's letter she asked me if I had any objections to her naming her next baby, if it is a boy after me. Of course I told her no and I feel very honored that she should want to do so.

I am reading "Gone with the Wind" now and I like it very much. I don't know why I never read it before. I am very thankful that I like to read and am given the opportunity to read. It makes the time pass faster and takes my mind off my troubles to a certain extent. I have also been given a Bible which I read every day.

I have just finished eating supper, "у ж и н" as it is spelled in Russian. I get more than enough to eat and always have tea to drink. In fact I am drinking tea and smoking as I write this letter.

The day is almost finished and after I finish this letter I will read a while and then go to sleep. I like to see night come for that means one more day less to wait. Always before I hated to see each day pass for that meant one day older.

Barbara, I would have written sooner but I kept thinking that each day I would get a letter from you so I kept waiting. I won't wait so long next time.

Darling, you know that I love you more than anything else in the world. I cannot find words to tell you how much. I miss you more than I can say and hope and pray that you are getting along all right.

Tell your mother to take care of herself and also to take care of you for me.

I often wonder if Eck misses me or if he has forgotten me already. I do miss him. Has he been good?

Well Darling, I will stop for this time since I cannot think of anything else to write. Take care of yourself and remember that I love you with all of my heart and I am always sending you . . .

All my love,

Gary

PS. I received a letter from Jean which I will answer soon.[30]

In a subsequent letter to Barbara, Frank wrote:

Darling, you say that I sound very dejected in my letters. You must make for some allowances for my being in prison. It isn't the best atmosphere in the world for writing gay letters. I don't like being here and I guess it reflects in my letters. Also Darling, there is no doubt in my mind that I will be found guilty in the trial. It will be more of a trial for determining the degree of guilt and the degree of punishment. This also reflects in my letters I suppose. Mine isn't a bright future no matter how you look at it. I only tell you this so you may be prepared for anything that might happen. Darling, I know you worry about me and I wish there was something I could do to set your mind at ease. But I won't lie to you and try to make things appear better than they are.[31]

He was prepared for the worst, and so was his wife. When the trial turned into an anti-American show, but Dad was able to escape with his life, he began to second-guess himself in his journal:

I will never know whether or not I did right by giving any evidence at all. I would have been convicted anyway on the evidence that they had. I felt bad about telling them anything at all and I am very thankful that I knew very little if any of anything of a strategic nature. It seems to me the primary interest of the court was to point out to the world what had happened and to use it as much as possible to put the US in an embarrassing situation. . . .

It seems to me that the prosecution did a good job of trying and convicting the United States and sentencing me because the US wasn't available. . . . All I can say about the trial is that it was a very hard three days for me. I was very keyed up all during this time and had to ask the doctor for sleeping powder at night. . . . I was both pleased and disappointed with the verdict. I was pleased that it wasn't the death penalty or a longer period of time. I was displeased for the number of years I received because it seemed fairly clear to me that the case was presented in such a way to make the US appear the guilty party and I was only a "tool." . . . Well I can't complain because I thought it would be the firing squad for me for sure. . . .[32]

Without specifically addressing the matter of his controversial statement immediately before his sentencing, he wrote:

I was asked during the investigation if I would do the same thing again had I had it to do over again. I said yea I would if it were necessary for the defense of my country. In answer to a question of whether or not I thought it (my flight) was wrong, I replied that I did not consider it wrong if it was necessary for the defense of the United States, but that I did think it was wrong if it was done without the necessity of defending the U.S. I said I believed such flights as mine were not only right but necessary if it saved the destruction of the people of the US and their property. Any nation in my opinion could do such things for their protection and not commit a crime. If they are done in the name of necessity when it isn't necessary then it is a different matter altogether and should be condemned.

I previously thought my flight was necessary at the time it was made. Now I don't know what to think. Of course I only get news from a Communist source now, but if the USSR said that they would accept any control if only the West would accept disarmament then there is no excuse for the arms race continuing. If the US does not accept this then I will begin wondering what is going on. With disarmament there would be no need for such flights for no country would be a threat to another but if all nations continue to build bigger and better weapons then flights such as mine will become the accepted thing and the only crime will be to be caught. . . .[33]

Especially after returning to the United States and seeing how the media had treated him, my father began to see himself as a scapegoat who was used to take the blame for a policy pursued by the political establishment.

Ruminating on his role in the failed summit, he said on the tapes:

I knew the incident was to blame but I didn't consider myself to blame because I assumed that whoever gave word that the flight was to take place was the responsible party. They should have taken this into consideration. If they didn't want this to happen or take the chance of this happening, then it was their responsibility to not take any chances. It was their fault, not mine. OK, I'm the instrument that caused it but I'm not responsible for . . . this Cold War business. I don't pretend to be an intellectual . . . but when someone comes up and tells you you've disrupted possible peace in the world it can sort of get to you.[34]

Facing a decade of confinement, Dad thought about escaping. The idea often occupied his dreams. So did suicide.

"Tried to think of ways to [escape]," he said on his tapes. "But it sure seemed like a hopeless situation. In fact, many times [I] got real despondent." He continued:

Most people would have a little difficulty killing themselves. You can think about it: Boy, if this happened, I'd want to kill myself. But it's a difficult decision to make when you come right down to it. And a good way to do it would be to escape and be shot. This would be one form of suicide. I don't see how you could get far enough to be shot.

During the trial I thought about it because I thought maybe I had an opportunity to run and get shot. They let me outside the court building, right in downtown Moscow, setting on the bench. There was always the hope that the person would live but it wouldn't have surprised me if they'd given me a death sentence. . . .[35]

Internalizing his words, I tried to relate to his difficult circumstances. The stress of the trial, having faced the possibility of a death sentence, the lack of support from Barbara, and the uncertainty of how long he would be in prison certainly took a toll on him. Through his writing you could see when he was depressed and when he was hopeful. I rode that roller coaster with him. By reading and copying the letters, I had a sense that I was learning things though my father that I otherwise never would have learned. It was like he was helping me understand what he was going through. I found myself thinking what it would be like to be in his shoes. For me this was like my own type of therapy.

Once incarcerated at Lubyanka, Frank composed a letter to Barbara:

5 September 1960

My Dearest Wife,

It has been only a week since I saw you last but it seems so much longer. When I heard that you were gone I all at once felt all alone. I do not know the words to tell you what it meant to me to see you.

I have not been moved to another prison yet. I suppose it won't be very long until I am moved. I would like to get it over with and get settled as much as I can under the circumstances.

I will enclose a list of the things you bought for me. I tried on all the clothes and they fit good. I have receipts for the money and the watch. All these things will be given to me when I leave here and get to the permanent prison.

So far my life has not changed much. I am still in the same cell but I have more time on my hands since there is no interrogation and preparation for a trial. I am glad all that is over. I hope I never have anything like that to go through again.

I am very depressed today. I don't know why so today more than any other day but that is the way it is. Just the thoughts of spending ten years in prison is getting to me. I am sure it would be the same if it were only for five years or even one year. The way I feel now I would much rather have stayed with the airplane and died there than spend any time in a prison. I know it is hard for you to understand this but you have never faced ten years in prison.

You may say I won't have to spend ten years in prison, that by behaving good I will get out sooner. That might knock off three years. Or you may think that there will be a pardon or some kind or exchange of prisoners, or that maybe something will happen through diplomatic channels to get me set free. I realize that maybe any of these things could happen but I cannot count on them. There is only one thing that is sure and that is my sentence is for ten years.

I doubt if I will ever be able to go to a zoo—that is if I ever get out of here—without having the desire to set all the animals free. I have never, before this, thought very much on the subject but I think all men and animals were born to be free. To take away one's freedom is worse than to take one's life, for death itself is a form of freedom.

Wasn't it Patrick Henry who said "Give me liberty or give me death"? He wasn't even speaking of his own personal liberty then— only of the liberty of a nation in which he was free at the time. How much more would he have said if he was locked in a cell at the time?

Darling, I probably shouldn't be writing all this to you. You have enough trouble of your own, because of me, and here I am trying to make you share my own personal moods and depressions. It is good to get these thoughts out of my mind though and writing to you is somewhat like talking to you.

No matter what happens to me or how long I stay here there is one thing that will never change, one thing I can depend on to last much longer than ten years, and one thing to keep my spirits up even though they do get low at times. That one thing is my love for you. You know that I love you very much and prison or nothing else except you yourself can ever change that.

Please try to tell your mother how very grateful I am that she accompanied you here and how much I enjoyed seeing her. She has been more like a mother to me than a mother-in-law and I love her like a mother. Tell her for me that as long as you are with her I know you are in safe hands.

Tell your sister Nell and her husband Fred that I think of them very often and miss them much. Tell them to take care of Tammy Gay. She will be a big girl when I see her again. Don't let her forget her uncle Gary. Tell Fred that he and I will go fishing again one of these days. When we do I hope we have as much luck as we had before. That was a good trip.

Well Darling, I guess that is about all for this time except once again I want to say, I love you very much. I wish our life could have been different but it is too late now to change what has happened. Don't worry about me for I will be okay. I will have my moods but that is all they are, they don't last too long. I know I will be okay as long as I know that you are. Take care of yourself and continue to love me and everything will work out all right.

All my love,

Gary

P.S. My address is the same as before until further notice.[36]

The prisoner was settling into his new cell at Vladimir by the time he received his next letter from his parents:

Sept. 12, 1960

My Dear Son,

If I had known you could receive letters we would have written several before this. We just recd your letter. You heard them tell us while there that you could write and rec. one letter a month. That is why I haven't written. Has Barbara wrote you. I talked to her on the phone Fri evening and she wanted to know if I had heard. She said she hadn't heard anything but would call me when she heard. We didn't know if you had moved or not. Sure hope we can hear from you once a month any way. It's so far to where she lives and we have no way to talk with her only by phone.

You can never know how we hated to leave you there. I'm so glad you got the testament. Read it and study it well and you can find great comfort from its teaching. The book of Acts tells how you are to be saved and the other books tell us how to live a Christian life. The first four books tell the teaching of Jesus so it's all the best book written if possible tell others of its teaching it would[n't] hurt anyone to learn the truths found in it.

We will do our best to stay well and pray that we can all be united again as soon as we can. God is our help and without him we can do nothing. So take him with you where ever you go. And pray that he will give you strength to stay well and keep you safe till we meet again.

Daddy plans to try to see Mr. K. [Khrushchev] in N.Y. around the 20th of this month. Don't worry too much. Everyone thinks everything will turn out OK. We sent two men home that was sentenced 10 and 20 years soon after their trial and maybe you won't have to stay the full time. Every one is for you and no one can be too far against you. Just remember how we have taught you to live and every thing will turn out all right.

I don't think Grandpa realizes the trouble. He always asks when you will be home. He can't remember things very long and asks over and over.

We have thanked every one that has helped us. We will thank them again.

Who has the pictures now? Does the lawyer have them yet? I wondered if you would get to see them.

We didn't have any trouble on our way back. Every one was so nice to us. I think air travel is the best way to go. It's so pretty up among the clouds.

If you need any thing, please let us know of if we can do anything. You know we would do any thing for you we could any time. So do let us know if we can see about anything or do anything any time. Try not to worry about us and remember every one is thinking and praying for you. May God bless all.

Write when you can. Everyone loves you. Let us know if you move and where to write.

All our love,
Your Mom and Dad[37]

Soon it became clear that Frank's budding friendship with Zigurd— whom he called "one of the finest people I have ever known"[38]—helped keep his mind occupied and his spirits up, as he explained in a letter to his wife:

21 September 1960

Dearest Barbara,

I am now at my permanent place of residence. I have been moved to a prison about two and one-half hours from Moscow by car at a city called Vladimir. I will remain here I suppose until my three years of prison are finished and then be transferred to a work camp.

The conditions here are very similar to the conditions in Moscow except I have a cell mate. He is a very nice person. He is thirty three years old and speaks English fairly well. He also speaks German and Russian. I don't think I could have done better if I had chosen him myself. He also is not a Russian.

He is a very interesting person to talk to and helps me a lot when I need any translating done. He is also helping me to learn Russian which I am sure is going to be a big job for him because it is very difficult for me.

I have been here a little over a week now and am getting into the routine. I don't think it is going to be too bad. Of course it could be a lot better but one cannot expect too much from a prison.

It sure is nice having someone to talk to. My cell mate says he hasn't spoken much English for the past eight years and says that as soon as he has had some practice it will come back to him. He has improved since I have been here and I think speaks good English. I wish I could speak Russian as good as he speaks English.

There is also a radio in the cell which helps a lot. Of course I cannot understand what is said but the music is very good. It is especially good after the long hours that I spent in solitary confinement in Moscow.

I will be allowed to write four letters a month, maybe two to you, one to my parents and one to a different sister each month. Things will be more or less routine and there will be very little for me to write about. I am sure my letters will soon become boring.

I suppose I should be getting a letter from you soon. I am anxiously awaiting one. It has been a long time since I heard from you. I would also like to know what arrangements you made about cigarettes, etc.

Darling they offered to let me wear my ring and watch but it is against the rules so I decided not to take them. I might lose them so I will give them to you to keep for me when I see you again. Time doesn't mean very much in prison and a watch would probably keep reminding me not only of the time but of the time remaining. I try to forget about that.

I am allowed to receive one package from you a month. I won't need too much but there are a few things which would come in handy. I would like to have an English dictionary, a couple of pipes and some pipe tobacco, cigarette paper for rolling cigarettes in case I run out at any time, chap stick of lips, a double edge razor with blades, shaving cream (tube), and after shave cream (not liquid), also a shaving brush. In the food line I could use some dried fruit (apples, peaches, etc.), some [Borden's] Eagle Brand milk (cans).

If I need anything else as time goes on I will let you know. Don't send too much at one time for there is very little space to keep it. I will let you know about other foods later.

Darling, I know you worry about me a lot but it is needless. The treatment is good and the food, although not as good as I was getting before, is plentiful and I won't be losing weight.

When you have time take some snapshots of yourself, your mother, Nell's family, and Eck and send them to me. I don't want to forget what all of you look like. No danger of that though for I think of all of you too often.

Darling—take care of yourself and don't worry about me. I will be all right. Where I am there is very little that can happen to me. I am safer here than in an airplane. Think of it that way.

Remember that I love you with all of my heart and I miss you very much. It seems like a long time but it will pass and then we can be together again and maybe find that there is happiness left in the world for us.

Bye for now.

All my love

Gary[39]

After a bleak Christmas—made slightly cheerier by the ninety-two Christmas cards he received from the San Francisco area, thanks to the kind suggestion of the influential columnist Herb Caen—my father allowed himself to believe that the new Kennedy administration might push for his release. He wrote in his journal:

On New Year's Day my cell mate translated the toast of Khrushchev to me. In it he stated that with the going of the old year and the government of the US and the coming of the new he thought it best to forget the U-2 Incident so that there might be better relations between the two countries. This toast of Khrushchev's set my hopes going. I kept thinking that it would be very hard for both countries to forget the incident with me still in prison. My cell mate was also very optimistic. He has always said I wouldn't be here too long.[40]

In a letter to Barbara dated January 16, 1961, he said, "I have great hopes of something very important happening soon. I don't want to build up your hopes but it is entirely possible that I could be released in the near future."[41]

Toward the end of the month, in a letter to his parents, he said, "I heard some excellent news on the radio this morning. The two Americans from the [R]B-47 have been released. It could have only been better if I had been with them but our cases were a little different. I am very happy for them and their families and I wish them the best. I personally think my chances of being released early are very good in view of the policy the new government has adopted."[42]

At about the same time, Oliver was writing to his son about the same news. Their letters crossed in transit. "If you could have been with them," he said, "my heart would have been so glad."[43]

When Frank learned that the Kennedy White House was doing nothing publicly to push for his release, his spirits sank. But this was not his only reason for despair. He was desperately worried about his wife and beginning to wonder about the future of his marriage, which could be seen in his twelfth letter to Barbara:

March 1, 1961

Dearest Barbara,

Today they returned a letter to me that I had mailed to you on the 23rd of February. It seems I am not supposed to tell you about my cell-mate. This means that you won't get a letter from me mailed in the month of February. I only wrote the one and it was returned and this one is to replace it.

I guess you know that I haven't received any mail from you since the twenty sixth of January. The one I received then was written by you on the ninth of January. I would like to know what is wrong that you aren't writing. If you don't want to write just say so and then I will not expect letters from you. As it is, each day I am waiting for a letter and when it doesn't come then I am very disappointed. Don't you think my situation is bad enough without you making it worse?

When I don't hear from you for a long time I get very despondent and start imagining all sorts of things. You could be dead for all I know.

I think your mother would have enough consideration for me to tell me if anything were wrong with you. I hope so anyway.

If it weren't for my mother and sisters I would not have received any mail at all in Feb. Thank goodness they care enough for me to write.

I guess you thought I stood a chance of being released with the RB 47 boys. I also thought this but we were mistaken. Things don't look near so bright any more. In fact it will probably be a long time before chances will be as good again as they were then. If they hadn't been here then maybe it would have been me.

I would like for you to start sending some magazines again also some books. Send anything you think I would like. I haven't received any of the magazines they told me they would give me starting in January.

Maybe you could get the Embassy to do this and save yourself a lot of trouble and also custom duties. Also you could have the Embassy cut the number of cartons of cigarettes to three a month. I have accumulated several cartons and don't need so many.

I would also like to have some more pictures if you have any. I only have the two that were taken at Nell's in November.

Why hasn't Nell answered my letter? Do you know? Tell her and Fred I said hello and hope they are fine. I'll bet the children are growing. I know I wouldn't recognize Tammy Gay.

Barbara, I want you to send my father one thousand dollars as soon after the receipt of this letter as possible. I am sure you have it available.

It was a very big disappointment to me to learn that Kennedy stated in one of his press conferences that my situation had not been discussed when the SU and US officials discussed the release of the other two pilots. I don't know why but I expected them to discuss it whether or not anything was done about it.

Darling, I want you to write more often. I have only received eight letters from you since you left Moscow in August. That is eight letters in seven months. Not a very good average no matter how a person looks at it. I expected and wanted you to write more without my having to ask you.

It certainly appears that you don't think very much of me if the number of letters are any judge. I can't imagine what you could be doing that occupies so much of your time so that you can not spare thirty minutes or so a week to write. I can only think that you don't want to write because I know you have the time.

I want you to be sure and start numbering each letter so that I can tell if any of them are lost or missing. Maybe there was one on the plane that crashed in Belgium. Only you know that.

Barbara, I am very sorry to have had to say so much about letters but I am very worried. You apparently don't realize how much mail from you means to me. The receipt of a letter is the only bright spot in my life. I am not begging you to write. I only want letters from you if you want to write them. If you do not want to write me then please let me know so that I won't worry when no letters arrive.

I guess that is about all for now. Please answer soon and remember I love you very much and can't help worrying when I don't hear from you.

All my love,

Gary

P.S. I don't know when this will be mailed. No one has been around to pick up mail for the last two days. I have asked someone to come today but so far no one.

P.S.S. I also need some stationery.[44]

Around this time, he addressed his feelings about Barbara in his journal:

I was almost sick with worry and I was extremely nervous and not able to sleep at all because my mind would not relax. (My cell mate put up with much during this time). It turned out that I had no need to be worried at all. On March 11th I received a letter from my wife with no mention at all of the fact that she had waited 45 days. (I know there was no letter in between because I had asked her and she said she would send me a copy of Kennedy's inauguration speech and she enclosed it in this February 21st letter. One month and one day after the speech was in the paper she mailed it to me. If she had written earlier she would have sent it for it was dated Jan. 20). She, in her letter, started as if she had only written the week before, mentioned she had been visiting relatives in North Carolina and had found someone, for the first time since May, to bowl and play golf with. Her letter jumped from one subject to another as if she couldn't think of anything to write or as if she were only performing a very unpleasant duty and anything would do to fill up the pages.

I must admit that I was very angry. That is putting it mildly. There is no excuse what-so-ever for her not writing more during this period of time. It only takes a few minutes to write a letter and let someone know that a person is all right.

Not counting the two letters I received before she came to Moscow in August I have received nine letters from her. Total I have received eleven that is an average of one a month. If the number of letters are any indication of the amount of love she has for me then we should have been divorced long ago.

Speaking of divorce, I am at the present time firmly determined to divorce her when I return to the States. It should have been done in fifty seven but for some reason I did not do it then. I don't know why now that I think back on it. I thought at the time that I loved her too much to let her go but now I don't know. I have never liked divorces and I hate the thoughts of getting one but I know that I can never make the kind of life I want with any woman who, while drawing her husband's pay which he has sacrificed several months of his freedom, so far, does not have enough consideration for him to write a few letters which takes very little time when one considers the fact that she is not working and has nothing to do.

I do not mind her enjoying herself while I am here as long as she conducts herself as a wife should. That is all right but I did not expect her to become so engrossed in seeking pleasure and forgetfulness that she forgets that she had a husband.

She has caused me since January, extreme mental suffering. Several times I became so nervous that my hands shake so much that my cell mate wanted to call the doctor. I wouldn't let him and it would pass after about thirty minutes. The things she has done since we have been married and which now I have plenty of time to remember and think about have made this last year almost unlivable. There have been numerous times that I have thought about stopping all these thoughts for good.

I can never have a future with her because the past will always be between us. I fooled myself for a while but I can not do so in the future. I want a happy home with children. I can never have it with her. There is nothing else to do. I only hope I am able to be firm about this when I am free. I cannot do anything at the present time because I foolishly left her with complete power of attorneys and she can take all I have.[45]

By the time these anguished words first assaulted me, I was a grown man who had known love and heartbreak, and I was able to experience my father's despair over his dying relationship as someone who understood the urge to try to save something that was dying. After all, love is a powerful emotion that affects people in different ways. In prison, Dad needed the emotional support of his wife through correspondence. But Barbara was having a difficult time handling the stress, notoriety, and front-page headlines, so she dealt with it in her own self-destructive way. Reading the letters and the journal, I could see how Dad was trying to convince himself that things would work out, but eventually he came to the realization that he could not repair the damage that had been done.

Rumors apparently concerning the pilot's troubled marriage reached his superiors long before the shoot-down, which the Prettyman inquiry addressed. A man whose identity was redacted but who had direct oversight of Powers, which may have been Colonel William M. Shelton, said, "I am confident in my own mind that this did not affect his flying."[46]

Trying to occupy his time with reading, rug-making, and following the moves of an important chess tournament in the Soviet media, Dad frequently played chess against Zigurd, who tutored him on the finer points of the game. "He beat me one time blindfolded," he said on his tapes. "Would sit with his back to the chess board and say, move such and such to here [and] I'd tell him where I'd moved. Still beat me."[47]

Prison life required many adjustments and offered few distractions, but Dad quickly learned that he could have had it much worse.

US Interrogator: From what you saw in the prison, would you say you were treated better, worse, or about the same as the other prisoners?

Powers: Well I thought better. But I asked them about this. I told them I didn't want to be treated any better than anyone else, and they said that they have three—what they call—three regimes, a severe regime, a normal regime, and a light regime. And they said that I was on the light regime and they treated all the prisoners who were on the light regime the same way. Now I don't know whether this was true or not. But supposedly the prisoners on the light regime receive better food, but you couldn't prove that by me. Two hours' walk a day instead of one, get to keep your hair, they didn't shave your head every 10 days or clip it all off, and you could shave daily if you had your own razor blades—and they let me keep razor blades in the cell, which surprised me. I heard that on the severe regime the people get 30 minutes' walk a day—well, it's a punishment—this severe. The normal prisoner received one hour['s] walk a day, their hair was shaved off every ten days, the food was supposedly worse, but I really don't know. . . . [48]

In a journal entry, he explained his daily routine:

It is the rule for all prisoners; get up at six o'clock in the morning. I haven't been a good keeper of this rule because I do not get up unless someone wakes me and it has been very seldom that anyone has awakened me in the mornings. I am usually up between six and seven but have sometimes slept longer. I don't like to do this but if they want me to get up all they have to do is say so. I suppose the reason I sleep late in the mornings is that most of the time I have a lot of trouble getting to sleep at night. It seems that the minute I prepare for sleep it is an indication for my mind to become filled with thoughts. There have been many times that I do not get to sleep before two or three o'clock in the morning. The average time I get to sleep would probably be around midnight when the guards change.

My cell mate does not wake me up. He lets me sleep and usually takes advantage of my being in bed and his having more room to move about in, to do his morning exercises. He also cleans the floor which takes two or three minutes. I feel bad about this because he does it all the time but even when I wake up he tells me to stay in bed so I won't be in his way while he is cleaning the floor. He says it is part of his exercise and won't let me do it even if I am up.

Depending on the time, we either go to the toilet before or after breakfast. Most of the time it is before. There is only cold water there and that wakes me up completely. I wash from the waist up each morning in the ice cold water.

Usually we do not have time to shave before breakfast and if we do we usually do not get hot water until breakfast so most of the time we shave after breakfast.

Breakfast is served usually between seven-thirty and eight o'clock and consists of either a soup or a porridge. There are usually two kinds of soups for breakfast, either fish soup or a vegetable soup made primarily from dried peas etc. There are several different kinds of porridge, cream of wheat, barley, millet, wheat, and oats. Each morning we are offered one of the above mentioned items. We also receive the bread ration for the day. I only take half my ration because I do not eat bread as much as everyone else seems to do here. I am also able to get a better bread occasionally from the commissary. There are two kinds of bread given each day, rye and whole wheat.

After breakfast and washing our dishes we usually have about one hour and one-half before walk. We shave and I either spend the time until the walk reading or studying Russian. Many months went by when I was so down hearted that, I am sorry to say, I did not study at all, I only read. Lately since July I have been spending an average of more than two hours a day on my studying but haven't made a tremendous amount of progress. I used to be a fairly good student but since

I have been in prison I cannot seem to concentrate and have a lot of trouble in remembering the words which it is necessary to remember in order to learn a language. I do not only have the trouble in Russian but many times when I am reading unless it is an exceptionally good book I sometimes have to reread pages more than once for my mind wanders to other things and I completely lose the meaning of the words that I am reading. Prison in my case is not conducive to good studying.

Usually about ten o'clock we go for a walk. My cell mate and I are allowed two hours a day. We usually spend two hours in the summer and one in winter. The court yard we walk in is about twenty by twenty-five feet and we walk in a circle. In summer we took a chess board with us and had a game of chess in the fresh air and the sunshine. In the winter we walk one hour only stopping for a few minutes to feed the pigeons if we have any bread.

After the walk we are brought back to the cell where we either read or study until lunch time which is usually about twelve thirty. This is the best meal of the day and consists of an excellent soup, a little light on meat though, and either a plate of cabbage, noodles, rice, manna, or mashed potatoes, and 250 grams of milk (it used to be 350 grams but was cut recently also the bread ration was cut).

After lunch we now take a nap of an hour or two. Before when we were making envelopes we spent the time working and also spent part of the morning working. Now we have no work to do. After the nap it is read or study until supper which is about six thirty. This is the worst meal of the day and usually consists only of potatoes.

I very seldom eat the supper that is given. My cell mate and I are lucky in that we receive help from outside. He gets some smoked meat each month that we use to supplement the meals. He also gets about a kilo of butter. We can buy margarine here but it doesn't take the place of butter.

After Supper we take another trip to the toilet and then either write letters, read or study until ten o'clock when it is time for bed.

At night there is always a light on in the cell. I have not slept in a dark room for over eighteen months. I usually put a towel or a handkerchief over my eyes. My cell mate most of the time goes right to sleep but I lay awake. This is sometimes the worst time of the day especially when I have some kind of bad news from home a little of which I constantly seem to have at all times.

It isn't a very pleasant life but it is much better than I expected and I am sure most Americans think conditions are worse than they are. I have never seen a prisoner maltreated here which is more than can be said of some of our prisons especially in the southern part of the U.S.[49]

One of the few regular distractions was his ability to go to a prison room periodically and watch Soviet -made movies, but he quickly soured on the predictable socialist themes. "It was usually pretty low class, what we would call a B movie. Story usually set on a collective farm, with some pretty girl who always sings really nicely."[50]

As the letters from Barbara began to arrive with greater frequency in the spring of 1961, Frank tried to stay positive. But he was a man who was clearly struggling with the same sort of suspicions that had provided tension for the entirety of his marriage.

30 April 1961

My Dearest Barbara,

Today is the thirtieth of April and I won't be able to mail this letter until after the holidays (May 1st + 2nd), but since I received this letter this afternoon I have been in a pretty good mood and thought I would start an answer anyway. Your letters certainly do a lot to cheer me up.

Since we neither one know how long we are to be separated it might be a good idea if you did buy a house. That way, instead of paying rent you could be paying for a house that we could probably sell later and maybe get the money back that would be completely lost as rent.

If I thought I would be home in the next few months I would advise against it but as it is it may be years so I suppose we should act as if it were going to be for nine more. I certainly hope it won't be but things do not look good.

The house you were telling me about sounds pretty good. Of course I have to rely on your judgment. Just make sure, for one thing, that the house you choose is high enough so that there is no danger of floods, etc. like you had there a few months ago.

It would be nice if I could see the plans of the house and grounds but since it takes so long for mail it would probably be best to go ahead without waiting for an answer from me.

I am sure Fred would be glad to help you and since he works for a Real Estate Agency he should know what to look for and how to choose and also if the price was reasonable.

You say that the man's equity is $7000. You should have enough with the money received from the sale of the Buick and what I had in the checking account to take care of that. Try not to touch the Calif. Saving account. Also you should have saved quite a lot from your allowance in a year's time so that there should be no need to put us in a tight place.

Maybe the house you mentioned is already sold. If not use your own judgment but be careful.

Does the house have a basement? What kind of heat? Just give me a complete rundown on everything. One other thing—buy it in both our names. Oh yes, how much property tax a year?

Who is the doctor you are going to who gave you the information about the house? Does he work at the State hospital? Also does he have anything to do with the house you were telling me about?

Well—just do as you think best. There is nothing I can do to help from here. You are on your own. I know of no one who I think could show more judgment in such things than you. Anything you do I am sure will be all right with me.

I am starting again where I left off last night. It is now the first of May and I have been in prison a year. It isn't a happy occasion so I would not be celebrating even if I were able to.

Darling, I hope you will not get angry at what I [am] about to say but I feel I must say it anyway. You have now experienced a year's separation. I know that it has been a very long, lonely, and difficult time for you. Probably more than for me since you are faced every day with temptation that I in my position do not have to worry about. In the face of these temptations and the fact that we may be separated for a much longer time, are you sure that you want to continue being married in name only? Have you met anyone who may already or in the future come to mean more to you than a husband who cannot be with you?

I want you to be honest to yourself and to me when you answer these questions. I want you to take into consideration that we very likely will be separated for several more years. Maybe not if there were an improvement in the international situation. There are in my opinion two ways that my situation could improve. One is for the US Government to strive for an improvement in international relations; the other would be for the Government to negotiate diplomatically on my behalf. It is quite obvious they have done neither so as I said before there is a very good possibility of our separation being for an extended length of time.

Darling, I am not thinking so much of myself as I am of you when I ask you to consider these things. You are still young and it isn't fair to you for me to ask you to waste the best years of your life in waiting for a husband who may be gone for a long time. I tell you truthfully Barbara that I would understand if you did not want to wait and I would not think bad of you if you decided not to do so. On the other hand I would never like to reproach you after being released for something which I am unable to forgive my wife. The consequences would be obvious but only delayed un-necessarily with disadvantages to both but mostly to you.

I don't want you to get the impression that I want you to do anything. That is very far from my mind and heart. The only thing is if the conditions are to be then it would be much better to either head that off or take steps that would be advantageous to both of us without making a bad situation worse.

I am sure you know that I love you and I am sure you realize I would never have married you if I thought I could not trust you. So don't think I am accusing for I am not. I only want you to know how I feel and I only want what is fair and right for you. Ours is far from being a normal situation and I do not feel that I have the right to make you think you are bound to me if you felt you would be happier free.

If I didn't feel I could trust you I would never agree to buying a house. I want you to know that I love you more now than before if that is possible. I know I will love you always even if I am required to stay here ninety more years instead of nine and it is because I love you so much that I want you to be happy.

As I said before, please don't be angry with me for stating what I feel. I only want to be fair with you in all respects.

Well. To get back to answering your letter, I have only read one of the sixteen books that you sent. I haven't received them yet but expect and hope they arrive about the sixteenth of this month when I usually receive the package from the Embassy. Don't worry about the selection of future books; the important thing is that I have something to read so that I can pass the time easier.

You ask about the temperature in Moscow in the hottest summer months. All I can go by is last summer's experience. July was uncomfortably hot. June was very nice a little cold around the latter part of May but comfortable. Around the middle of August it began getting cool again as you know. The sun has been shining a lot during the last two or three weeks of April. It snowed a little on the first of May (yesterday) but when the sun is shinny [*sic*] it is nice but rather cool in the shade or when it is cloudy.

Well, Darling, I guess that is all for this time. Thanks for bringing up the buying of a house. I guess we should have considered it earlier but up until lately I thought that we might have the opportunity to do it together.

Bye for this time. Remember Barbara, I love you very much and want your happiness above all else. Take care of yourself and tell all I send my love,

All my love,

Always,

Gary[51]

With his marriage crumbling, Dad was confronted with a news report that left him angry and feeling even more powerless than usual.

4 May 1961

Dear Mom & Dad,

I was quite shocked when I read the news clipping you sent in your number 9 letter, (which you forgot to number), written on April 10th.

You seemed worry that it was true even though in the article you said you didn't believe it. Well you can set your mind at rest on that account. I do not intend to stay in the Soviet Union when I am released. I have never said to anyone that I intended to do so. I am a citizen of the United States and am proud to be one. I might not like all the policies of the US government but I feel sure there are many millions of people in the States who disagree with them also.

I cannot imagine where the correspondent John Mossman got his information unless he invented it himself. You may rest assured that I will return home, where I belong and want to be, as soon as I am released. Remaining here has never entered my mind.

I noticed in the article that "John Mossman quoted no source for his story." Apparently he had none.

Once again I want to state that I do not intend to remain in the S.U. when I am released. No one has asked me if I wanted to and I don't even know whether or not I would be allowed to.

As far as Barbara coming to Russia I have heard nothing about it. She said earlier that when I was transferred to a work camp and if I were allowed to see her often, she would want to come and live near the camp until my sentence was up. If I could see her often enough to make it worth while then I would allow it. But you can rest assured that even if it were allowed, we both would return as soon as my sentence was up.

Don't worry about my doing anything or giving any cause for my country to doubt me. It looks as if this British correspondent is trying, for some reason I don't know, to tell the people that I have renounced my country. I would never do this. I was born an American and intend to die an American.

You wrote on the back of your envelope "Remember what Patrick Henry said." He is remembered, much to his credit, for what he said. It looks as if I will be remembered, much to my discredit, for what some correspondent writes even though there is not one word of truth in what he wrote.

I wish there was some way to force him to disclose where he got his information. I know my friends and family will not believe this but probably many Americans will. I certainly hope not.

You asked me to let you know if your note was censored. All mail coming and going is censored but there has never been anything marked or cut out of your letters since I have been in Vladimir. I think all prisons all over the world censor mail so that there can be no plans of escape etc.

I suppose Jean has her new baby boy by now. I am very anxious to hear about it. I am keeping my fingers crossed.

Everything here is the same. The weather is becoming very nice. Still a little cool when the sun isn't shining and we had a little snow on the morning of the first of May. Even though John Mossman said I would be released, I am still occupying the same cell in the same prison.

Well I guess that is all for this time. Please don't worry about the article in the paper. It isn't true. In fact I have been wondering just how much that is written in papers can be believed. Very little apparently.

Love,

Francis

P.S. This is primarily a letter to you but you may use it to refute the story if you think it necessary.[52]

Emphasizing the point in a letter to his sisters Jess and Jan, Frank said, "When I am released I intend to return home even if I have to walk and try to swim the Atlantic. . . . I have no idea what the purpose of such a lie could be, but it will be believed by many American people much to my future disadvantage."[53]

When the summit meeting between Kennedy and Khrushchev produced no movement on his issue, Dad's dashed hopes could be felt in his June 15 letter to Barbara: "Darling, I am sorry that I wrote that I might be released after the meeting between K+K. I cannot help grasping at each little ray of hope and amplifying it into a beacon of optimism but I can keep from telling you and maybe raise your hopes also. . . . One thing that makes me pretty sad is if nothing happens as a result of this meeting then I have very little chance of being released at all. If a meeting between the two will not do it then what will?"[54]

Around this time he became aware of his father's communicating with Rudolf Abel. "I know nothing will come of the negotiations," he wrote to Barbara on August 10, 1961, "because as far as I know, Abel is not a Soviet citizen and why should the SU agree to an exchange for a non citizen? It is just that my father is grasping at straws."[55]

Frank kept writing to Barbara, not realizing the level of her distress. He was painfully aware of his wife's alcohol problem, but he did not know she was dealing with significant psychological problems. The news of her commitment back in Georgia left Frank reeling, as his journal entry of October 14, 1961, made clear:

> According to the letter [from Mrs. Brown, Barbara's mother] she has been under a great mental strain. My mother-in-law stated that when my wife was drinking that she [my wife] could not stand her mother and would have to go somewhere out of her sight. . . . I am almost completely in the dark. . . . I can only assume that alcohol has a lot to do with it. . . . I cannot understand how such a drastic action could be taken without consulting me. . . . I am worried to death and feel so helpless that I don't know what to do.[56]

When Barbara wrote to him without mentioning the situation, Dad recognized it as part of a larger pattern of dishonesty. In a letter dated November 1, 1961, he said:

> I expected you to be honest with me and tell me what has been happening since the latter part of September but you never mentioned it at all. You seem to have made a habit of forgetting to tell me many of the things I have a right as your husband to know. Even though I am in a prison in another country, the fact remains that I am still your husband

and cannot help but be interested in all you do and all that happened to you. When you do not tell me things and I find out from other people I cannot help but wonder how many things there are I should know that neither you nor other people tell me. . . . I will not hesitate to get a divorce when I return to the States if your conduct has been such that it merits such an action.[57]

After her next letter, in which she admitted to the commitment to the psychological ward, Dad wrote back, having caught her lying about the timing of her release. Despite continuing to profess his love for her, he wrote:

I am not proud of you at all. I know something was wrong for a long time but I didn't expect you to go to such extents that legal commitment to a hospital would be necessary. . . . Now maybe you realize why I said I don't have the confidence in our marriage that I had before. Can you blame me? Well, I have decided that the only way you can help yourself is to stop drinking completely or you will end up back in the same place for the same reason. . . . Barbara, between now and the time I return home, no matter how long it is, I do not expect to hear that you have drank a single drink. I am not asking you this time. I am telling you. If I ever hear you are drinking again the first act I will do when I return to the States is get a divorce. . . . Now it is up to you to decide whether or not I mean more to you than drink. I hope it isn't a hard decision for you to make and I hope I mean more to you than drowning your sorrows. . . .[58]

Addressing the matter in his journal, he wrote:

I fear that she and I will never be able to live together again. I love her very much and I do want us to have a happy life together but I do not intend to remain married to a woman who has not had enough respect for herself or for me to live as a woman should live when placed under the circumstances we have. It is my opinion that she will pay no attention to what I said even though I told her it was either drink or me. I feel that she thinks she will be able to charm me into forgiveness when we are together again. . . . She seems to think she can do anything she wants to do as long as she can get away with it.[59]

Even as he tried to plan for some sort of future, with or without Barbara, my father began angling to improve the conditions of his confinement. He would soon be eligible for a transfer to a work camp, which would allow him to be out in the fresh air.

"This camp business has me worried," he wrote in his journal.

Here in the prison I have been relatively isolated. I have contact only with my cell mate. In a camp it is my understanding that all the prisoners were free to mingle and more or less govern themselves in the camp. Of course there are guards outside. It is my impression that they are set up somewhat like concentration camps before the war. I have heard that there are fights and groups who oppose each other and I do not know how I will fit into such a situation since I cannot speak the language. I don't fear any harm to myself because I don't think the Soviet government would want to cause an international event by exposing a citizen of the US to such conditions in which he might be harmed in any way.[60]

After marking his second Christmas at Vladimir, Frank wrote his thirty-third letter to his parents:

26 December 61

Dear Mom & Dad,
    I haven't had a letter from you since the ninth of this month. I hope all of you are well.
    I have been thinking about all of you a great deal today (25 Dec). I guess it is because of the time of the year. I hope everyone had a good Christmas.

This has been just another day for me and I can't say that I have much Christmas spirit. I have spent a big part of the day thinking about past Christmases. The ones that I remember best are the ones we all spent together when all of us children were small.

I remember that most all of this year I have had hopes of being able to spend this Christmas with you. There were a couple of times that I felt almost certain that I would be able to do so but it didn't turn out that way.

There is always the possibility that things may be better next year but I am afraid that I am not too optimistic. Things look too bad for me to have much hope of being released anytime soon. Actually I can not see any reason why the Soviet Union should release me and on the other hand I can see no reason why I should be kept. One thing for certain they will never have to worry about my flying over their country again. I have been taught a lesson that I don't expect to forget any time soon no matter where I may be.

I had great hopes that there would be some constructive talks on the Berlin and German problems and that tensions would relax in the world but it looks as if things are not going to improve much. I suppose that it wouldn't change things very much anyway because it seems to me that as soon as things get better in one part of the world, they immediately get worse in another part.

I remember how much hope I had last January when I heard of Khrushchev's toast that was made New Year's eve. He was going to forget about the U-2 event and hoped that relations between the countries would get better. Of course I interpreted that to mean that I might be released but that has been one year ago and I am still here. Maybe he has forgotten the event and it appears that Kennedy has also forgotten it but it still remains very strong in my memory.

Then there was the time in June when the meeting between the two K's took place. If I had had a bag to pack I would probably have packed it then. I was almost positive I would be released as a result of that meeting, but nothing came of it but an increase in tension in the world because of Berlin.

We will probably never know but I feel that I could have been released if Kennedy had made any efforts to have it done. I may be doing him a wrong by thinking that way because I don't know for certain that he hasn't but if he has he has certainly been secretive about it.

Now in a few days a new year will begin. Who knows, maybe something will happen then. I have no reason to think that anything will happen but I have hopes. If I didn't have such hopes I would probably go crazy.

Well, I guess that will be all for this time. Take care of yourselves.

Love,

Francis[61]

As Oliver continued to try to push his case with officials in Washington, and his appeal for clemency lingered with the Presidium of the Supreme Soviet, the prisoner tried to remain optimistic. "I certainly hope this year brings my release," he said in the journal entry dated January 28, 1962. "I have no particular reason to think it will do so but if there are better relations between the US and SU, I think I stand a good chance of being released. From what I have heard things are not too good at the present time. I am very much afraid that if there is not some kind of disarmament soon there will be a war. There has been no period in history when an arms race has not ended in a war."[62]

Eight days later, the KGB colonel asked the rhetorical question that changed my father's life.

The next letter he wrote would be as a free man.

When the pilot was repatriated, the doubts continued to swirl at Langley.

"After we managed to get Powers back," McMahon said, "and after all the debriefing of Powers, it proved that he did exactly what he was told, and sure enough he was shot down. McCone didn't want to accept that. . . . It was too bad that Powers was not heralded as the hero that he was."[63]

His home life remained troubled as well.

Settling into his job at CIA headquarters, while trying to make his marriage work, Dad headed off to bed. Barbara said she was going to stay up a while and write a letter to her mother.

He reported on his tapes the events that followed:

> Late in the night, she woke me up, said, "Gary, I've just taken a whole bottle of sleeping pills." Had no idea she would ever attempt anything like this. [I told her] I know you're just lying to me. Then she fell on the floor. Thinking she was play-acting, I tried to wake her up. Shook her. Slapped her face.
>
> So I contacted a doctor I knew in the agency. Called ambulance. Took her out. Couldn't revive her. Just a few more minutes she would have been dead. . . .
>
> Went to hospital. Put a tube down her throat. Transferred her to Georgetown [Hospital], where she became alright, sometime after daylight. Got her out of danger. . . .
>
> This same man [from the agency] got word [somebody in the media] got word that she had attempted suicide, and I denied it. I hated to lie, but I did. Told him she had a bad oyster or something.
>
> I think she saw what she was and didn't like what she saw.[64]

When I started trying to learn about my father's life, Mom insisted that I not attempt to contact Barbara as long as my mom was alive. For whatever reason, she didn't want that connection to my Dad's previous life. I honored Mom's wishes but always regretted that I never got the chance to talk with Barbara.

Of course, I will always be connected to my dad's first wife through his 1960 220SE Mercedes convertible, which Barbara drove while Dad was in prison. The automobile remained in the garage at the Sherman Oaks house for several years after Dad died, fortunately avoiding serious damage when an earthquake destroyed the house in 1994. It belongs to me now. In recent years, I have spent about $12,000 on repairs, but it still needs plenty of tender loving care.

When I take the Mercedes out for an occasional spin, to keep it lubricated, I sometimes flash back to those tender moments when Dad would hold me on his lap and let me steer while we were heading up the last mile to our home in Sun Valley. Since it is the only thing Dad specifically left me in his will, it is very special to me.

Chapter Eight

THE LAST ECHO

On the morning of June 14, 2012, I walked into the Pentagon feeling the full weight of my family's complicated history. It had not been easy living in the shadow of all those doubts. But I was not easily deterred by long odds or setbacks.

In the years after founding The Cold War Museum and becoming its first full-time executive director, I faced a series of formidable obstacles. While working full-time as the president and CEO for the Vienna-Tysons Corner Chamber of Commerce to support my family, I put in an additional 20–40 hours per week to promote the museum to civic clubs, military officials, and media outlets. I used my traveling U-2 Incident exhibit as a catalyst for a permanent museum, while searching and negotiating for artifacts, pitching for governmental and corporate funds, and spearheading an oral-history project involving Fairfax County public-school students.

"The whole point of The Cold War Museum was to educate future generations in what that time period was all about," I told the media.[1]

Embracing the concept, Virginia social studies teacher Patti Winch said, "It's hard for our students today to understand the Cold War. I don't think they connect with the fear factor."[2]

In 2006, after I had raised enough money to work for the museum full-time, the nonprofit entered into a partnership agreement with the Fairfax County Park Authority to build a permanent museum on the site of an old Nike missile-launch facility in Lorton, Virginia. We began signing up sponsors, but the agreement ultimately fell apart in 2009, when Fairfax County Park Authority walked away from the negotiating table after the museum had lined up donors who had pledged to write checks to get the facility up and running.

The donors wanted to see the lease signed first, and the park authority wanted to see the money in the bank. It was a catch-22, with neither side wanting to take the first step.

Local politicians and community leaders developed great hopes for the museum, which they envisioned as a significant tourist draw.

"I'm very disheartened," said Irma Clifton, the president of the Lorton Heritage Society.[3] "I think it was the perfect opportunity to tell the story of that part of our history where it actually happened."

The disintegration of the deal was a crushing blow. My failure was plastered all over the front page of the *Washington Post*.[4]

Thirteen years of my life had been invested in making this museum a reality. And we got so close. Then we were shot down. Seems to run in the family.

But then my telephone started to ring. That's when I learned the truth behind the hackneyed PR phrase "There's no such thing as bad press."

Alerted by the news story, representatives from several other northern Virginia localities called to express interest in creating a home for the museum. My board and I eventually secured a deal with the Vint Hill Economic Development Authority in Fauquier County, which provided a facility suitable for renovation and very favorable terms.

With funding sources drying up in the wake of the severe recession, I resigned from my staff position, to preserve the organization's finite resources. I became Founder and Chairman Emeritus and turned the operation over to the volunteers. No one was prouder than me to watch the new leadership, chaired by John Welch, negotiate the final hurdles of turning my dream into a reality.

Utilizing a facility once used by the NSA, CIA, and US Army Security Agency, The Cold War Museum opened in 2011 at what used to be known in intelligence circles as Vint Hill Farms Station, featuring an estimated $3 million in rare artifacts—including but not limited to a Stasi prison door; the US Postal Service mailbox used by spy Aldrich Ames to contact his Soviet handlers; a prisoner's outfit worn by a member of the captured USS *Pueblo*; a sailor's uniform from a USS *Liberty* crewmember; and the largest known collection of civil defense memorabilia in the United States. The frequent tours of schoolchildren and history buffs validated my original vision, preserving and teaching about the milestone events of the epic clash between East and West.

By this point in my life, I was a family man with mounting responsibilities, learning to balance my personal life with the powerful urge to educate the world about my father and the Cold War.

Though I started out as a young man who always heard the voice of his mother ringing in his head, telling him to be skeptical of other peoples' motives, I endeavored to embrace a certain amount of vulnerability. But my scars ran deep. I remained very guarded. Truthfully, I always felt like I had to hold something back, until I met Jennifer.

The beautiful daughter of a business associate, Jennifer Webber, came into my life in late 1995. She could sense that the business-like vibe I was projecting was clearly a defensive mechanism to keep people at a distance. On one of our first dates, she said, only half joking, "I don't know whether to call you 'Gary' or 'Mr. Powers.'" This was also because she was ten years younger. Had she called me Mr. Powers when we first met, I would probably not be writing about her now.

Jennifer remembers learning about Francis Gary Powers from her older brother, Bo, and feeling sorry for his parents. When she later studied the U-2 Incident in school, she never learned that he had survived the shoot-down.

When she was twenty, her mother asked, "Do you know who Francis Gary Powers is?"

Aware of the historical figure but still unsure of herself, she said no.

It turned out that her mother, Binnie, who served on the Downtown Fairfax Coalition's Festival of Lights and Carols committee, knew the pilot's son, who was the executive director of the coalition at the time.

"I couldn't wrap my head around the son's age, thinking his father died in 1960," she said.

Sometime after this, during an event at the Old Town Hall, I noticed this beautiful blond standing next to my friend Binnie, who just happened to be Binnie's daughter. I was immediately smitten, and one thing led to another.

Soon Jen became very knowledgeable about the pilot and the U-2 Incident.

On her first trip to my condo, she noticed a picture of the U-2 inscribed by Kelly Johnson. She looked at the date next to the signature. It was the day she was born.

"Must have been fate," she said with a laugh, many years later.

Jen quickly grasped the significance of her future husband's enduring relationship with his late father.

"Gary was deprived of something most of us take for granted," Jennifer said. "The impact that loss has had on his life is hard to overstate. But when you add the fact that he didn't know the truth about this controversial figure. . . . Gary is the kind of person who needs to know the truth. Otherwise it would have haunted him for the rest of his life."

Through the years, Jennifer has indulged my determination to chase every conceivable lead and press my father's case. We often planned family trips around speaking engagements, air shows, media interviews, conventions, and meetings with Dad's friends and colleagues. She tried to understand why I put so much of my heart and soul into the effort, sometimes worried that my quest was developing into an unhealthy obsession.

"Every time he achieves one goal to honor his father, there is another one waiting in the wings," she said. "Sometimes I would like to see him put the same effort that he puts toward his father's memory to his family at home. But I have also never been in Gary's shoes. I have never been told my father was a traitor or a coward, so I can't say his 'obsession' is anything other than normal."

I don't need anybody to tell me I'm a lucky man. Jen's support and understanding through the years has been incredible. I can't imagine my life without her.

Even before we learned that we were going to have a son, I had given the issue of names serious thought. As with so many things in my life, the choice was fundamentally shaped by the realization that the world viewed my father through a distorted lens.

My mother was adamant: She wanted us to name the boy Francis Gary Powers III. She had her reasons, and I understood them. She wanted her son to make a statement to the world. I liked the idea of Francis Gary Powers III, but did I really want to burden my son with all the misinformation associated with the name?

In the end, the decision turned partially on a piece of advice offered by Gregg Anderson during our trip to Moscow in 1990. "If you name him after your father, you're doing it for the wrong reasons," Gregg said. "But if you're naming him after yourself for your own accomplishments, then you may be doing it for the right reasons."

By the time our little boy arrived on July 2, 2002, I had earned my master of public administration degree from George Mason University, was managing the Vienna-Tysons Corner Regional Chamber of Commerce, and had founded The Cold War Museum.

In my mind, naming him Francis Gary Powers III was not the act of a man defiantly shaking his fist at the world. It was, instead, a symbol of how I was well on my way to transcending my father's lingering shadow and establishing my own legacy.

To us and his friends, our son headed into his teenage years known as Trey. In the years ahead, he will have the opportunity to choose how he presents himself to the world. In time, I hope the name will become less of a burden and more a source of acknowledged pride.

Even as I pursued my father's story with an insatiable desire to know more and spread the truth, I spent many of those years as the primary caregiver to Trey—making sure he did his homework and handling many of the household chores—while Jen worked a full-time job in the legal profession. "If he had a lecture or had to go out of town to set up the exhibit, Gary was the one who arranged for someone to get Trey on or off the bus," Jen said.

Because they understood how important the quest was to me—and because I often involved them in the process—my wife and son never felt neglected. "If anything, we have grown because of it," Jen said. "What his journey has taught me is to never give up. Every time a door was shut in Gary's face, he would open another door. I don't have that perseverance. I don't think many people do. It's a trait I really admire in Gary."

On May 1, 2010, the fiftieth anniversary of the U-2 Incident, I was back in Moscow, telling an audience of soldiers and cadets at the Central Armed Forces Museum: "In order to understand the world today you must understand how we got here, and we got here through the Cold War."[5]

Describing myself as "walking, living, and breathing Cold War history,"[6] I give at least four dozen presentations a year—sometimes accompanied by the exhibit—telling my father's story and how it fit into the larger conflict.

"A lot of people have heard of Francis Gary Powers and know he was shot down, because there was quite a furor over it," said Adam Smith, the director of the Experimental Aviation Association's Air Venture Museum in Oshkosh, Wisconsin, where the I drew a big crowd in 2002.[7] "But if you ask people what else they know about it, they don't know."

Refuting the conventional wisdom about Francis Gary Powers and the moment that defined him became a central part of my life.

The crowds who showed up for my speeches enjoyed hearing about the little boy who once asked, while being tucked into bed: "Dad, how high were you flying?"

The answer hit them like a punch line: "Not high enough! Or I would not have been shot down."

"Gary, I can't tell you how high I was flying," the father then said. "It's a secret."

Especially in the wake of the 1998 Declassification Conference and my various other efforts to learn the truth, the people who attended my lectures were let in on the secrets of altitude and other once-classified details, pulling back the veil of the fast-fading Cold War.

Sometimes I encountered young people who expected me to talk about U2, the Irish rock band fronted by Bono.

Standing before groups large and small, I attacked the myth of the self-destruct button and poison-tipped pin.

Questioned by well-intentioned people who believed the false news they had read in the press or had been told during a time of inconvenient truths, I explained the reality about the self-destruct buttons.

"I have seen Gary handle the misperception about his father with dignity and grace," Jen said. "He has never yelled or shown anger toward anyone who believed the misinformation circulating in the public. He would simply state the facts and move on."

It took years and years of seemingly disparate events, bouncing off each other, for the federal government to begin casting a new eye on my father's story. It took years and years of accumulated knowledge, allowing me to know the right questions to ask and the right buttons to push. It took a very supportive wife who loved me and understood. Sometimes, it took me becoming a pain in the ass.

"It was pretty inspirational to watch," said my friend Bob Kallos. "Very methodically, Gary attacked these assumptions about his dad and proved them to be false."

My friends and family often wondered why I was pushing so hard to vindicate my father.

"Gary was absolutely driven on the subject [and] stuck with it a lot longer than most people would have," said his friend Chris Means.

Every time someone pushed back against the facts and insisted that my father should have committed suicide, or suggested that he spilled his guts to the Russians, I was forced to confront the doubts that had shadowed my entire life. It mattered not that I knew the truth. It mattered not that I believed with every fiber of my being that my father was a hero who did his best in very difficult circumstances. One uninformed person who bought into those myths gave them an enduring power over my father's story. I was determined to reclaim that power.

Knowing how my father suffered—while in captivity, and after his ambivalent repatriation—filled me with a powerful resolve. I felt a sense of duty to set the record straight.

In 2010, I read a magazine article that mentioned that RB-47 crew members John McKone and Bruce Olmstead had been awarded the Silver Star, the military's third-highest honor. Naturally, I was happy for the colonels, who had been held captive at Lubyanka at the same time as my father. They were personal friends.

I had first met McKone and Olmstead in Omaha, Nebraska, at the newly opened SAC Museum in September 1998, during one of the first public displays of the U-2 Incident exhibit. We were all part of a panel discussion on Cold War reconnaissance.

But something about the wording of the citation really pissed me off. It noted that McKone and Olmstead had not been subjected to a show trial. This struck me as another slap at my father. That wording and reference did not need to be in the official award's citation. But it goes to show how the misinformation, rumors, and speculation continued to negatively influence Dad's reputation.

Now I had a new mission.

First I consulted with Buz Carpenter, who advised me on how to navigate through the bureaucracy. After I gathered the necessary materials, including a supporting letter from Congressman Eric Cantor and the head of the Air Force Association, Buz told me: "I think you have enough of a case to go for it." So I submitted a detailed application, including this cover letter:

January 16, 2011

DoD Civilian/Military Service Review Board
1535 Command Dr., EE Wing, 3rd Floor
Andrews AFB, MD 20762-7002

Dear DoD Civilian/Military Service Review Board Members:

I am writing to request a determination by the DoD Civilian/Military Service Review Board for my father's eligibility to be awarded the USAF Silver Star posthumously.

It has recently come to my attention that Colonels Bruce Olmstead and John McKone were awarded the Silver Star in October 2004 and it is unfortunate that my father was not considered for the same recognition at that time since all three men were shot down by the Soviets in 1960, held at Lubyanka Prison during the same time period, and awarded the POW Medal subsequent to their return home to the United States after their imprisonment.

On May 1, 2000, my father was posthumously awarded by the USAF and the CIA the POW Medal, the Distinguished Flying Cross, the National Service Medal, and the CIA Director's Medal. My father's service records were updated at that time to show that his time spent in the U-2 program between approximately 1956 and 1962 should count as military service.

I have attached the redacted files on my earlier AFBCMR [Air Force Board of Correction of Military Records] determination for issuance of his POW Medal and update of his military service records as supporting documentation for this request.

In conclusion, the awarding of the Silver Star to Colonels Bruce Olmstead and John McKone in and of itself should be enough evidence and set the necessary precedence for my father's eligibility to also be awarded the Silver Star. I look forward to hearing from you soon with a favorable determination. If you should have any questions or need additional information, please do not hesitate to call.

Thank you for your assistance.

Very truly yours,

Francis Gary Powers, Jr.[8]

Truthfully, I thought, after the POW Medal and the others Dad received in 2000, we were done. I never imagined any additional honors from the government. I knew this was a much bigger deal.

For months, paperwork shuttled back and forth between me, various military officials, and Congressman Cantor's office. In recommending the honor up the chain of command, Lieutenant Colonel Cheryl Beineke, Deputy Director of the Secretary of the Air Force Personnel Council, concluded: "Due to the clandestine and sensitive nature of the overflight operations that Powers was engaged in, global political tensions of the day, and other ongoing negotiations, no medals were presented when Powers was released and returned to the United States."[9]

After being forced to repeatedly make the case for Dad to receive the POW Medal, I expected resistance from the Air Force. So I was rendered virtually speechless on December 15, 2011, when I went to my mailbox and tore open the latest letter from the Air Force.

December 8, 2011

MEMORANDUM FOR THE CHIEF OF STAFF

Under the authority of Section 1552, Title 10, United States Code and Air Force Instruction 36-2603, and having assured compliance with the provisions of the above regulation, the decision of the Air Force Board for Correction of Military Records is announced, and it is directed that:

The pertinent military records of the Department of the Air Force relating to FRANCIS G. POWERS (DECEASED) . . . be corrected to show that he be awarded the Silver Star for gallantry in action during the period 1 May 1960 to 10 February 1962.

Phillip E. Horton

Deputy Executive Director

Air Force Board of Correction of Military Records[10]

Not only was the honor nearly a half a century in the making, but it would not have been possible if I had not vigorously argued a decade earlier for Washington to consider my father's time with the CIA as part of his military service. This bureaucratic achievement was the foundation on which the Silver Star was bestowed.

It was the best Christmas present of my life.

Many young people suffer the loss of a parent. The tragedy hits us all differently, and, one way or another, we all try to cope. My search to find meaning in my father's life also served a deeper purpose. It was my way of dealing with the unfinished business Francis Gary Powers left behind on the first day of August in 1977.

Assembling the pieces of the jigsaw puzzle became a kind of therapy. I wasn't just seeking redemption for my father. I was also seeking a measure of peace for myself.

My sister, Dee, observed my journey from a unique perspective.

Especially after she moved out at age eighteen to pursue a career in the military, Dee felt distanced from me. "For a long time, I think our mother made sure we weren't friends," she said. "I can't really explain why. But fortunately we became closer through the years and eventually got to where we have a good relationship."

She understood what a triumphant moment the Silver Star was for me. "I think Gary wandered without a voice for a while," she said. "But he found that voice in making sure our dad was remembered the way he should have been. It made me very happy to watch him find that inner peace."

My private battle to recast our father's place in the history books culminated inside the Pentagon's ornate Hall of Heroes, where a small group of relatives and friends gathered alongside various high-ranking officials of the military and intelligence establishment.

"Never seen so much brass in my life," said Bob Kallos, who made the trip from Philadelphia with his twelve-year-old daughter. "It was pretty intimidating and humbling."

Chris Conrad watched closely as I moved through the crowd, greeting the invited guests, before the program began. "I remember being so proud of Gary, not just for this incredible accomplishment, which would not have happened without him pushing for it, . . . but also to see this guy who had once been kind of awkward and unsure of himself mature into this very polished guy who's confident and quite a good public speaker," recalled Conrad, who flew in from California. "Several of his closest friends were there. We all have busy schedules, but we wanted to be there for Gary. We all understood what a profoundly wonderful moment this was for him."

Former U-2 pilot Carl Overstreet wished his old friend Frank could be there to see the big fuss.

As part of my effort to learn about my dad, I had gotten to know Carl and his wife, Elizabeth. "Carl thought very highly of [Frank] and he was able to tell Gary about his dad," Elizabeth said. "Carl always said he was a good guy, a good pilot, and a hero."

Seated in the front row, Jen fretted about nine-year-old Trey, who was about to play an important role in the ceremony. "I was worried that he would have stage fright and would be intimidated by all the cameras," she said.

After speaking for a few minutes about Francis Gary Powers's service to his country, General Norman Schwartz, the Air Force chief of staff, presented the box containing the medal to the grandchildren the pilot never got to know: Dee's grown daughter, Lindsey, and Francis Gary Powers III, who impressed everyone with his poise and manners.

"I was just so proud," Jan Powers Melvin said. "So many emotions pouring over me in that special room, which most people never get to see. I just wish Francis could have been there."

All those years after my father returned home amid such ambivalence, the citation acknowledged that he was "interrogated, harassed, and endured unmentionable hardships on a continuous basis by numerous top Soviet Secret Police interrogation teams," while "resisting all Soviet efforts through cajolery, trickery and threats of death," and exhibiting "indomitable spirit, exceptional loyalty, and continuous heroic actions."[11]

Welling up with emotion, I felt a satisfaction I had been pursuing for much of my adult life. My father was now vindicated. Finally. "It's never too late to set the record straight," I told the packed auditorium. "Even if it takes fifty years."

Closure comes in many forms. Sometimes it washes over you when you experience a moment that exceeds your wildest expectations. Vindication is especially sweet when it fills up a hole in your heart.

"To see Gary's triumph on behalf of his dad was just so moving and inspirational," said my friend Joe Patterson.

The Silver Star was an admission that Washington had treated Francis Gary Powers unfairly, that it had left a patriot out in the cold for far too long. It was a concession that the Cold War was a real war fought by men who made great sacrifices and sometimes got caught up in situations that forced the country to debate the meaning of heroism.

"These events," wrote Adam J. Herbert in *Air Force* magazine, "are reminders that sometimes justice comes slowly."[12]

More than twenty-two years after the fall of the Berlin Wall, when Francis Gary Powers officially became an American hero in the eyes of the military establishment, the delayed recognition felt like something even more profound: The last fading echo of the Cold War.

Chapter Nine

UNFINISHED BUSINESS

In June 2014, I heard rumors of a major motion picture in the works concerning the exchange on the Glienicker Bridge. Eventually I confirmed that Steven Spielberg was directing the film, a discovery that filled me with new anxiety on an old subject. Was Hollywood planning to smear my father?

After sending out a series of blind emails, expressing the Powers family's "concern" at the potential negative impact of basing the movie off of debunked misinformation, I eventually heard back from Mark Platt, one of the producers, who is best known for his Broadway production of *Wicked*. This led to an hour-long telephone conversation in July 2014. After many of my fears were allayed, I signed on as a technical advisor as the $40 million film moved into production.

Although the Silver Star ceremony represented the dramatic completion of my decades-long battle to restore my father's good name, I continued to make speeches and seek the still-hidden details concerning my father's life. There was still plenty of unfinished business.

Realizing that a film "inspired by true events" could potentially reverse all of the gains we achieved, I worked closely with the Amblin Entertainment team to try to influence the picture's portrayal of my father.

A staffer wanted to know if my father was tortured. When I said he was not, the staffer said: "That's too bad. Not for your father, but for the suspense of the interrogation scenes in the movie."

Some of my suggestions wound up informing the narrative, including when I told Spielberg that the United States had hidden a sniper in the trees near the Glienicker Bridge, aimed at Abel, in the event that something went wrong with the exchange. This became part of the climactic scene of the film, through the character of Tom Hanks, who portrayed James Donovan.

I also landed a cameo as an agency man walking out of a hangar, next to the actor portraying my dad, Austin Stowell. Along with other members of my family, I attended different premieres of *Bridge of Spies*, which opened to critical acclaim in October 2015.

The Powers family really liked the movie. However, one scene bothered me. During a briefing, the pilots were told to "spend the dollar," an obvious reference to the use of the poison pin, which was not accurate. But beyond a few such instances of artistic license, I was gratified that the film portrayed my father accurately and pointed out at the end that he had been recognized as a hero for his service to his country.

The film is historically accurate in the big picture, but the details in each scene are not 100 percent accurate. That's Hollywood.

As the production team wrapped the final day of shooting at California's Beale Air Force Base, Dee and I were touched when Spielberg toasted Francis Gary Powers as an American hero. That meant an awful lot to me, for Mr. Spielberg to acknowledge my dad and show the respect he had for him.

Not long after the film completed a successful domestic run, I returned to my father's roots to take another bow.

In March 2016, I represented the family when the terminal building at the tiny Lonesome Pine Airport in Wise, Virginia, just down the road from Pound, was dedicated in my father's honor. "This is a very deep privilege," I said, adding that I was "honored and humbled" by the gesture.[1]

I shared a bit of my own personal journey with the home folks, and hinted at the mission that gave me purpose. "Through classified files and FOIA requests," I said, "I was able to show that he did everything he was supposed to do, that he served this country honorably, that he did not betray the country."[2]

The decision to place Dad's name on the building was Wise County's way of saying it was proud of the U-2 pilot, which once would have been a rather-controversial stand for local politicians. It was yet another reminder that the world was a very different place.

"This, to me, is about family and community," said Kim Mullins, who spearheaded the effort as a member of the Cumberland Airport Commission. "Francis Gary Powers left here a hero, came back a hero, and died a hero. And don't let nobody tell you any different."[3]

In 2012, I filed a FOIA request seeking information concerning a long list of additional issues about my father. It took five years for some items to finally be released, and they provided some interesting news.

Nine years after he was rebuffed in his attempt to rejoin the Air Force, Frank hired an attorney to press his case for military retirement benefits.

In a letter addressed to President Richard Nixon on August 31, 1971, Jerry K. Staub, of the Glendale, California, firm Edwards, Edwards, and Ashton, argued:

> I am unable to understand why Mr. Powers, who has made such a tremendous sacrifice for his country, is being denied those benefits on retirement that are being conferred to others under similar circumstances. Mr. Powers has played by all the rules. He has lived, since 1960, with the personal tragedy of the U-2 Incident. He has foregone substantial personal economic reward [by turning down his first offer of a $150,000 book deal, in 1962] at the request of the government. Why, then, has the government refused to honor its commitment to Mr. Powers? . . . I refuse to believe that his country is so entirely ungrateful.[4]

The declassified documents revealed that some officials in the government were prepared to offer Dad three choices:

1.) Retirement from the Air Force at the rank of lieutenant colonel . . . crediting him with his time in the Air Force, CIA, and working on government contracts with Lockheed.

2.) Crediting him with his CIA and Air Force active duty time totaling twelve years and reinstating him in the Air Force for the next eight years until twenty years' federal service are completed.

3.) Reinstatement with assignment as to CIA as a U-2 mission planner.[5]

According to an October 19, 1971, memorandum written by CIA general counsel Lawrence R. Houston, the agency authorized as much as $250,000 for Powers's settlement, with the Air Force agreeing to assume half of the cost.

"The Air Force has determined that they cannot see their way clear to restore him to active duty," the memo said. "In lieu thereof, a proposal has been approved by Secretary of the Air Force Seamans and Secretary of Defense Laird whereby a sum of up to $250,000 would be offered to Powers in lieu of all claims. This sum would be placed in a trust to be administered by a corporate trustee. The mechanics of the movement of money and arrangements for the trust will be accomplished by the agency so that there will be no traceable record back to the Government."[6]

Three days after his death, evidence of the confidential deal consummated six years earlier was confirmed in a secret CIA memo:

4 August 1977

MEMORANDUM FOR: John F. Blake
Acting Deputy Director of Central Intelligence

FROM: [REDACTED]
SUBJECT: Francis Gary Powers

1.) A trust was established with $175,000 on 27 October 1971, which was to provide Mr. Powers with $8,750 per annum. This trust was established in lieu of Powers' having been reinstated on active duty in the Air Force. When the trust was established, Mr. Powers signed a release and discharge. Included in that release are the essential elements of a secrecy agreement, to keep forever secret any information relating to the trust agreement and all other classified information gained by virtue of Mr. Powers' association with the U.S. Government. The release states specifically that any disclosure of classified information could result in the revocation of the trust with the reversion of the monies in the trust to the grantor.

2.) The general terms of the trust agreement are that upon Gary Powers' death the income will be paid to his wife unless they are legally separated or estranged. Upon his wife's death, payments shall be made to the issue of Francis Gary Powers.

3.) Originally, the trustee was a Los Angeles lawyer by the name of [REDACTED] was subsequently appointed a judge in a Los Angeles County court and the Agency agreed that a corporate trustee would be substituted for [REDACTED]. On 11 October 1974 the CIA General Counsel wrote to [REDACTED] setting forth the relationship of the Bank as trustee for the CIA.

4.) Please comment on the following:

(1) I think we should contact the trustee and present him with written notification of the death of Gary Powers and of the change in beneficiary. This would normally require a death certificate and is in according with the terms of the trust agreement.

(2) [REDACTED]

(3) I think we should also discuss with Mr. Powers' attorney how we might enforce the secrecy agreement with Mrs. Powers since she did not sign the release.

(4) What do you think about an official Agency representation at the Powers funeral which is now scheduled for Arlington Cemetery?

(5) I have talked with Major General Harold R. Vague, Air Force Judge Advocate. (He participated with John Warner in meeting the attorney in California.) General Vague has

no objections to our proceeding with the above actions. General Vague has cleared the following responses with the Air Force Vice Chief of Staff: The only Air Force participation in the funeral will be the Honor Guard at Arlington Cemetery. No high ranking Air Force personnel will attend. The Air Force has no objection to any CIA representation at the funeral.[7]

This was a shocking revelation. I never thought these documents would see the light of day.

During my high-school years, Mom had told me about the trust, which helped pay my private-school tuition. After Dad died, she was afraid that the money would be revoked and she would lose out on the monthly stipend at a time when the family needed it the most.

At her request, the money was eventually moved to her personal bank account, alleviating her fear that it would eventually disappear.

While the documents demonstrated the Air Force's unwillingness to take my father back, I was gratified to learn that the Air Force and CIA had worked together to try to help my family. These backroom deals done in secret almost fifty years ago need to be taken in context of the time period of the Cold War and not through a modern lens.

Another once-secret document suggested something I had been told but could never prove.

A memo dated October 27, 1972, stated, "After Lockheed felt it could no longer support Powers, the Agency funded an extension to enable Powers to alleviate his own situation."[8]

This passage raised more questions than it answered, but it appeared to confirm my longtime belief that the CIA had paid part of Dad's salary while he was employed at Lockheed.

Exactly why Kelly Johnson fired my father was one of those questions I continued to wonder about: Was it because of budget cutbacks, Johnson's sensitivity to the publicity generated by Frank's book, or pressure from Washington?

A top secret document provided as part of the 2017 FOIA release showed the CIA reporting on my father's comments during a 1971 appearance at California State University–Northridge, my alma mater, concerning his separation from Lockheed:

> Mr. Powers talked about his experiences and said in the course of his talk in about 1970, two weeks after having submitted his book to CIA for review before publishing, he was laid off at Lockheed. He was asked if he meant that CIA had pressured Lockheed to fire him; his answer was something like, "Yes, I do, but you can draw your own conclusions for these facts."[9]

This left me with another question unlikely to ever have answered: Was the CIA violating American law by spying on an American citizen on American soil?

Mom told me that our home phone was tapped, and that during Dad's book tour, he was convinced that he and Curt Gentry were tailed. Noticing an agent at an airport, and eager to have some fun, Frank walked up to the young man, introduced himself, and told him where they were going that day. The man appeared flustered and eventually disappeared into the crowd.

I still didn't have all the answers, of course, which is one reason why I arranged to return to Moscow in early December 2017, after putting together a couple of business deals to offset expenses.

After the breakup of the Soviet Union, Russian authorities finally acknowledged a long-concealed instance of friendly fire: One of the MiG fighters dispatched to try to shoot Powers out of the sky had been hit by an SA-2 missile, killing the pilot, Sergei Safronov. Always determined to chase every lead, I was happy when the pilot's son contacted me through The Cold War Museum. We shared a long conversation.

He said his mother did not blame my father for her husband's death. She understood that her husband was following orders and my father was following orders, and that it was not my father's fault that her husband had died. I was very touched by this.

I wanted to show my respects to the MiG pilot, so on the day after attending a conference, as snow drifted from the sky, I walked up the steps to the granite memorial to the fallen Soviet hero, adorned with his photograph and a portion of the plane's tail section.

They told me not to smile. If I smiled, it would be an insult to the Russian people.

Dressed in a suit and with a very solemn look on my face, I dropped to one knee and placed ten red roses in tribute.

I lingered for a few moments, thinking about what the pilot's family must have gone through, how they had surely struggled to deal with the loss, and wondering how they suffered for all those years not knowing the truth of how he died.

Continuing to trace my father's journey, I visited a local history museum in Yekaterinburg, once known as Sverdlovsk, where I sat in the back seat of the car my father rode in after being captured, and where I saw additional artifacts from the U-2 Incident, including a fragment of the plane. "It is now history," I told the assembled reporters.[10] "We can reflect on it and learn from it."

I visited one of the old missile bases where the SA-2s were fired that blasted the U-2 out of the sky; the site where the wreckage crashed; and the place where Dad parachuted to Earth. The former collective farm was now a high-end housing development.

Most everyone seemed happy to greet me, including the mayor of Yekaterinburg, Yevgeny Roizman, as well as one of the nearby village mayors who hosted me for lunch and vodka shots. However, another mayor publicly announced that he wanted nothing to do with the son of the American spy and preferred that I not visit his village. I still stopped in the little town.

That was the only real animosity I felt on the whole trip. Everyone else was very nice and accommodating. I believed we helped foster a good relationship with the Russian people.

After learning I was going to be back in Moscow, I reached out to journalist Svetlana Tumanov, a onetime KGB agent (also married to a onetime KGB agent) whom I had met on a previous trip. Svetlana told me she was going to take me to an event. She didn't elaborate.

During the taxi ride into the heart of Moscow with an interpreter and a business associate, I recognized a big green building in the distance. It was the Hall of Columns where my father's show trial was orchestrated, the mysterious place that had often occupied so many of my thoughts. Soon the driver pulled up to the majestic building, and I learned that Svetlana, who was on her way, had arranged to take me inside the auditorium where my father had once been put on trial for his life.

We basically had to sneak in the back door, because we didn't have official invitations for the event.

In the lobby, while sipping champagne, Svetlana introduced me to several dignitaries, including politician Serge Baburin, who would unsuccessfully seek the Russian presidency in 2018. "Baburin was thrilled [like] a little boy to meet Gary Powers Jr.," she said.

Hard-liner Sergei Stepashin, a longtime Russian government official, was not so welcoming. "Oh, the son of the spy," he said to Svetlana, before turning away.

Realizing the significance of the moment, as we prepared to enter the auditorium for a classical-music concert hosted by a pro-Palestine organization, Svetlana leaned in and told me, "Please compose yourself and think for the moment: what happened behind those doors in 1960!"

While the orchestra played Tchaikovsky and Rachmaninov, my mind drifted back to those difficult days. I could imagine my father in the dock on the stage. I could feel his fear.

It was truly a moving moment. I was walking in my father's footsteps, and I felt a close connection to him.

Still, the lingering tension of my father's life could be seen when *CBS News Sunday Morning* aired a segment in 2017 celebrating the birthday of the late Ian Fleming. After telling its audience that Francis Gary Powers "let himself be captured alive by the Soviets,"[11] the news program ran an old tape of Fleming, asking what James Bond would have done in such a situation. "I hope he would have taken his pill," Fleming said.[12] Stunned by the insult on Memorial Day weekend, I wrote a letter of protest. This made me feel better, especially when it prompted CBS to air, the following Sunday, a correction stating that my father was under no orders to take his own life if captured. In 2018, about the time this book began moving through the editing process, a review for another book in the *Wall Street Journal* included a comment influenced by the still-swirling misinformation.

Some people who watched my father's show trial and bought into the mythology attached to the U-2 Incident will always see Francis Gary Powers as a tainted figure. Some minds can never be changed. But I know the truth, and after devoting so much of my life to searching for it, the truth has set me free. Now more than ever, I am a man at peace.

ACKNOWLEDGMENTS

On the morning of June 15, 2012, Keith Dunnavant fired up his laptop and, while sipping his first cup of coffee, began scanning the headlines of the *New York Times'* website. One item immediately caught his eye: "Powers, U-2 Pilot Captured by Soviets, Awarded Silver Star."

As a student of history who had grown up during the Cold War, Dunnavant was familiar with the story of Powers and was aware that the pilot had died many years before.

But it was the posthumous Silver Star that caught his attention.

Why . . . after so much time?

He smelled a good story.

Dunnavant visited with Francis Gary Powers Jr. and began to understand and appreciate the long journey Gary had taken to learn the truth about his father and, ultimately, to set the record straight, which culminated with the military's third-highest honor.

The road to this book began formally in 2013.

The authors are grateful for the help of a long list of individuals, starting with Steven L. Mitchell and all the good folks at Prometheus Books for providing a home for this book and believing in it.

We were also blessed by the expert guidance of agents David Black and Jennifer Herrera of the David Black Literary Agency, who took great care in helping us shape the story.

The research included dozens of interviews and contributions from various others who assisted in other ways. They all have our sincere thanks for helping us get the story right.

To flesh out Francis Gary Powers's formative years in southwest Virginia, we benefited from the generosity of spirit and the keen memories of a long list of folks, especially Joan and Walton Meade, Jack Goff, and Jan Powers Melvin.

To understand Kelly Johnson, the Skunk Works, Area 51, and the U-2, we turned to Tony Bevacqua, Bob Gilliland, Pete Law, Jake Kratt, Robert Gilliland Jr., Harry Andonian, Steve Justice, and Buz Carpenter.

To bring the CIA days to light, we were aided by Joe Murphy, Ken Bradt, Jeannie Popovich Walls, Frank Murray, T. D. Barnes, Jim Herbert, and Steve Betterton.

To illuminate Gary's story, we leaned on the good memories of his lovely wife, Jennifer, as well as friends Chris Conrad, Joe Patterson, Chris Means, Jon Teperson, and Bob Kallos.

Fortunately for us, Winston Skinner loves history and is devoted to keep it alive in the pages of the *Newnan Times-Herald* in the suburban Atlanta town of Newnan, Georgia. Through the years, Skinner has written several articles about the marriage of Francis Gary Powers at a little parsonage just a few blocks from his newsroom. He pointed us to Frank's best man, Johnny Estep. Thanks for all the help, Winston.

We are indebted to Trishia Thompson and her mother, Betty Baugh, who granted us access to Dr. James Baugh's unpublished manuscript and correspondence concerning the events of 1960–1962 and gave us permission to quote from these historic documents.

Aviation historian Carol Osborne offered several of her video interviews of important figures from the past, including the late Tony LeVier. Thanks, Carol.

Rosa Anne Speranza helped us learn about the important role her parents played in the Powers saga.

In addition to reviewing the journal, letters, and audio tapes Francis Gary Powers left behind, Gary has spent nearly three decades gathering mounds of research concerning his father's journey, much of it classified until recent years, including the transcript of his CIA debriefing after his release from prison. Several government reports proved extremely helpful, including the NSA's "The Final Overflights of the Soviet Union, 1959–60," and the CIA's "History of the OSA," "The May Day 1960 Incident," and "The CIA and the U-2 Program, 1954–1974." Gary expresses his sincere gratitude to the CIA for all of their help over the years to assist with his research.

Gary would like to take this opportunity to acknowledge the many friends and family members who supported his search and helped in various ways through the years: his aunts, uncles, and cousins, as well as his close friends Brandon, Chris, Joe, Jon, Bob, Mike, Randy, Topher, and Jay (RIP).

A long list of people helped Gary work through the federal-government bureaucracy, to find the truth and honor his father, and/or to assist with his efforts. He would especially like to thank Chris Pocock, Pat Halloran, and Buz Carpenter, as well as the following:

Jim Connell for obtaining access to his father's prison cell at Vladimir, and various other assistance.

Gregg Anderson (RIP) for all his work he did on behalf of the Powers family when Gary's father passed away in 1977, and for helping with Gary's first trip to the Soviet Union in May 1990.

Leonov Minin for helping with his visit to Moscow in June 1997.

Svetlana Tumanov for helping him to access to the Hall of Columns.

Anton Vladimirovich, Natalja Pavlovna, and Andrew Guselnikov, who helped Gary to visit U-2 Incident–related sites in Sverdlovsk in December 2017.

Rainer Hunger and Vaclav Vitovec from Vienna, Austria, and Prague, Czech Republic, respectively, who are fellow Cold War historians, collectors, and friends who assisted with travels in Europe over the years.

Doug Campbell for his help with another project concerning Gary's father.

The Cold War Museum Board of Directors, staff, volunteers, and docents, who helped with the creation of the museum, especially co-founder John Welch.

Dave Baldwin (RIP), Werner Juretzko (RIP), Chris Sturdevant, Baerbel and Horst Simon, Kevin Fleckner, Richard Neault, and Jason Smart, who helped with the creation of The Cold War Museum chapters.

Carol Bessette (RIP) and John Bessette, who helped with the creation of the Spy Tour of Washington, DC.

The extended U-2 community, including Sam Crouse, Tony Day, and Chuck Wilson, who have supported Gary's efforts to find out the truth over the years.

The CIA for allowing Gary in to photocopy declassified files from the Historical Intelligence Collection, and Linda McCarthy, who helped with the creation of the U-2 Incident exhibit.

Attorneys Mark Zaid and Bradley Moss for their help with filing the FOIA requests, which became an integral part of the book.

All of Gary's Cal Nu fraternity brothers (1983–1987) who helped him to come out of his shell.

Keith thanks his brothers—Bill, Tom, Ron, and Jim—and various other family members and friends for their support of this project, with a special thanks to his beloved mother, who encouraged it for years but passed away before getting to see it published.

We are sure that we have left off some names of individuals to whom we are indebted for their help and support over the years. We thank you too.

The published record concerning the U-2 Incident and various parts of the story is extensive, and we benefited from a significant amount of outstanding newspaper, magazine, and book journalism, which helped us understand the players, the times, the technology, and the controversy.

Specific quotations are listed in the notes, but several books were especially helpful, including *Operation Overflight*, by Francis Gary Powers with Curt Gentry; *Mayday: Eisenhower, Khrushchev, and the U-2 Affair*, by Michael R. Beschloss; *Strangers on a Bridge*, by James B. Donovan; *The Craft of Intelligence*, by Allen W. Dulles; *The U-2 Spyplane*, by Chris Pocock; *Kelly: More Than My Share of It All*, by Clarence L. "Kelly" Johnson with Maggie Smith; *Reflections of a Cold Warrior*, by Richard M. Bissell Jr. with Jonathan E. Lewis and Frances T. Pudlo; *The Brothers*, by Stephen Kinzer; *Skunk Works*, by Ben Rich and Leo Janos; *Eisenhower: Soldier and President*, by Stephen E. Ambrose; *Memoirs of Nikita Khrushchev*, vol. 3, edited by Sergei Khrushchev; and *The Crisis Years*, by Michael R. Beschloss.

LIST OF INTERVIEWS CONDUCTED BY KEITH DUNNAVANT

Gary Powers Jr. (In person, telephone, and email) Multiple, 2013–2018
Harry Andonian (Telephone) August 18, 2016
T. D. Barnes (In person) October 7, 2015
Betty George Baugh (In person) April 26, 2018
Michael Betterton (In person) October 7, 2015
Tony Bevacqua (In person) October 6, 2015
John Birdseye (Telephone) September 4, 2018
David Boyd (In person) January 12, 2018
Liz Boyd (Telephone) November 12, 2017
Kenneth Bradt (Telephone) March 26, 2018
Buz Carpenter (Telephone) February 12, 2017
Chris Conrad (Telephone) March 2 and 4, 2018
Robert Conrad (Telephone) June 5, 2018
Frank Cruz (Telephone) August 9, 2018
Johnny Estep (In person) February 17, 2015
Mary Finch (Telephone) October 18, 2016
Bob Gilliland (In person) April 14, 2015
Jack Goff (In person) March 12, 2016
Jim Herbert (Telephone) August 7, 2018
Deborah Jaffe (Telephone) May 22, 2018
Steve Justice (In person) February 2, 2018
Bob Kallos (Telephone) March 4, 2018
Sergei Khrushchev (Telephone) April 14, 2018
Jake Kratt (Telephone) November 14, 2017
Pete Law (Telephone) July 22, 2017
Walton Meade (In person) March 12, 2016
Chris Means (Telephone) March 1, 2018

Joe Murphy (Telephone)	April 2, 2018
Carol Osborne (Telephone)	September 12, 2018
Elizabeth Overstreet (Telephone)	April 11, 2018
Joe Patterson (Telephone)	March 1, 2018
Norman Polmar (Telephone)	September 27, 2018
Jeannie Popovich Walls (Email)	March 5–May 13, 2018
Dee Powers (Telephone)	April 10, 2018
Jan Powers Melvin (Telephone)	April 6, 2018
Jennifer Powers (In person and email)	Multiple, 2014–2018
Joan Powers Meade (In person)	March 12, 2016
Rosa Anne Speranza (Telephone)	April 11, 2018
Jon Teperson (Email)	July 10, 2018
Trisha Thompson (In person)	April 26, 2018
Svetlana Tumanov (Email)	March 30–April 16, 2018

NOTES

CHAPTER ONE: THE RESTLESS HEART

1. Francis Gary Powers and Curt Gentry, *Operation Overflight: A Memoir of the U-2 Incident* (New York: Holt, Rinehart, and Winston, 1970), p. 4.
2. Ibid.
3. Ibid.
4. Personal tapes of Francis Gary Powers, 1969.
5. Ibid.
6. Ibid.
7. Ibid.
8. Ibid.
9. Winston Skinner, "The Marriage of U-2 Spy Pilot," *Newnan-Coweta Magazine*, September/October 2011, pp. 78–79.

CHAPTER TWO: OPEN SKIES

1. Evan Thomas, "Spymaster General: The Adventures of Wild Bill Donovan and the "Oh So Social" O.S.S.," *Vanity Fair,* March 2011, https://www.vanityfair.com/culture/2011/03/wild-bill-donovan201103.
2. Stephen Kinzer, *The Brothers*: *John Foster Dulles, Allen Dulles, and Their Secret World War* (New York: St. Martin's, 2013), p. 1.
3. Michael R. Beschloss, *Mayday: Eisenhower, Khrushchev, and the U-2 Affair* (New York: Harper & Row, 1986), p. 126.
4. Allen W. Dulles, *The Craft of Intelligence* (Guilford, CT: Lyons Press, 2016), pp. 157–58.
5. Ibid., p. 194.
6. Nikita Khrushchev, *Memoirs of Nikita Khrushchev, vol. 3,* ed. Sergei Khrushchev (University Park, PA: Pennsylvania State University Press, Thomas J. Watson Institute for International Studies, Brown University, 2013), p. 241.
7. Stephen E. Ambrose, *Eisenhower: Solider and President* (New York: Simon & Schuster, 1990), p. 378.

8. Clifford Johnson, in video interview with Carol Osborne, June 6, 1993.

9. Clarence L. "Kelly" Johnson with Maggie Smith, *Kelly: More than My Share of It All* (Washington, DC: Smithsonian Institution Press, 1985), p. 97.

10. Tony LeVier, in video interview with Carol Osborne, September 18, 1982.

11. Johnson with Smith, *Kelly*.

12. Chris Pocock, *The U-2 Spyplane: Toward the Unknown* (Atglen, PA: Schiffer Military History, 2000), p. 9.

13. Ibid., pp. 9–10.

14. Clarence L. "Kelly" Johnson, Skunk Works Program Log, Project X, December 1953.

15. Ibid., December 19, 1954.

16. Ibid.

17. Pocock, *U-2 Spyplane*, p. 27.

18. Johnson, Skunk Works Log, April 13, 1955.

19. Richard M. Bissell Jr., with Jonathan E. Lewis and Francis T. Pudlo, *Reflections of a Cold Warrior* (New Haven, CT: Yale University Press, 1996), p. 23.

20. Nick Sabides Jr., "A Spymaster's Son, Bangor Man Seeks Traces of His CIA Dad," *Bangor Daily News*, August 25, 2013.

21. Johnson, Skunk Works Log, July 15, 1955.

22. Bissell with Lewis and Pudlo, *Reflections,* p. 99.

23. Ben R. Rich and Leo Janos, *Skunk Works* (New York: Little, Brown, 1994), p. 134.

24. Ibid., p. 135.

25. Ibid.

26. Ibid., p. 140.

27. Francis Gary Powers and Curt Gentry, *Operation Overflight: A Memoir of the U-2 Incident* (New York: Holt, Rinehart, and Winston, 1970), p. xi.

28. Ibid., p. xii.

29. Ibid., p. xiv.

30. Bissell with Lewis and Pudlo, *Reflections*, p. 107.

31. Powers and Gentry, *Operation Overflight*, p. 10.

32. Personal tapes of Francis Gary Powers, 1969.

33. "Eisenhower Presents His 'Open Skies' Plan," History.com, last updated August 21, 2018, www.history.com/this-day-in-history/eisenhower-presents-his-open-skies-plan.

34. Johnson, Skunk Works Log, May 3, 1956.

35. Pocock, *U-2 Spyplane*.

36. Rich and Janos, *Skunk Works*, p. 146.

37. Powers and Gentry, *Operation Overflight*, p. xv.

38. Beschloss, *Mayday*, pp. 136–39; Ambrose, *Eisenhower*, pp. 424–26; Pocock, *U-2 Spyplane*, pp. 54–56.

39. Powers and Gentry, *Operation Overflight*, p. 39.

40. James B. Donovan, *Strangers on a Bridge* (New York: Atheneum, 1964), p. 189.

41. Ibid., p. 260.

42. Kurt Loft, "Sputnik Began Space Race 40 Years Ago," *Tampa Tribune*, October 4, 1997, p. 1.

43. Carl Nolte, "Warm Welcome during Cold War," *San Francisco Chronicle*, May 26, 1990, p. C9.

44. Pocock, *U-2 Spyplane*, p. 160.

45. Dulles, *Craft*, p. 195.

46. Powers and Gentry, *Operation Overflight*, p. 57.

CHAPTER THREE: MAYDAY

1. *The Last Overflights of the Soviet Union, 1959–60* (Washington, DC: National Security Agency Report, June 25, 2013), chap. 4, p. 170.

2. Nikita Khrushchev, *Memoirs of Nikita Khrushchev, vol. 3*, ed. Sergei Khrushchev (University Park, PA: Pennsylvania State University Press, Thomas J. Watson Institute for International Studies, Brown University, 2013), pp. 236–37.

3. George B. Kistiakowsky, *A Scientist at the White House* (Cambridge, MA: Harvard University Press, 1976), p. 328.

4. Richard M. Bissell Jr., with Jonathan E. Lewis and Francis T. Pudlo, *Reflections of a Cold Warrior* (New Haven, CT: Yale University Press, 1996), p. 121.

5. Chris Pocock, *The U-2 Spyplane: Toward the Unknown* (Atglen, PA: Schiffer Military History, 2000), p. 167.

6. Francis Gary Powers and Curt Gentry, *Operation Overflight: A Memoir of the U-2 Incident* (New York: Holt, Rinehart, and Winston, 1970), p. 49.

7. *Last Overflights*.

8. Personal tapes of Francis Gary Powers, 1969.

9. Bissell with Lewis and Pudlo, *Reflections*, p. 124.

10. *Last Overflights*, chap. 4, pp. 175–76.

11. Powers and Gentry, *Operation Overflight*, p. 57.

12. Bissell with Lewis and Pudlo, *Reflections*, p. 126.

13. Michael R. Beschloss, *Mayday: Eisenhower, Khrushchev, and the U-2 Affair* (New York: Harper & Row, 1986), p. 33.

14. Bissell with Lewis and Pudlo, *Reflections*, p. 126–27.

15. Powers and Gentry, *Operation Overflight*, p. 59.

16. Khrushchev, *Memoirs*, p. 237.

17. Ibid., pp. 237–38.

18. Ibid.

19. Powers and Gentry, *Operation Overflight*, p. 60.

20. Ibid., p. 61.

21. Pocock, *U-2 Spyplane*, p. 55.

22. Clarence L. "Kelly" Johnson, Skunk Works Program Log, Project X, December 17, 1956.

23. Pocock, *U-2 Spyplane*, p. 64.

24. Johnson, Skunk Works Program Log.

25. Ibid., November 17, 1955.

26. Pocock, *U-2 Spyplane*, p. 34.

27. Powers tapes.

28. Powers and Gentry, *Operation Overflight*, p. 67.

29. Powers tapes.

30. Ibid.

31. David Wise and Thomas Ross, magazine excerpt from *The U-2 Affair* (New York: Random House, 1962).

32. Powers tapes.

33. Powers and Gentry, *Operation Overflight*, pp. 69–70.

34. Powers tapes.

35. Wise and Ross, *U-2 Affair*.

36. Khrushchev, *Memoirs*, pp. 237–38.

37. Ibid., p. 238.

38. Powers tapes.

39. Powers and Gentry, *Operation Overflight*, p. 73.

40. Powers tapes.

41. Ibid.

42. *The May Day 1960 Incident* (Washington, DC: Central Intelligence Agency Report), p. 2.

43. Bissell with Lewis and Pudlo, *Reflections*, p. 127.

44. Ibid., p. 127.

45. Ibid., p. 128.

46. Stephen E. Ambrose, *Eisenhower: Solider and President* (New York: Simon & Schuster, 1990), p. 508.

47. *May Day Incident*, p. 4.

48. Beschloss, *Mayday*, p. 38.

49. *May Day Incident*, p. 6.

50. Ibid., p. 7.

51. Beschloss, *Mayday*, p. 39.

52. Khrushchev, *Memoirs*, p. 239.

53. Associated Press, "Reds Say They Shot Down U.S. Plane," *Washington Daily News*, May 5, 1960, p. A1.

54. *May Day Incident*, p. 7.

55. Ibid., p. 8.

56. Ibid., p. 9.

57. Powers tapes.

58. Ibid.

59. *May Day Incident*, p. 33.

60. Ibid.

61. David Wise, "The Russian Behind the Downing of Powers' U-2," *Los Angeles Times*, April 30, 1995, p. 18.

62. Osgood Caruthers, "Khrushchev Charges Jet Was 1,200 Miles from the Border," *New York Times*, May 8, 1960, p. A1.

63. Beschloss, *Mayday*, p. 243.

64. Ambrose, *Eisenhower*, p. 511.

65. Ibid., p. 512.

66. Staff, "The Nation: Summit and Consequences," *Time*, May 30, 1960, p. 18.

67. James Reston, "What Kind of President Do You Want? III," *New York Times*, May 11, 1960, p. 38.

68. Editorial, *Toledo Blade*, May 10, 1960.

69. Editorial board, "Crisis in the Cold War," *New York Times*, May 8, 1960, p. 28.

70. Ambrose, *Eisenhower*, p. 509.

71. Powers tapes.

72. Ibid.

73. Ibid.

74. Ovid Demaris, "Going to See Gary," *Esquire*, May 1966, p. 90.

75. Ibid., p. 91.

76. Staff, "Nation."

77. A. M. Rosenthal, "3 Leaders Fly from Wreckage of Summit," *New York Times*, May 20, 1960, p. 4.

78. Allen W. Dulles, *The Craft of Intelligence* (Guilford, CT: Lyons Press, 2016), p. 195.

79. Demaris, "Going to See Gary," p. 92.

80. Dr. James Baugh, unpublished manuscript, 1960–62. Reprinted with the permission of Baugh family.

81. Ibid.

82. Ibid.

83. Associated Press, "U-2 Pilot Urges Wife to Visit Him in Moscow," *New York Times*, June 15, 1960.

84. Associated Press, "U-2 Pilot Denies He Spied," *New York Times*, May 10, 1960, p. 1.

85. Baugh, manuscript.

86. Ibid.

87. Ibid.

88. *Richmond Times-Dispatch*, May 11, 1960.

89. Oliver Powers, letter to Nikita Khrushchev, May 10, 1960. Powers Family Archives.

90. Nikita Khrushchev, telegram to Oliver Powers. Powers Family Archives.

91. Peter Hahn, "Wealthy Immigrant Pays Tab for Trip of Powers Family," *Boston Globe*, August 18, 1960, p. 4.

92. Baugh, manuscript.

93. Hahn, "Wealthy Immigrant.'"

94. Associated Press, "Moscow Says Trial Indicts U.S.," *New York Times*, p. 11.

95. *Richmond Times-Dispatch*, August 7, 1960.

96. Seymour Topping, "U-2 Pilot's Father Pleads for Khrushchev Sympathy," *New York Times*, August 14, 1960, p. 1.

97. *May Day Incident*, p. 31.

98. "U.S. Issues Statement," *New York Times*, August 10, 1960.

99. *New York Times*, August 12, 1960.

100. Ibid.

101. *May Day Incident*, p. 26.

102. Ibid., p. 27.

103. Jason Caffrey, "Gary Powers: The U-2 Spy Pilot the U.S. Did Not Love," BBC World Service, January 3, 2016, https://www.bbc.com/news/magazine-35064221.

104. Associated Press, "Pilot Calls Treatment Better than Expected," *New York Times*, August 18, 1960, p. 23.

105. Excerpts from trial transcript, *New York Times*, August 18, 1960.

106. Ibid.

107. Unnamed correspondent, "Two Soviet Witnesses Are Questioned by Powers," *New York Times*, August 19, 1960, p. 4.

108. Ibid.

109. Ibid.

110. Ibid.

111. Associated Press, "Washington 'Pilliored,'" *New York Times*, August 18, 1960, p. 16.

112. Ibid.

113. Ibid.

114. Trial transcript.

115. Powers and Gentry, *Operation Overflight*, p. 154.

116. Associated Press, "Powers' Soviet Lawyer Sees Hope for Leniency," *New York Times*, August 19, 1960, p. 4.

117. Beschloss, *Mayday*, reprinting of FBI file, p. 331.

118. Trial transcript.

119. Beschloss, *Mayday*, p. 334.

120. Trial transcript.

121. Baugh, manuscript.

122. Powers and Gentry, *Operation Overflight*, p. 158.

123. Seymour Topping, "U.S. Pilot Rejects Attacks on U.S.," *New York Times*, August 20, 1960, p. 1.

124. William J. Jorden, "President Voices Regret at Ruling," *New York Times*, August 19, 1960, p. 1.

125. Baugh, manuscript.

CHAPTER FOUR: REPATRIATED

1. Francis Gary Powers and Curt Gentry, *Operation Overflight: A Memoir of the U-2 Incident* (New York: Holt, Rinehart, and Winston, 1970), p. 232.

2. Personal tapes of Francis Gary Powers, 1969.

3. Ibid.

4. Associated Press, *Atlanta Constitution*, February 6, 1962.

5. Nikita Khrushchev, *Memoirs of Nikita Khrushchev, vol. 3*, ed. Sergei Khrushchev (University Park, PA: Pennsylvania State University Press, Thomas J. Watson Institute for International Studies, Brown University, 2013), p. 293–94.

6. Michael R. Beschloss, *Mayday: Eisenhower, Khrushchev, and the U-2 Affair* (New York: Harper & Row, 1986), p. 302.

7. Michael R. Beschloss, *The Crisis Years* (New York: HarperCollins, 1991), p. 35.

8. Ibid., p. 36.

9. Dario Leone, "55th Wing RB-47 Co-Pilot Shot Down and Imprisoned by Soviets Will Be Buried in Arlington National Cemetery," Aviation Geek Club, July 26, 2017, https://theaviationgeekclub.com/55th-wing-rb-47-co-pilot-shot-imprisoned-soviets-will-buried-arlington-national-cemetery/.

10. Adam Taylor, "This Kremlin Leader Bragged about Tipping a U.S. Presidential Election," *Washington Post*, January 6, 2017, https://www.washingtonpost.com/news/worldviews/wp/2017/01/06/this-kremlin-leader-bragged-about-tipping-a-u-s-presidential-election/?utm_term=.4133a24956ea.

11. David Lawrence, "Khrushchev Believes Kennedy Victory Represents Apology for U-2 Incident," *LaCrosse* (Wisconsin) *Tribune/New York Herald Tribune* syndicate, January 4, 1961, p. 6.

12. Powers tapes.

13. Ibid.

14. Powers and Gentry, *Operation Overflight*, p. 235.

15. Unnamed staff, "Powers, in Letter from Soviet, 'Sure' U-2 Itself Did Not Explode," *New York Times*, September 27, 1960, p. 1.

16. Francis G. Powers, letter to the editor, *New York Times*, September 27, 1960.

17. Beschloss, *Mayday*, p. 356.

18. Unnamed contributor, "Dr. James B. Donovan, 53, Dies; Lawyer Arranged Spy Exchange," *New York Times*, January 20, 1970, p. 43.

19. James B. Donovan, *Strangers on a Bridge* (New York: Atheneum, 1964), p. 264–65.

20. Garrett Epps, "The Real Case Behind Bridge of Spies," *Atlantic*, November 17, 2015, http://www.theatlantic.com/politics/archive/2015/11/abel-bridge-of-spies/416325/.

21. Oliver Powers, letter to Rudolf Abel, June 2, 1960. Powers Family Archives.

22. Powers tapes.

23. Jeff Gammage, "Swarthmore Prof Was Snared in 'Bridge of Spies' Case," *Philadelphia Inquirer*, October 25, 2015, http://www.philly.com/philly/education/20151025_Swarthmore _prof_was_snared_in__Bridge_of_Spies__case.html.

24. Powers and Gentry, *Operation Overflight*.

25. Powers tapes.

26. *Washington Daily News*, February 10, 1962.

27. Peter Braestrup, "U-2 Pilot Is Reunited with Parents under Extreme Security," *New York Times*, February 11, 1962, p. 1.

28. Associated Press, "Predawn Telephone Calls Bring Powerses Surprising, Good News," *Courier-Journal* (Louisville, KY), February 11, 1962, p. 1.

29. Associated Press, "I Can't Sleep . . . I'm Too Excited," says Powers' wife in Georgia," *Redlands* (California) *Daily Facts*, February 12, 1962, p. 1.

30. Powers tapes.

31. Ibid.

32. John D. Morris, "Powers Fulfilled His Contract, U-2 Inquiry Thus Far Shows," *New York Times*, February 22, 1962, p. 1.

33. Powers and Gentry, *Operation Overflight*.

34. Ibid.

35. *New York Times* News Service, "Pilot Blasted for Attempt to Save Self," *Los Angeles Times*, August 26, 1960, p. 1.

36. Paul Healey and Jerry Greene, "Powers Talks: The U-2 Story," *Washington Daily News*, March 7, 1962, p. 1.

37. Beschloss, *Mayday*, p. 354.

38. Staff, "Text of CIA Chief's Report on Powers Inquiry and Excerpt from Pilot's Statement," *New York Times*, March 7, 1962, p. 12.

39. Executive Sessions of the Senate Foreign Relations Committee, Volume 12, 86th Cong., *Report on the U-2 Incident*.

40. Ian Fleming, "Gary Powers and the Big Lie," *Sunday Times* (London), March 11, 1962.

41. Baugh, manuscript.

42. Ibid.

43. Ibid.

44. Ibid.

45. Dr. James Baugh, letter to Francis Gary Powers, November 25, 1961. Reprinted with permission of Baugh family.

46. Powers and Gentry, *Operation Overflight*, p. 287.

47. Tom Fitzpatrick, "Another Scapegoat Talks, but Few Listen," *Chicago Sun-Times*, July 1, 1973.

48. Powers tapes.

49. Fitzpatrick, "Another Scapegoat Talks."

50. Don Page, "Former U-2 Pilot Reconnoiters Freeways Now," *Los Angeles Times*, March 1, 1973, part 4, pp. 1 and 24.

51. Ibid.

52. Francis Gary Powers, letter to the Church Commission, September 17, 1975.

CHAPTER FIVE: LOST IN A CROWD

1. Dale Fetherling, "Wreckage of Powers Helicopter Examined," *Los Angeles Times*, August 2, 1977, part 1, p. 3.

2. Ibid.

3. Ibid.

CHAPTER SIX: SEARCHING FOR THE TRUTH

1. Greg E. Norman, "Son of the Cold War Won't Let Era Be Buried," *Los Angeles Times*, March 6, 1997, part 3, p. 1.

2. Francis Gary Powers Jr., letter to Department of Defense Civilian/Military Service Review Board, August 7, 1997. Powers Family Archives.

3. James D. Johnston, letter to Francis Gary Powers Jr., Powers Family Archives.

4. Ibid., chap. 4, p. 178.

5. Colonel R. Philip Deavel, letter to Francis Gary Powers Jr., November 22, 1999. Powers Family Archives.

6. "Bob Gilliland Intro to Gary Powers 2000 Hall of Fame," 2000 enshrinement ceremony, Kentucky Aviation Hall of Fame, YouTube video, 4:48, September 18, 2017, https://www.youtube.com/watch?v=vn7kqDZcQno.

7. Ibid.

8. Mrs. Francis Gary Powers, letter to General J. R. Dailey, April 17, 2004. Powers Family Archives.

CHAPTER SEVEN: VOICE FROM THE GRAVE

1. Personal tapes of Francis Gary Powers, 1969.

2. Ibid.

3. CIA de-briefing transcript of Francis Gary Powers, February 1962. (Very lightly edited, for ease of readability.)

4. *The Last Overflights of the Soviet Union, 1959–60* (Washington, DC: National Security Agency Report, June 25, 2013), chap. 4, p. 185.

5. John McMahon, CIA interview, December 4, 1997, and February 4, 1998. Declassified 2010.

6. Harry Cordes, Oral History, Roadrunners Internationale, http://roadrunners internationale.com/cordes_u-2.html.

7. CIA de-briefing transcript.

8. Prettyman Board investigation into the U-2 Incident, transcript of interviews, 1962.

9. CIA de-briefing transcript.

10. Francis Gary Powers, letter to Oliver and Ida Powers, September 6, 1960. Powers Family Archives.

11. Ida Powers, letter to Francis Gary Powers, September 17, 1960. Powers Family Archives.

12. CIA de-briefing transcript.

13. Powers tapes.

14. Francis Gary Powers, personal journal, written while being confined in Soviet prison, 1960–62.

15. CIA de-briefing transcript.

16. Cordes, Oral History.

17. Powers, personal journal.

18. CIA de-briefing transcript.

19. Prettyman investigation, transcript of interviews.

20. CIA de-briefing transcript.

21. Powers tapes.

22. CIA de-briefing transcript.

23. Francis Gary Powers, letter to Barbara Powers, May 26, 1960. Powers Family Archives.

24. Francis Gary Powers, letter to Oliver and Ida Powers, June 21, 1960. Powers Family Archives.

25. Powers, personal journal.

26. Francis Gary Powers, letter to Barbara Powers, June 28, 1960. Powers Family Archives.

27. CIA de-briefing transcript.

28. Powers, personal journal.

29. Powers tapes.

30. Francis Gary Powers, letter to Barbara Powers, July 19, 1960. Powers Family Archives.

31. Francis Gary Powers, letter to Barbara Powers, 1960. Powers Family Archives.

32. Powers, personal journal.

33. Ibid.

34. Powers tapes.

35. Ibid.

36. Francis Gary Powers, letter to Barbara Powers, September 5, 1960. Powers Family Archives.

37. Oliver and Ida Powers, letter to Francis Gary Powers, September 12, 1960. Powers Family Archives.

38. Powers, personal journal.

39. Francis Gary Powers, letter to Barbara Powers, September 21, 1960. Powers Family Archives.

40. Powers, personal journal.

41. Francis Gary Powers, letter to Barbara Powers, January 16, 1961. Powers Family Archives.

42. Francis Gary Powers, letter to Oliver and Ida Powers, Undated 1961, Powers Family Archives.

43. Oliver and Ida Powers, letter to Francis Gary Powers, January 27, 1961. Powers Family Archives.

44. Francis Gary Powers, letter to Barbara Powers, March 1, 1961. Powers Family Archives.

45. Powers, personal journal.

46. Prettyman investigation, transcript of interviews.

47. Powers tapes.

48. CIA de-briefing transcript.

49. Powers, personal journal.

50. Powers tapes.

51. Francis Gary Powers, letter to Barbara Powers, April 30, 1961. Powers Family Archives.

52. Francis Gary Powers, letter to Oliver and Ida Powers, May 4, 1961. Powers Family Archives.

53. Francis Gary Powers, letter to sisters Jean and Jan, May 4, 1961. Powers Family Archives.

54. Francis Gary Powers, letter to Barbara Powers, June 15, 1961. Powers Family Archives.

55. Francis Gary Powers, letter to Barbara Powers, August 10, 1961. Powers Family Archives.

56. Powers, personal journal.

57. Francis Gary Powers, letter to Barbara Powers, November 1, 1961. Powers Family Archives.

58. Francis Gary Powers, letter to Barbara Powers, November 9, 1961. Powers Family Archives.

59. Powers, personal journal.

60. Ibid.

61. Francis Gary Powers, letter to Oliver and Ida Powers, December 26, 1961. Powers Family Archives.

62. Powers, personal journal.

63. McMahon, CIA interview.

64. Powers tapes.

CHAPTER EIGHT: THE LAST ECHO

1. Maria Glod, "Students Help Museum Collect Cold War History," *Washington Post*, October 12, 2006, http://www.washingtonpost.com/wp-dyn/content/article/2006/10/10/AR2006101001546.html.

2. Ibid.

3. Fredrick Kunkle, "Fairfax, Virginia Breaks Off Talks on Cold War Museum," *Washington Post*, April 15, 2009, http://www.washingtonpost.com/wp-dyn/content/article/2009/04/14/AR2009041402885.html.

4. Glod, "Students Help Museum Collect Cold War History."

5. Associated Press, *Lansing* (Michigan) *State Journal*, May 2, 2010.

6. *Kentucky Post*, December 8, 2001.

7. Ibid.

8. Francis Gary Powers, letter to Department of Defense Civilian/Military Service Review Board, January 16, 2011. Powers Family Archives.

9. Air Force Board of Correction of Military Records, Memorandum, November 16, 2011. Powers Family Archives.

10. Air Force Chief of Staff, Memorandum, December 8, 2011. Powers Family Archives.

11. Citation, Air Force Silver Star awarded to Francis Gary Powers, June 14, 2012.

12. Adam J. Hebert, "Long Roads to Redemption," *Air Force*, July 2012, p. 4.

CHAPTER NINE: UNFINISHED BUSINESS

1. Robert Sorrell, "Heart in the Sky: Lonesome Pine Airport Dedicates Terminal to Wise County Veteran," *Bristol* (Virginia) *Herald Courier*, March 12, 2006, https://www.heraldcourier.com/news/local/lonesome-pine-airport-dedicates-terminal-to-wise-county-veteran/article_e905b0a1-33be-57fa-8dfc-26af27494580.html.

2. Ibid.

3. Stephen Igo, "Lonesome Pine Airport Terminal Dedicated in Honor of Cold War Spy Plane Pilot," *Times News* (Kingsport, TN), March 14, 2016, http://www.timesnews.net/News/2016/03/14/Airport-terminal-dedicated-in-honor-of-Cold-War-spy-plane-pilot-1.

4. Jerry K. Staub, letter to President Richard Nixon, August 31, 1971. Released by the CIA after a Freedom of Information Act request.

5. Memorandum for Executive Officer, "Items for General Cushman's Black Book," September 16, 1971. Released by the CIA after a Freedom of Information Act request.

6. Memorandum from Lawrence R. Houston, October 19, 1971. Released by the CIA after a Freedom of Information Act request.

7. Memorandum for John F. Blake, August 4, 1977, Released by the CIA after a Freedom of Information Act request.

8. Memorandum from John Parangosky, October 27, 1972. Released by the CIA after a Freedom of Information Act request.

9. Memorandum to Director, Special Projects Staff, October 24, 1971. Released by the CIA after a Freedom of Information Act request.

10. Associated Press, "Son of US Spy Pilot Views U-2 Artifacts at Russian Museum," *Air Force Times*, December 7, 2017, http://www.airforcetimes.com/news/your-air-force/2017/12/07/son-of-us-spy-pilot-views-u-2-artifacts-at-russian-museum.

11. "Almanac: Ian Fleming," CBS Sunday Morning, May 28, 2017, https://www.cbsnews.com/news/almanac-ian-fleming/.

12. Ibid.

INDEX

INDEX